How to Sail

JOHN FISHER
author of *Sailing Dinghies*

Copyright © 2013 Read Books Ltd.
This book is copyright and may not be
reproduced or copied in any way without
the express permission of the publisher in writing

British Library Cataloguing-in-Publication Data
A catalogue record for this book is available from the
British Library

Sailing

Sailing is the propulsion of a vehicle and the control of its movement with large (usually fabric) foils called sails. By changing the rigging, rudder, and sometimes the keel or centreboard, a sailor manages the force of the wind on the sails in order to move the vessel relative to its surrounding medium (typically water, but also land and ice) and change its direction and speed. Mastery of the skill requires experience in varying wind and sea conditions, as well as knowledge concerning sailboats themselves and an understanding of one's surroundings. While there are still some places in the world where sail-powered passenger, fishing and trading vessels are used, these craft have become rarer as internal combustion engines have become economically viable in even the poorest and most remote areas. In most countries sailing is enjoyed as a recreational activity or as a sport. Recreational boating or yachting can be divided into 'racing' and 'cruising'. Cruising can include extended offshore and ocean-crossing trips, coastal sailing within sight of land, and day-sailing.

Throughout history, sailing has been instrumental in the development of civilization, affording humanity greater mobility than travel over land, whether for trade, transport or warfare, and the capacity for fishing. The earliest representation of a ship under sail appears on a painted disc found in Kuwait dating between 5000 and

5500 BC. Advances in sailing technology from the Middle Ages onward enabled Arab, Chinese, Indian and European explorers to make longer voyages into regions with extreme weather and climatic conditions. There were improvements in sails, masts and rigging - and navigation equipment vastly improved. From the fifteenth century onwards, European ships went further north, stayed longer on the Grand Banks and in the Gulf of St. Lawrence, and eventually began to explore the Pacific Northwest and the Western Arctic.

Recreational boats (sometimes called pleasure craft, especially for less sporting activities) fall into several broad categories, and additional subcategories. Broad categories include dinghies (generally under 16 feet powered by sail, small engines, or muscle power), paddlesports boats (kayaks, rowing shells, canoes), runabouts (15-25' powerboats with either outboard, stern drive, or inboard engines), daysailers (14–25-foot sailboats, frequently with a small auxiliary engine), cruisers (25–65' powerboats with cabins), and cruising and racing sailboats (25–65-foot sailboats with auxiliary engines). Boating for pleasure might involve a singlehanded vessel, or the boat may be crewed by families and friends. Sailing vessels may proceed on their own, or join a flotilla with other like-minded voyagers. They also may be operated by their owners, who often also gain pleasure from maintaining and modifying their craft to suit their needs and taste, or may be rented for the specific trip or cruise. A professional skipper and even crew can be hired along with the boat in some cases.

Cruising trips of several days or longer can involve a deep immersion in the logistics and navigation of sailing, as well as meteorology, local geography and history. Once the boat is acquired it is not all that expensive an endeavour, often much less expensive than a normal vacation on land. It naturally develops self-reliance, responsibility, economy, and many other useful skills. Besides improving sailing skills, all the other normal needs of everyday living must also be addressed. There are work roles that can be done by everyone in the family to help contribute to an enjoyable outdoor adventure. A style of casual coastal cruising called 'gunkholing' is a popular summertime family recreational activity. It consists of taking a series of day sails to out of the way places and anchoring overnight while enjoying such activities as exploring isolated islands, swimming, fishing, etc. Many nearby local waters on rivers, bays, sounds, and coastlines can become great natural cruising grounds for this type of recreational boating. Casual boat trips with friends and family can become lifetime bonding experiences.

Long-distance voyaging, such as that across oceans and between far-flung ports, can be considered the near-absolute province of the cruising sailboat. Most modern yachts of 25–55 feet long, propelled solely mechanically, cannot carry the fuel sufficient for a point-to-point voyage of even 250–500 miles without needing to resupply. But a well-prepared sail-powered yacht of similar length is theoretically capable of sailing anywhere its crew is willing to guide it. Even considering that the cost benefits are offset by a much reduced cruising speed, many people traveling distances in small boats come to appreciate the more leisurely pace and increased time spent on the water. Since the solo circumnavigation of Joshua Slocum in the 1890s, long-distance cruising under sail has inspired thousands of otherwise normal people to explore distant seas and horizons. The important voyages of Robin Lee Graham, Eric Hiscock, Don Street and others have shown that, while not strictly racing, ocean voyaging carries with it an inherent sense of competition, especially that between man and the elements. Such a challenging enterprise requires keen knowledge of sailing in general as well as maintenance, navigation (especially celestial navigation), and often even international diplomacy (for which an entire set of protocols should be learned and practiced).

This element of competition brings us onto 'Racing and Regattas'; a common activity in the sub-culture of boaters owning larger (twenty-five foot plus) small boats and larger Yachts, and are frequently organised around a Yacht club or Marina organisation. The National Marine Manufacturers Association, the organization that establishes several of the standards that are commonly used in the marine industry in the United States, defines 32 types of boats, demonstrating the diversity of boat types and their specialization. In addition to those standards, all boats employ the same basic principles of hydrodynamics. Sailboat racing can be done on conventional family sailboats racing under one of the simpler handicap formulas (PHRF, or Performance Handicap Rating Formula is one such rule), or can be done on specialized boats with virtually no accommodation or compromises for comfort.

Racing is generally either one design, where the boats are close to identical, or handicapped where the boats' finishing times are adjusted based on their predicted speed potential. It is further broken down into ocean racing, where boats start at one port and race in the ocean and back to the same port or a new destination, or buoy racing where boats race around prescribed courses and return to port at night. Several famous races cross oceans, like the 'biennial Transpac Race' from Los Angeles to Honolulu, or the 'Newport-Bermuda Race' from Newport, Rhode Island to Bermuda. Other races actually circumnavigate the globe, like the 'Volvo Ocean Race' or 'Vendee Globe race'. The 'America's Cup'– established in 1851, this is the oldest, and arguably the most prestigious event in yacht racing. Participants are restricted to a measurement formula for the boats, and the rules concerning the same have been controversial ever since 'Australia II' took the cup away from the U.S. with a secret winged keel.

The formal racing of boats is believed to have started with sailboats in the Netherlands sometime in the seventeenth century. Soon, in England, custom-built racing 'yachts' began to emerge and the Royal Yacht Squadron was established in 1815. In 1661 John Evelyn recorded a competition between *Katherine* and *Anne*, two large royal sailing vessels both of English design, '...the wager 100-1; the race from Greenwich to Gravesend and back.' One of the vessels was owned, and sometimes steered by Charles II, the King of England. The king lost.

In the present day, as yacht racing has become more prevalent, and yacht design more diverse, it has become necessary to establish systems of measurements and time allowances due to the differences in boat design. Longer yachts are inherently faster than shorter ones; therefore, in the interests of fairness, in the 1820s a 'primitive system of time allowance was introduced on the Solent.' Larger yachts were handicapped; but owners with the biggest vessels obviously resented these attempts to lessen their wins. As a result both ratings and 'one-design' competition were developed. Today, the major races can be classified as offshore, ocean, around the world and inshore racing, all adhering to one set of rules, but diverse handicapping standards. Boating for both races and recreation is an immensely popular past time all over the globe, and it is showing no signs of abating. We hope the reader enjoys this book.

[Photo: Eileen Ramsay

1. A day for single-handed sailing. National 12 ft. on the Thames

CONTENTS

Chapter		Page
	ACKNOWLEDGEMENTS	13
	INTRODUCTION	15
I	WHY THEY ENJOY IT	17
II	WHAT KIND OF SAILING?	22
III	PICKING THE RIGHT BOAT	37
IV	GOING AFLOAT	50
V	KNOTS AND OTHER NOTIONS	67
VI	MANAGING MORE SAILS	77
VII	CARE OF SAILS	93
VIII	CLASS DISTINCTIONS	98
IX	CAN I BUILD HER?	116
X	LONG LIFE TO THE BOAT	128
XI	GOING RACING?	134
XII	WINNING MOVES	147
XIII	YOU ARE OFFICER OF THE DAY	160
XIV	TIDES AND TIDAL STREAMS	169
XV	MEET THE WEATHER MAN	172
XVI	IS HE GOING TO HIT ME?	192
XVII	STOPPING AND STARTING	200
XVIII	SAFETY FIRST	209
XIX	GOING CRUISING	219
XX	PILOTAGE AND NAVIGATION	227

Appendix

| | ON BUYING A BOAT | 255 |

PLATES

Plate		Facing Page
I	A day for single-handed sailing. National 12 ft. on the Thames. *(Photo. Eileen Ramsay)*	Frontispiece
II	A Five-O-Five planing with the trapeze in use	66
III	Black Soo, a modern hard-chine design ocean racer with a fin-keel	67
IV	Swallow Class yachts racing at Cowes. The 6-metre K 47 in the background appears to have gone aground. *(Photo. Beken & Son)*	98
V	A day for a good crew—a Firefly at Whitstable *(Photo. Eileen Ramsay)*	99
VI	Yachting World Cadet Class in action. *(Photo. Group Captain Haylock, R.A.F. [retd.])*	162
VII	Shearwater Catamaran	163

DIAGRAMS

Figure		Page
1	Sails of a dinghy	45
2	(1) Sloop. (2) Cutter. (3) Ketch. (4) Yawl	47
3	Parts of a dinghy	52
4	Parts of a cutter	53
5	Beating, reaching, running	59
6	Reef knot	68
7	Reef knot for rapid untying	68
8	Double bend	68
9	Bowline	68
10	Clove hitch	69
11	Rolling hitch	69
12	Sheet bend	69
13	Topsail sheet bend	70
14	Figure of eight knot	70
15	A slippery hitch	70
15A	Slippery hitch for halyard	70
16	Fisherman's bend	71
17	Bowline on a bight	71
18	Topsail halyard bend	71
19A	Whipping the end of a rope	72
19B	Whipping rope in middle	72
20	Short splice	73
21	Eye splice	73
22	Reefing and furling gears	82
23	Use of kicking strap	84
24A	Gybing the spinnaker	87
24B	Hoisting the spinnaker	89, 90, 91, 92
25	Repairing a sail	96
26	Building at home	122-124

DIAGRAMS

Figure		Page
27	Showing theoretical action of wind on sails	142
28	Choosing the right tack	152-3
29	A mark boat drifts out of position	165
30	Starting marks poorly arranged	166
31	Tide level diagram	171
32	A depression moving north-eastwards, showing clouds to be expected	186
33	Shipping weather forecasts	190
34	Lights, etc., shown by ships at sea	196
35	Coastal navigation buoys	228
36	Lead line for sounding	232
37	Compass roses	235
38	Allowing for the tide	240
39	A running fix	243
40	Calculations for a noon Sight	247
41	Position line obtained from an assumed position	249
42	From a typical Admiralty chart	251

ACKNOWLEDGEMENTS

I SHOULD like – without making them in any way responsible for what appears – to thank many kind friends for valuable suggestions which they have made.

I owe a particular debt of gratitude to Miss Mary Blewitt, author of that admirably clear and concise book, *Celestial Navigation for Yachtsmen*, for her help, and to Mr. Guthrie Penman, of the Royal Ocean Racing Club and of Itchenor, Sussex, whose experience of international class racing, added to his knowledge of the design, construction and handling of boats both large and small in many different parts of the world, have made his advice invaluable.

My thanks are also due to the Royal Yachting Association for permission to publish the rules of International 14-ft. Class, and to the following who have allowed me to reproduce copyright illustration material: The Admiralty for permission to reproduce a portion of Coastal Chart No. 2172 (Fig. 42); Messrs. Beken of Cowes for Plates III and IV; The Bell Woodworking Company of Leicester for Fig. 26; Messrs. Brown, Son and Fergusson for Figs. 3 and 5; Messrs. Peter Davies, Ltd. for Fig. 24; The English Universities Press for Figs. 6, 9, 16 and 20; Everyman's Yachting, Hutchinson's Scientific and Technical Publications for Fig. 22; Group Captain Haylock, R.A.F. (retd.), Editor of *Yachting World* for Plate VI; Messrs. Methuen and Co. for Figs. 7, 8, 13, 14, 18, 19 and 34; Messrs. Muller for Fig. 32; Messrs. John Murray, Ltd. for Fig. 20; Messrs. G. L. W. Oppenheim of Amsterdam for Plate I; Pelican Books for Figs. 2, 10, 11, 12, 15, 17, 32 and 36; Mr. Ian Proctor and Adlard Coles Ltd. for Fig. 23; Miss Eileen Ramsay for Plates I, V and VII; Reed's Nautical Almanack for Fig. 35; and the *Yachting World* for Fig. 25.

Figs. 3, 5, 15A and 24B have been re-drawn by Mr. Roy Glanville, R.B.A., S.M.A.

JOHN FISHER.

INTRODUCTION

"I do not know anything more glorious or exciting than to stand at the tiller of a noble yacht, with a slashing breeze making her leap through the seas, the spoondrift flying out from her lee side in showers of flaky foam, feeling oneself the master of her every motion, and she like a thing of life answering every thought of the brain and every movement of the hand; topping the white-crested waves like a bird, gliding swiftly down the hollows, nipping now and again little foam wreaths over her snowy deck, and anon cleaving through a giant billow, scattering rainbows of sea froth like pearls, and rubies, and sapphires around her; agreeable companions on the quarter-deck; a stalwart, active crew forward, a full bread locker, a damp beef cask, and the grog tub brimming, with a pleasant port and kindly friends looming at the end of the bowsprit."

These words, by Vanderdecken, are as true to-day as when they were written eighty years ago.

And we can prove it with figures.

In Britain, the number of sailing clubs has nearly trebled since the end of Hitler's war. Several of the best-known classes of standard small boat have passed the two thousand mark. New fleets are being started every month. But still more people might like to go sailing if only they knew how to set about it. Possibly they fancy the idea of yachting but have never been in a boat in their life.

Or perhaps they sailed a long time ago in someone else's boat without learning enough to strike out on their own.

Or they are not sure whether sailing is expensive and whether yachtsmen are "stuck-up".

Or they wish to join a club without knowing any of the members. This book is written for them.

CHAPTER I

WHY THEY ENJOY IT

As a first approach to the open-minded we shall claim a few special advantages for the sport of sailing. Recollect first that the scientists have failed to discover exactly how the wind moves a boat over the water and to what extent the sail is drawn rather than pushed ahead by the mysterious and invisible currents of air.

There is magic in sailing; and the feeling that you are being propelled by a mysterious unknowable force never completely vanishes however often you go afloat. Nor does the sensation of moving silently ahead without any exertion of one's own. This must be one reason why people are prepared, year after year, to get themselves cold and wet (though later, perhaps, full of hot rum) in order to go afloat. For sailing does not always consist of sunshine and fashion-plate girls on the deck and iced champagne all around.

Often the sky is paper-coloured and the sea looks like lead, and the rain pours down your neck as from a vast barber's hose. Yet on such a day you find almost as many people afloat as in picture postcard weather.

As sailing's second most important attraction we would list the change which it provides. For instance, on dry land the ground, we hope, moves only during an earthquake. Yet afloat it happens all the time, with the result that you feel on a new world and the sight of a spinney of masts bobbing up and down – even in one's mind's eye on a cold winter day at the office – recalls a completely different existence, an Arcadia, cleansed from buildings, from the roar of engines and from the smoke of car exhausts. Sailing is restful, precisely because it provides that contrast. Moreover each trip afloat is different from the others. You may sail day after day from the same jetty and traverse the same two or three channels, flanked, perhaps, by a mud-bank with some reeds, an old wreck; a cornfield and some houses with thatched roofs. Yet the landscape never twice looks the same. For if ever the wind blows twice at the same speed and from the same direction, the set of the tide and the waves are different; or the temperature is hotter or colder than we remember; or the light, which depends on the sun's position and its declination, alters the scene. The angle from which we view the land changes as the tide rises or falls. So does the speed of the tide on which we are carried or against which we must struggle. Sometimes the wind blows against the tide to raise white horses in a few minutes.

At others the wind is so light that it scarcely stirs the sail and the boat drifts with the tide so quietly that you hear the voices of children playing in the fields.

The picture is framed in clouds which can change in an afternoon from feathery white billows to hard and angry thunder clouds. Thus in sailing you can always count on the unexpected as a contrast to a week of routine.

Next advantage: sailing is the least commercial of any sport we can recall. The prize money, even in a National Championship, is peanuts. Afloat you find no transfer fees, no cheer leaders, no pool forecasts nor any of the blemishes which can turn sport into a commercial business. There are no professionals (apart from paid hands, and you will not be wanting these yet awhile), and no gate. In a yacht race the boats may start near the club house, but they soon draw away and, when they do, you can seldom see what happens unless you are in the race yourself. This, we believe, helps to encourage the type of helmsman who goes sailing because he likes sailing for its own sake and not for what the gallery will say. The standard of sportsmanship amongst yachtsmen is extremely high and the helmsman who is prepared to win against the spirit of the rules rapidly finds himself frozen out.

There is, on the other hand, considerable camaraderie

amongst yachtsmen, all of whom have at some time or other suffered misfortunes, such as running aground, breaking masts, or splitting a sail. In these emergencies they need help and they get it; and whereas on the London to Brighton road you might not find one car stopping to help another over a puncture repair, at sea, where there may be danger, perhaps to a ship, perhaps to a life, one helmsman never passes by on the other side when he sees a fellow yachtsman in trouble. This "help your neighbour" principle holds good even on shore, where "X" helps lift "Y's" boat on to the jetty because he knows "Y" will some day do the same for him.

Sailing is one of the few sports which you can enjoy on your own without feeling lonely. It is not only that there is always something to do aboard. We are not being fanciful in saying that when sailing alone you feel that two other people are with you all the time – the boat and the wind. Each of these have kept the personalities they had in the days of Homer, who was one of the world's finest yachting correspondents.

Contrary to general belief, yachtsmen ashore do not permanently wear peaked caps, even during Cowes Week, nor are they all equipped with 22-carat gold cigar piercers and diamond cuff links. They are usually far from being stand-offish; they are more interested in whether a helmsman sails a sporting race than in whether he knows the wine list, and they respect the owner who goes sailing in spite of his bank balance rather than because of it.

While on the subject of money we should mention that running a small boat (which is the liveliest kind of boat to run) costs a good deal less than running a car; less even a year than some people spend on tobacco. And it is by no means necessary to own a boat in order to sail. In these days the owners of large boats are giving up the idea of manning them with paid hands and are relying on amateur crews. These amateur crews consist of people who are able to go on cruises or in races only in vacation time. They cannot keep on throughout the season. Often in these days of crisis their plans have to be changed at short notice. A plentiful and regular supply of them is therefore needed. So there is a chance for the newcomer, when he has learnt the rudiments of sailing, to join a big ship as crew, first as a substitute and later as a regular, under which conditions sailing becomes a very much cheaper method of going abroad than taking a plane or Channel steamer.

Another advantage of sailing is that for small boats it has now become an all-the-year-round sport. The season no longer begins in May and ends in August. It starts in January and finishes in December. This is not because we in Britain have become a very much harder and fitter race, but because we are going in for smaller and smaller boats. These can be sailed in inland waters where it would be impossible for a larger boat to manœuvre – even if there were sufficient depth of water. Such waters are well protected from the gales which close down winter activity on the coast, and include not merely rivers and sheltered estuaries, but lakes, quarries, meres which have been left after salt has been excavated, and similar pitches. At the beginning of 1951 a new field was opened to the small-boat sailors through the efforts of the Royal Yachting Association. This body persuaded the British Waterworks Association to agree to allow boats to sail on compensation reservoirs (the reservoirs which are used to keep up the level of rivers and canals in dry months, but not for supplying washing or drinking water). Clubs wishing to use compensation reservoirs are now sponsored by the Royal Yachting Association and are usually required to pay for the wages of the Water Company official who is present at sailing times. They are asked to guarantee that fish and wild birds and their nests will be undisturbed. In many cases they have to instal a boat-house, launching equipment, proper sanitary conveniences and, if necessary, an approach road of hard core sufficiently strong to stand up to the weight of the boats and trailers which will use it. But these concessions provide chances of sailing near home which no generation before has had.

The word "generation" reminds us to point out that sailing

happens to be one of those sports which you can take up late in life and keep up late. Naturally, those lucky people who have sailed since they were children have certain automatic reactions which make sailing easier for them than it is for older people who have to think what they are doing. Also experience counts, particularly in racing, where often you see a situation developing on the lines of something that happened before and can profit thereby. But this certainly does not prevent a man in his late thirties from taking up sailing – even in a small boat – for the first time and making a go of it. One such man whom we know did so after Hitler's war and soon won a British National Championship trophy for his mantelpiece. Yachting can be kept up very much longer than many other sports; it is not strenuous; it does not call for the kind of effort that is made in boxing or athletics; there is no wear and tear on the "bellows" or heart, and you do not finish up any sailing race panting for breath. So it is possible to keep on at the helm long after tennis and cricket have become matters for the photograph album.

Part of the fascination of sailing consists in the spark of peril which it provides, or seems to provide. For one thing you seem to go so fast through the water. A speed of six knots in a small boat, where you are close to the waves, seems like sixty, and can bring the same feeling you get on those giant switchbacks at fun fairs. Each emergency becomes more, rather than less, interesting as you realize more easily what you ought to have done in order not to get into it. We have heard people say that the expert skipper never puts to sea in conditions unsuitable for his boat and the crew she carries; and we agree that, with weather forecasts and ship-to-shore radio, the dangers of going to sea have been very much reduced. But they still exist. Scarcely a year passes without news of some fresh adventure, and even on the very calmest day it is as well to remember that one is usually sailing out of swimming distance from land. It is to keep such feelings of anxiety to exactly the right proportions that most of the following chapters are written.

CHAPTER II

WHAT KIND OF SAILING?

THERE are several ways of going afloat, and no agreement among yachtsmen is likely to be reached on which is the most pleasurable – day sailing, or day racing, or off shore cruising, or ocean racing. So let us examine these in turn and see what each has to offer.

Day sailing

Day sailing is the simplest and least expensive way of going afloat. Starting from scratch, you are committed to nothing more than hiring a boat. There is no trying to beat the other fellow; there are no ambitious journeys; there is nothing strenuous except, perhaps, at worst, taking to oars when the wind drops. The sails of boats used for day sailing are usually small in area and demand little attention, so that it is possible to keep everything well in hand. The boat is likely to be comfortable and roomy. The picnic basket can be packed and taken, as also the camera (in a waterproof case). Sun glasses are worn and swim suits and towels carried. The beer is trailed in a string bag over the side to keep it cool. (Would that people would do the same with the gramophones and portable wireless sets.) There is all the time in the world. The charm of day sailing is that you can explore. You are not tied to a course or a programme except perhaps by the tide.

Here, while we think of it, is a trick which is of great importance in mastering the tide on such picnic trips. Imagine the skipper preparing for his afternoon's rest in the sun. The boat is at rest by the water's edge. But the skipper looks anxious and worried. He knows that the tide is falling, that when he wakes after his doze he may have to drag the boat across thirty yards

WHAT KIND OF SAILING? 23

of sand or mud in order to get it into the water again. (Equally, if the tide is rising, the skipper may wake and find that the boat is now afloat twenty yards off shore, where it can be boarded only after a swim.) All these troubles can be avoided if the skipper does as follows:

He should have a small anchor attached at the anchor ring to a line at least three times the depth of the water at high-tide. The loose end or fall of the line is made fast to the stem of the boat. In addition, a second and thinner line is attached to one of the flukes of the anchor. This second line can be conveniently wound on a small reel or stick. When wishing to anchor the boat on a falling tide, the skipper unwinds, let us say, 100 feet of line from the reel and places the anchor with both lines attached on the deck of the boat near the stem. He then gives the boat a powerful push out into the water, taking care to keep hold of the reel in his hand. When the boat has glided out a suitable distance, the skipper jerks the reel line which pulls the anchor off the deck of the boat and the boat then anchors itself. The skipper then retires ashore and, provided that his line is long enough, can sleep undisturbed by the receding tide. When he wishes to go aboard again he pulls up the anchor with his line and heaves it ashore with the boat following.

For a rising tide the technique is similar, except that the skipper can put the anchor in the ground in advance before the tide has begun to float his boat.

So far we have assumed that the would-be sailor is going to hire a boat. This is probably the best way he can start, particularly if he finds himself on holiday several hundred miles from his home. The charges for the hire of boats vary a good deal according to the time of the year (mid-season is naturally more expensive) and according to the day of the week (week-ends are more expensive than weekdays). It should be possible, however, at most times of the year to hire a small boat suitable for one or two people for around about six guineas per week. The chances are, however, that anyone who goes out once or twice in a hired boat and likes it will want to own a boat of his own, which he can cherish from week to week. If so, a simple arrangement is to keep the boat in the garage or under cover in the garden and sail from home. Boats of up to 12 feet in length can conveniently be put on rubber rollers or padded chocks on the top of an ordinary 10 h.p. saloon car, a procedure which avoids the expense of a separate trailer behind the car, such as is used for transporting larger dinghies. As will be seen later, one type of small family boat is especially designed for being carried on the top of a car. A boat of this kind should have the mast designed for easy stowing, if necessary in pieces.

Sailing from the garage makes it possible to use several pieces of water instead of only one – and to pick the area which suits the weather conditions for that particular day. Suppose, for instance, that the weather forecast says that the winds will be moderate to strong in one coastal area, then you may prefer to sail inland, perhaps in a river protected by houses, or lakes surrounded by trees. But if the forecast is light to moderate on the coast, then you make for the sea.

A small family boat not belonging to any recognized class is the cheapest form of sailing craft, since it does not have to be made to specified measurements or weight or with specified materials, as racing boats are. Moreover, a boat designed for day sailing can take more people than the same length boat used for racing. Racing boats tend to be narrow for their length, whereas day sailing boats for picnicking are broad in the beam with more room in them. They require less managing, which is just as well if there are children in the boat. It is the difference between the carthorse and the racehorse.

A "knock about" picnic boat saves you money. You avoid the extra gadgets and refinements that have to be fitted to a racing boat. You can do without that second suit of sails which the racing man has, and which he keeps on one side, perhaps for use in light weather only. The owner of a knock about boat saves money, too, because he is less hard on his gear than he would be if he raced. Everything, including the sails, which account for perhaps one-fifth of the cost of the boat, lasts longer. The family boat does not need the fine finish that a racing boat must have if it is to slip through the water in the way it should. In fact, the family boat used for picnicking offers a very easy and pleasant life. Let us, however, not overlook other forms of sailing, none the less pleasant but far less easy.

Day racing

The difficulties and disadvantages of day racing are easily seen. In the first place, it is necessary to join a club. This club will have its racing programmes on fixed days and at fixed times of the day. Even if the date and the time entirely suits you, you may have difficulties in getting the crew. A puncture or a last-minute overtime order may mean that the crew whom you had hoped would do a sterling job in the front end of the boat cannot be present. Another difficulty is that some boats can be sailed with two-up in light weather, but need a third in heavier winds. Other boats which normally take two can be sailed singly in light airs. It follows that on some days someone may have to be left ashore if the boat is to sail at its best, and at other times you may be short of your third man.

Then there is the fact that the club decides the course in advance, so that on a day when you may feel like going on a short trip up-country amongst the water meadows you may find yourself banished on an eight-or-ten-mile stretch to the open sea and back. On joining a club you are tied to the other people who belong to it. In most cases you are pretty sure to be lucky, but one cannot always tell.

Then you are limited not only to the people who belong to the club, but to the boats they have chosen to sail. Most clubs occasionally have handicap races in which any type of boat can join, but because of the difficulties of handicapping, clubs usually adopt a number of classes of racing boat to which one's choice is consequently limited. Some of these class boats may cost more than one would care to spend; others may be pure racing machines unfitted for any other purpose. But there it is.

The decision will have been made, in all probability, long before you thought of joining the club, and there is little that can be done about it.

We have not yet finished with the list of difficulties. Racing boats are less comfortable than others used for knocking about. Often a racing boat, because it travels faster through the water, is wetter, and because its sail area is large it is harder work for the helmsman and crew. One's hands at the end of a sailing season feel and look quite different from what they were at the beginning, and the skin pads of one's palms become toughened and leathery from hauling and heaving the various ropes. Nor is the hard work confined to the race itself. There is more to be done on shore in maintaining a racing boat. And there is more to be read about, too. It becomes advisable, for instance, to study magazines such as *Yachting Monthly*, *Yachting World*, and *Light Craft* (all monthlies), the *Yachtsman* (bi-monthly), and *Yachts and Yachting* (fortnightly). It is also necessary to master the complicated series of rules by which yachts when racing are prevented from fouling each other.

Then, apart from the extra expenses of racing due to bigger and better equipment, racing insurance rates are higher than ordinary rates, and the budget may also have to provide for trips away from one's own sailing area to other clubs.

The last few pages have listed a formidable set of drawbacks, which might deter anyone from approaching the starting-line of a race. But we do not hesitate to recommend racing as a form of sailing in preference to ordinary day-boat work, for when once the elements of how to sail have been mastered this question "How good am I?" is bound to assail you. It can be answered only by racing.

Yacht racing is by no means all of a kind, the two broad classifications being (i) Class Racing and (ii) Handicap Racing. In class racing the boats fall between the measured limits of one class and race level, i.e. their times are actual and not adjusted after the race is over. Handicap racing is the opposite. Handicap systems vary from the complicated calculations made from the boat's measurements for off shore races by such organizations as the Royal Ocean Racing Club in London and the Cruising Club of America in New York to those of local regattas, where often the form book says no more than that "Alice, length 16′ 3″, is not quite so fast as Mr. Spindrift's Blue Jean but better than Mr. Heaver's Cloud".

Handicapping in ocean races has reached a fine art, but even the most superior mathematicians have found it difficult to devise the perfect handicapping system for small boats in short races, for, during a short race on any one particular day, there is seldom time for the weather to average up. For instance, you may get high winds or light airs, but rarely both on the same afternoon, and different weather suits different designs of boats. Some designs are good light-weather boats, but hard to manage in a blow, and others vice versa. Many small boats demand a light crew in light weather and a heavy crew in strong winds. All these factors make it hard to fix a handicap for small boats that will work fairly for different classes of boat and for all sizes of crew on any particular day.

However, it is clearly a pity that the man who cannot afford to buy a class boat built to exact measurements should be debarred from all racing, and a number of attempts have been made to provide a system under which Menagerie Races, in which many different types of boat take part, can be run off on a handicap.

One of the best known of these systems has been introduced in the South of England by the Portsmouth Harbour Racing and Sailing Association. The system caters not only for boats of different classes in the same club which may want to race against each other, but for boats from different clubs. Under the Portsmouth system each boat is handicapped by its local club, not on its average speed, which may vary from course to course according to the strength of the tide, the wind, wave formations and other factors, but on its performance as compared with some well-known standard racing class in which the boats are alike, or nearly so. These standard classes in turn are rated against each other and a comprehensive table is thus prepared. In assessing the performance of any boat in his area the handicapper takes into account whether that boat is being sailed by novices or by experienced helmsmen. Mr. S. Zillwood Milledge, who has done much of the groundwork on which the Portsmouth system is based, has calculated that a champion helmsman can be expected to sail 10 per cent faster than the average, while a novice may be 20 per cent slower.

Typical ratings at the time of writing are as follows:

Shearwater Catamaran	78
International 10 sq. M. Canoe	83
Flying Dutchman	84
Jollyboat	86
International 14 ft. Dinghy	89
Y.W. Hornet	89
National Flying Fifteen	90
Finn	91
International 12 sq. M. Sharpie	91
National Swallow	91
National 18 ft. C.B. Dinghy	91
National (Merlin-Rocket) 14 ft.	91
Swordfish 15 ft. O.D.	94
X Class One Design	100
National Redwing	101
Enterprise	103
National Firefly O.D.	103
Yachting World G.P. 14 ft.	107
Graduate	108
Island 14 ft. O.D.	114
Hamble Star	115
Fleetwind	116
British Moth	121
West Wight Scow	129
Yachting World Cadet	132

NOTE. These ratings are a guide only. They are subject to

variation especially if any modification has been made to the hull, sails or rigging of the class concerned.

These ratings or factors can be applied to boats either according to the length of the course or the time taken by the leading boat. Fuller details, for which we have no space here, can be obtained from the Portsmouth Harbour Racing and Sailing Association.

While no handicapping system can be absolutely faultless, the Portsmouth system goes some way towards allowing the family boat to enter for regatta races with the least possible embarrassment, and if extended sufficiently would allow a man to take his family boat far afield and yet be sure of being able to enter for races at a prearranged handicap without injustice to himself or to his rivals.

Boats of the same class racing level usually take part in points races in addition to regattas and special cup races. In points races the helmsman gets a number of points calculated according to the number of boats starting the race and his own position at the finish. Often points racing consists of a series of, say, eight races from which the helmsman can pick his six best results and discard the two races in which he did worst. A typical points scoring table is given on page 30.

A different type of system is used in class racing to distribute prizes as evenly as possible throughout the season, and to avoid the situation where most of the awards in each class go to the three or four best helmsmen to the discouragement of the rest of the fleet. Under this system, each time a boat wins it incurs a penalty based on 5 seconds for each completed 5 minutes of the race (based on the elapsed time of the first boat home). This penalty is added to the finishing time of this boat in subsequent races.

A further success, despite this handicap, incurs a further penalty of 5, and so on, until some other boat becomes the winner.

POINTS FOR CUP RACES

Starters:

Position	1	2	3	4	5	6	7	8	9	10	11	12	13	14	15	16	17	18
1st	3	4	5	5	6	7	7	8	9	9	10	11	11	12	13	13	14	
2nd		1	2	3	3	4	5	5	6	7	7	8	9	9	10	11	11	12
3rd			1	2	2	3	4	4	5	6	6	7	8	8	9	10	10	11
4th				1	1	2	3	3	4	5	5	6	7	7	8	9	9	10
5th					1	1	2	2	3	4	4	5	6	6	7	8	8	9
6th						1	1	1	2	3	3	4	5	5	6	7	7	8
7th							1	1	1	2	2	3	4	4	5	6	6	7
8th								1	1	1	1	2	3	3	4	5	5	6
9th									1	1	1	1	2	2	3	4	4	5
10th										1	1	1	1	1	2	3	3	4
11th											1	1	1	1	1	2	2	3
12th												1	1	1	1	1	1	2
13th													1	1	1	1	1	1
14th														1	1	1	1	1
15th															1	1	1	1
16th																1	1	1
17th																	1	1
18th																		1

WHAT KIND OF SAILING?

For simplicity, the system is worked in multiples of 5, and the following example may help to explain the scheme. Assume three boats in a race with handicaps as follows:

> Boat A   +10
> Boat B   +35
> Boat C   +50

On past form boat C is the fastest (hence the handicap) and, true to form, completes a race in 23 minutes 15 seconds.

The nearest complete number of 5-minute intervals below this elapsed time is $\frac{23}{5}=4$.

The penalties incurred are therefore:

> C   50×4=200 secs.=3 mins. 20 secs.
> B   35×4=140 secs.=2 mins. 20 secs.
> A   10×4= 40 secs.

The actual finishing times (elapsed times) were:

> C=23 mins. 15 secs.
> B=24 mins. 7 secs.
> A=25 mins. 53 secs.

which on corrected time becomes:

> C   23 mins. 15 secs.+3 mins. 20 secs.=26 mins. 35 secs.
> B   24 mins. 7 secs.+2 mins. 20 secs.=26 mins. 27 secs.
> A   25 mins. 53 secs.+0 mins. 40 secs.=26 mins. 33 secs.

Boat B is therefore the winner and receives a handicap of 40 for the next race. This system may not be ideal, but is there any system which can deal fairly in a variety of weathers with a mixture of boats of different lengths, rigs and weights – in fact, designed to meet entirely different performances and conditions?

Cruising

Cruising is a third possibility for a man who is thinking of going afloat. It may mean anything from crawling along the coast in an open boat with camping equipment to crossing the Atlantic. Even a short-distance cruise, however, needs rather more organization than a day race, and consequently calls for more of the owner's spare time. The cruising man has much to learn. He must know the Board of Trade "Traffic" rules as well as the workings of the compass and the methods of determining the boat's position at sea He must use planning and foresight when steering a large boat; dropping and weighing anchor sometimes calls for special skill. The skipper will have to deal with food and freshwater problems, and be able to interpret weather from the forecast and local signs.

If instead of buying a small cabin cruiser or camping boat with a tarpaulin rigged over it for sleeping at night the newcomer prefers to act as crew with someone else, that is all right, too. He will have a good time and perhaps at first not too much responsibility, but he will have to learn very much more seamanship than he would need in his own little craft.

Ocean racing

Here is rough sailing at its best. Ocean racers are built to be driven hard through all weathers into areas where there may be no suitable harbour to run to in bad weather. During an ocean race the boats are often completely alone for days at a time. There is not let-up – it's twenty-four hours a day. Take, for example, the Fastnet, one of the classic ocean races of the world, organized by the Royal Ocean Racing Club. It is sailed over a course of 630 nautical miles from Cowes to the Fastnet Rock (the last you see of Ireland before America appears on the horizon) and back again to Plymouth. In the Fastnet race in 1949 two of the yachts lost their masts soon after the start; on the third day the wind rose to gale force. The yacht Olivier Van Noort broke its rudder; in Golden Dragon the tiller was smashed; Farewell lost a cross-tree; and Gulvain, then an almost brand-new all-metal yacht, broke a forestay support mast close to the Lizard, and might well have been driven ashore on the rocks if the wind had not changed. Twenty

WHAT KIND OF SAILING? 33

boats had to retire. In the 1957 Fastnet, Maze was dismasted, Inschallah's deck-house and ports were stove in and more than half the competitors had to retire.

Ocean racing really began in 1905 when the schooner Atlantic won the race from Sandy Hook to the Lizard in the record time of 12 days, 4 hours 1 minute 19 seconds, competing against five other yachts.

To-day the Atlantic is divided into two bites: the first bite being the Bermuda race of about 635 miles from Brenton Reef off Newport, Rhode Island, to Bermuda; the second leg (if there are enough entries) covers the last 2,800 miles to Plymouth. The Bermuda race, the most cherished of all off-shore races amongst American yachtsmen, and the Transatlantic race (entries permitting) are run every other year, in the non-Fastnet race years. "Down under" there is the famous Sydney to Hobart race over a course of about the same distance as the Fastnet.

But let's face it, you are in for a tough time if you go ocean racing, and you will have to work hard on a boat built for speed rather than comfort. There may be none of the comforts you find in a cruising boat such as a permanent hot-water system, or a refrigerator in which beer and other delicacies are kept cool. An ocean racing boat cannot afford the extra weight or bulk of such luxuries. Even doors in some boats are replaced by canvas curtains in order to save weight. Yet, despite these hardships, ocean racing has a very definite fascination of its own. Nine times out of ten one has to beat not only one's competitors but the weather, and in spite of the long distances covered there are often very close finishes. In 1931, for instance, Captain J. H. Illingworth won the Forsyth Cup for the first home in the Channel Race of 230 miles by 55 seconds. In the same year Patience beat Highland Light in the Fastnet event by about the same difference; and in the 1937 race from St. Nazaire to Benodet, Illingworth's boat Maid of Malham finished only two lengths ahead of Ortac, another famous racing yacht. In the 1950 Transatlantic race Mr.

Adlard Coles' yacht Cohoe was placed first, having won by a margin equivalent to only 2 seconds per mile. When Coles arrived at Plymouth he found that one rival, Samuel Pepys, had come in 4 hours 57 minutes ahead, a difference of 6 seconds a mile. But on handicap Samuel Pepys had to allow Cohoe 8 seconds a mile. So you never quite know in an ocean race who is ahead of you and who is behind. You may even think that you are last and that everyone else is ashore drinking champagne, and then it turns out that yours is the first boat home.

Anyone who wants to take up ocean racing seriously needs to have plenty of free time. In the first place, it is not always easy to know how long the race itself will take, for a course which under one set of weather conditions could be run in four days might, under different circumstances, take nearly a fortnight. Then there must be preparation before the race. The crew must know the way around the ship, and the navigator must study the course and the weather and tide forecasts. Such matters cannot very well be left until you are going up to the start of the race. At the end of the run there are festivities, and these, too, cannot easily be skimped. In most cases the yacht club where the race finishes holds a dance, after which the owner and his crew may well need further time for recovery. Then on the way back you have the same uncertainty about how long the voyage will take. It can be reckoned even that a race of, say, 400 miles to some such place as Santander, in Spain, and the journey back, cannot comfortably be accomplished in less than three weeks. Four is better still.

Of course, there are many shorter trips. Most of the ocean races are slightly over 200 miles, but even so attendance on them soon runs away with the average ration of holiday. The standard of seamanship required for ocean racing is higher than that needed for cruising. Often the crew is picked for special qualifications: one, perhaps, may be a good cook capable of serving up hot meals under any conditions of hard weather; another is an expert radio mechanic or can repair sails, wood or metal. Others can get the boat along exceptionally well, particularly at night. All should be long-sighted, for often a boat's finishing time depends on observing the right buoy at the right moment. The crew must all be practically immune from sea-sickness. This weakness vanishes to some extent with practice. Occasionally, at the beginning of the season, a hard-boiled crew member, of rubbery constitution, will succumb in circumstances he could completely ignore in his second or third race. Acidity and poor elimination are said to be contributory causes, for which the remedy is the traveller's favourite brand of laxative. Lack of exercise, combined with the change of routine and the cramped positions one takes up when bracing oneself against the motion of the ship, seem to slow up the digestive system practically to stopping point. Experts add that warmth and plenty of ventilation help to prevent sea-sickness. Good ventilation depends on the design of the boat; the crew member must take care of the warmth. There are excellent sea-sickness remedies on the market and we advise a thorough testing beforehand to see which of these suits best. We have known cases where one crew member has borrowed another's favourite remedy, with disastrous results. No ocean-racing skipper wants to sail with one of his crew out of commission.

The newcomer will naturally seek to start his ocean racing with an apprenticeship as crew. Once this standard has been reached he may look forward to a good deal of free sailing. In Britain he will probably hope to join the Royal Ocean Racing Club. If he has not already sailed in an ocean race he can join as a provisional member and qualify later for full membership. Like several other clubs, the Royal Ocean Racing Club has, at the time of writing, its own boat Griffin, on which crews can sail for very moderate fees. Arrangements for cruising can often be made through the Little Ship Club or through advertisements in the yachting press.

Enthusiasts in Britain who like ocean racing but have neither the time nor the money for large boats, have now formed a

Junior Off-shore Group of boats of around twenty feet length overall which are too small to be handicapped satisfactorily in Royal Ocean Racing Club events. J.O.G.'s programme consists of races of mainly less than 100 miles in length which can be run during a week-end. The Junior Off-shore Group has strict regulations, to ensure that its boats are seaworthy and stable. Each member of the crew of two or three plays a much greater part in the race than would be the case in a larger boat.

Now we have had a general survey of the advantages and disadvantages of four different approaches to the sport of sailing, and it is time that we looked at some boats.

CHAPTER III

PICKING THE RIGHT BOAT

IT is our opinion that the perfect boat has never been built, since one that is ideal for sailing on Monday may be mulish or awkward on Tuesday under different conditions. We would not expect an Admiralty whaler to go well on a balmy June evening on the upper reaches of the Thames, nor should we expect a Thames "A" rater to excel in rough weather in the Solent.

Quite apart from the weather, the nature of the terrain affects our choice of the ideal boat. For instance, if the boat is to be launched from a suitable jetty or a kindly tideless river bank, it pays to go for a light craft which can easily be loaded on to a trolley and launched from that, or lifted bodily into the water. If, on the other hand, the boat has to be launched from an open beach the construction may have to be heavier and more robust.

The weather conditions which we are likely to encounter will influence not only the shape of the boat and the amount of sail carried, but the type of rig. The international 12-metre "Sharpie" is a good example of what we mean. Here is a boat with a length of 19 ft. 7 in. She is far too heavy to be pulled out of the water in comfort, therefore she has to be kept on moorings. But if Bermudian rig were adopted, the mast would have to be so tall that the Sharpie, being a narrow boat for its length and having no fixed keel, would almost certainly be blown over at moorings through the windage in the rigging, even if there were no sail up. Therefore the mast must be made up of two parts, only the lower of which is kept permanently standing. With only that short stump showing it is perfectly safe to leave the Sharpie on moorings.

Next we have to consider the waters on which the boat is to be sailed. If, for instance, the depth of your channel dries out at low-tide to 3 ft. 6 in., it is unwise to have a boat which draws 5 ft. and which can manœuvre only at certain states of the tide. And if you want to keep a keel boat in a harbour which partly dries out every tide, you will have to choose something with a good strong hull that will settle comfortably on the mud without canting right over. Otherwise your mooring will have to be placed in deep water, giving you a lengthy row to and from the boat at high-tide.

The centre plate does a great deal to solve this kind of difficulty. It is essentially a sheet of wood, metal or plastic material which can be lowered or raised through a slot in the bottom of the boat. It is used instead of a fixed keel. Like a fixed keel, it prevents the boat from skidding sideways. The four-sided well in which the centre board moves up and down prevents the water from the slot flooding the boat.

There are at least four advantages to be gained by using a centre board boat: (i) you get more sailing – you can visit harbours and creeks at all stages of the tide which may be closed to deeper-draught vessels except at high-tide; (ii) you can cheat awkward tides by sailing through the shallows where there is often no tidal current and where you may find a favouring eddy; (iii) your boat can take the mud without canting over on to one side as a keel boat might; (iv) she can more easily be taken out of the water than a fixed keel boat, which may need a special cradle to get it ashore and "legs" to support it when it gets there. You might well ask why, under these conditions, everyone does not go for centre board boats in preference to boats with fixed keels. There has indeed been a recent trend in this direction and some boats have two centre boards, or bilge-boards as it would be more correct to call them, one on each side of the keel. One drawback in the larger boats is that the centre board and its casing take up a good deal of room in the cabin. Some people, too, are influenced by fears of centre board failure. Perhaps the tackle breaks and you cannot get it up, or the slots get blocked and then you cannot let it down. Designers sometimes safeguard themselves by giving their centre board boats a small fixed keel through which the centre board works. Such a boat can be sailed, though not very efficiently, even if the plate "packs up". Even so, the centre plate has the disadvantage that if much strain is put on it water may eventually work in around the casing, in which case the leakage, though small, may be difficult to stop. But these items on the debit side have not stopped successful ocean-racing owners from using centre plate boats in really tough races.

The main object of both keel and centre plate, as already mentioned, is to give the boat a grip of the water and prevent it from slipping sideways. But when the boat is heeled the fixed keel which is made of iron or lead and is far heavier than the centre board exerts an increasingly great leverage towards righting the boat as the angle of heel grows larger. The hull of a flat beamy boat will also counteract the heeling effect of the wind up to a certain critical angle. But once this angle has been passed and the boat is nearly on its side, resistance becomes a minus quantity, for the flat hull has nothing in reserve to stop the wind blowing it right over. Designers say that such boats have good initial stability to distinguish their behaviour from that of fixed-keel boats, whose resistance increases steadily with the angle of heel.

The waves which we are likely to meet with will also affect our choice of boat. Open boats can be sailed for considerable distances at sea, but it is wiser and more comfortable to have some decking to keep water and spray out of the boat. Most small boats sailed in the open sea, therefore, have foredecking as far as the mast, and sidedecking, too, so that even when the boat is heeled over heavily water will not come over the gunwales. Since the war several designers have favoured the idea of producing a small boat which it would be almost impossible to swamp. The decking of the original post-war 14-ft. Merlin class boats made it possible to turn the boat right over on its side in the water with comparatively little risk of filling. The

Yachting World Cadet and the International Five-O-Five are too more generously decked dinghies. But there are some disadvantages too. In the first place, the decking occupies so much space that there is very little room in the well of the boat. Boats designed in this style could hardly be used for anything but racing. They would be no good for family work. One wonders, too, whether it is desirable to encourage helmsmen to buy the kind of boat in which it does not matter if you sail in such a way that the boat capsizes. Perhaps there is something to be said for the kind of boat which teaches you to be more careful. But there is more than one point of view about this.

Now we shall come to the shape of the hull. Here length is an important factor, as the speed of the boat varies in proportion to the length or, to be more exact, to the square root of the length. But breadth or beam in a boat is needed as well as draught for stability. This stability must be sufficient to support the sail area needed to allow the boat to make full use of its length. But again, if we concentrate too much on stability, then the resistance to the boat's movement through the water is likely to be larger. In short, as Lord Dunraven wrote, ". . . a yacht must be broad, narrow, lengthy, short, deep, shallow, tender, stiff. She must be self-contradictory in every part. . . ."

No wonder that yacht designing is a pursuit of absorbing interest.

Cost comes into the picture, too. The modern owner looks for a boat with plenty of accommodation for the money. Without going into too much detail it can be said that this has led modern designers to concentrate on boats of light displacement; that is, boats that are large for their weight.

One of the most remarkable hull developments of this century has led to the arrival of the dinghy or small sailing boat which "planes". A dinghy when travelling sufficiently fast builds up a powerful bow wave. In the case of a modern planing dinghy, the front part of the boat eventually becomes supported out of the water on this bow wave. When this happens the wave-making which normally holds back the boat is enormously reduced, and the speed of the boat is raised perhaps to two-and-a-half times what might otherwise be expected from the length of the boat.

The modern planing dinghy was originally "discovered" by Uffa Fox, perhaps the most famous designer of small boats in the world. Uffa Fox was once an apprentice in a seaplane building firm in the Solent, and his ideas on how small boats could be made to plane came from observations that he had made on the behaviour of wooden seaplane floats. In 1928, when the second race was held for the famous Prince of Wales Trophy for "14-footers", Uffa Fox appeared with his own planing hull boat Avenger, the first of its kind. He won the trophy easily and in this single race rendered old fashioned the boats of nearly all his competitors. Dinghies are almost alone in their ability to plane. Larger boats which are capable of carrying the necessary sails are usually too heavy to lift themselves out of the water on to a plane. The dinghy is unique inasmuch as it carries adjustable ballast in the form of human bodies. Seated in the centre of the boat the helmsman and crew weigh, perhaps, 20 stone, but when sitting outboard on the windward side of the boat the effect of their weight is greatly increased by leverage. Larger boats cannot adjust their ballast in this way; they have to carry it in one place all the time.

But shifting weight is not the only way of getting extra stability. Catamarans, which have become more and more popular in recent years, achieve this in a different way. These craft consist of two hollow floats connected by a bridge deck on which the helmsman and crew sit. Only the floats, not the deck, touch the water. As the floats are unsinkable and are placed six or seven feet apart, the catamaran has tremendous stability without the vast increase in wetted area which you would get in an ordinary boat of the same righting capacity. This allows the catamaran to carry the same area of sail as a bigger boat and to travel very much faster. A good catamaran can easily travel at 20 knots or more under favourable conditions.

Recently, builders have paid a good deal of attention to discovering the best type of construction for sailing boats. Metal craft made of various alloys have appeared. These alloys compare favourably with wood for strength and lasting qualities. The best types resist corrosion and, unlike wood, are not subject to rot. They absorb no water and the weight of the boat is therefore the same at the end of the season as at the beginning. Metal has the further advantage of not "drying out". If a planked wooden boat is left in the sun for some time there are chances of cracks developing, and the wood may alter shape to some extent. Then, when the boat is put back into the water, it will leak until the planks have "taken up" again. A metal boat avoids all troubles of this kind.

Since the war, metal has been used for constructing not only small dinghies such as those kept on a hard or gravelly beach, where there is a good deal of bumping and boring, but also larger boats for day and ocean racing.

Many people, however, do not feel quite as much at home in a metal boat as they do in a wooden one. Perhaps the noise of sea on metal has something to do with it; aided, perhaps, by the feeling that one is entirely dependent on one's buoyancy tanks for keeping afloat in an emergency. Also, it is not quite so easy on a metal boat to make little adjustments here or put in an extra cleat there, in the rather off-hand way one does with wooden boats.

Fibreglass is another material which has become popular since the war. Fibreglass boats are moulded from a mixture of synthetic resins and glass fibres which solidify with the help of a catalyst. They are extremely strong, and a small boat with a skin of only $\frac{1}{16}$ in. thickness can be hit hard with a hammer or run on to a concrete ramp without any apparent damage. Fibreglass, like metal, is impervious to heat and damp. It will not warp or absorb water.

It can be produced either in colour or supplied transparent

for putting over the top of the skylight, as is the practice with cruising boats. In the fibreglass moulding process mats of glass fibre are laid out on a male mould shaped like the inside of the boat. A female mould (slightly larger) is then placed over the glass matting on the male mould, leaving a slight space between the two. The edges of the moulds are sealed and resin is then drawn into the space between them under vacuum and allowed to set. Manufacturers claim that fibreglass boats are cheaper to produce than wooden boats of the same type, but the prospective buyer cannot, of course, save money by building them at home. Also, they are slightly more difficult to work on than wooden boats.

Illogically, perhaps, the wooden boat still remains the favourite. It may need repainting every time you bump into the buoy or the stage. It sometimes cracks and splits, but it is still the most popular material.

Most wooden boats to be seen in British harbours are of plank construction and are built by one of two processes – clinker or carvel. In the first method (clinker construction) each plank in the boat overlaps the other and is joined directly to it with nails. Thus the planks help to support each other and the framework of the boat can be comparatively light and therefore inexpensive. Carvel-built boats, on the other hand, have the planks laid flush and smooth with one another. They are fastened to a more closely spaced and solid framework, which adds to the cost and the weight. Double-skin planking, a variation of the carvel method, is used on some racing boats in Britain. In this process the inner skin is laid diagonally and an outer one, rather thicker, is laid fore and aft with a layer of oiled calico between. The two skins strengthen one another, so that less timber is required and a lighter boat is produced.

Sheet marine plywood made from veneers has become more and more popular in the last few years for use instead of planks for boat building. By joining these sheets together the hull can be formed far more easily than by using individual planks. Many plywood designs are of the hard-chine type, for example, the Hornet, Enterprise, Graduates and International Stars that is, the boat, instead of being gradually rounded at the sides, has a sharp angle or chine where the sides of the boat join the floor. Some boats such as the Enterprise have two chines or angles on each side. They are known as double-chine boats. Hard-chine boats may not be attractive to look at, but some, despite the extra wetted surface which is inevitable, give a good account of themselves in the water and are comparatively easy for amateurs to build. Round-hulled boats can be made of plywood veneer moulded to the correct form, either piecemeal with the aid of glue and small tacks or under pressure. Moulding processes under pressure were successfully developed in the aircraft industry during the war for making the wooden wings of the Mosquito plane. To-day the National Firefly (length 12 ft.) and the Swordfish (length 15 ft.) Class boats are all pressure moulded and so are most of the newer International fourteen ft. Class boats. Moulded boats are sufficiently tough not to need the timbers (ribs) which are used in carvel and clinker boats, and therefore are delightfully easy to keep clean. They absorb little water, so that your racing boat at the end of the season weighs little more than at the beginning; they also stand up very well to extremes of heat in such places as the Persian Gulf, since they do not dry out as a plank boat does.

Before leaving the subject of boats in general it is perhaps desirable to list the main types that one is likely to meet and the way by which they can be identified. The most simply rigged boat seen in British waters is the one with single mast and single sail. The Americans call this a cat-rigged boat. In these boats the sail will most probably be some form of four-sided lugsail. The simplest form of lugsail, when ready for hoisting, is attached to two poles, the larger of which (the boom) is at the lower edge or foot of the sail. The second pole (or yard, as it is called) is attached to the upper edge or head of the sail. The leading edge of the sail between these two poles is known as the luff, and the after (hindmost as the boat travels) edge of the sail between the other ends of the two poles is the leech. When it is desired to hoist the lugsail the yard is attached in the middle to one end of a halyard (the rope which hauls the yard up). This halyard passes through a sheave or pulley

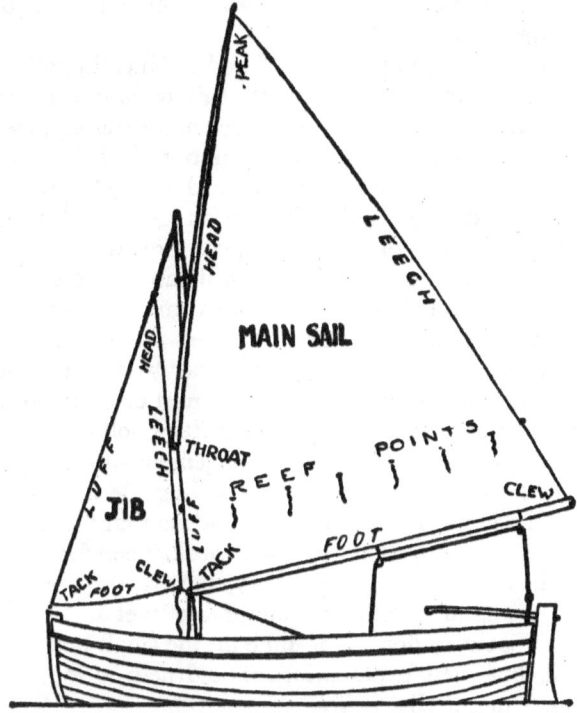

Fig. 1. SAILS OF A DINGHY
Standing lug-sail and jib

in the mast and down to the deck again. When the halyard is pulled, the yard rises till its centre is right up against the mast. In this position, because the luff of the sail is fairly short, one end of the yard inevitably points downward and the other, to which the peak of the sail is attached, necessarily points almost vertically upwards. Balance lugsails carry the tack (lower front corner) of the sail forward of the mast. Standing lugsails carry the tack abaft (behind) the mast.

The upper front corner of the sail, the one between the luff and the head, is known as the throat and the lower aft corner (hind) is the clew.

As we have seen, both standing and balance lugsails have the throat and part of the head of the sail forward of the mast, an arrangement which is not very efficient for sailing to windward. An improved performance is obtained with a gunter yard. This gunter is rather like the yard we have previously discussed, but its lower end is fitted with jaws which slide up the mast so that none of the sail projects forward of the mast.

The Bermudian rig is, however, still more efficient when sailing to windward than the gunter. In this case the sail, instead of having four edges, has but three; and the luff of the sail is attached directly to the mast, either by means of slides which run in a metal track fixed to the mast or by the rope to which the luff of the sail is sown which fits a hollow groove in the mast – a simpler and better arrangement unless the sails are normally left on the boom after sailing. Bermudian sails are tall and narrow, for it has been found that sails with a long leading edge are better for windward work. Therefore, to prevent the boat from being top-heavy, light hollow masts are used, sometimes of wood and sometimes of metal.

We have spent rather a long time on the small boat and its single sail, but these explanations should help to explain the larger boats more fully.

Moving on from the single-sail boat, we have first the sloop. This has a single mast and a single three-cornered foresail, commonly called a jib. With the wind split up over two sails it is possible to control the boat more easily. The boat has a better-balanced sail area. Frequently in a single-sail boat the mast has to be stepped fairly far forward if the sail is to draw at its best when going to windward. The result is that when

PICKING THE RIGHT BOAT 47

running before the wind the nose of the boat is pressed down on to the water, which slows progress and may even be dangerous.

Going one step further, we have the cutter which has a mainsail and two headsails; that is, a jib and a staysail, the latter so called because it is attached to the main forestay (wire rigging which is the forward support of the main mast). Because of this extra foresail the mast of the cutter is placed farther aft than that of the sloop; the staying is easier and more convenient to handle in heavy weather.

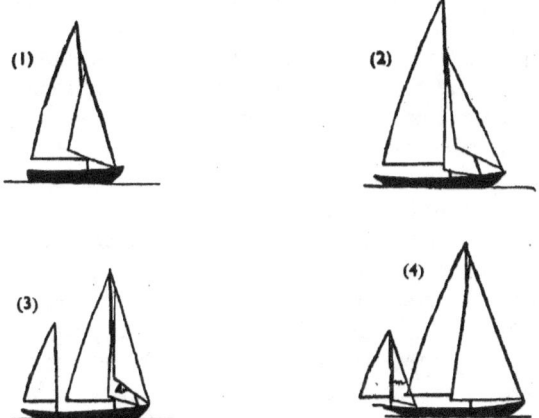

Fig. 2. (1) SLOOP. (2) CUTTER. (3) KETCH. (4) YAWL

Some cutters and sloops, particularly the older ones, are gaff-rigged. They have a four-sided mainsail, the head of which is attached to a gaff standing back at an angle of about 45 degrees from the mast. This is easily handled and good for running but, like the lug, not so efficient to windward.

Next we come to boats with two or more masts. Again, the job of the extra mast is to split up the sail area and so make the boat more easily manageable. Both yawls and ketches have their smaller mast, namely the mizzen, stepped abaft the main mast. A ketch's mizzen mast is forward of the rudder post, whereas in the yawl the mizzen is abaft the rudder post.

In the ketch the mizzen replaces the mainsail to some extent, so that the latter is more easily handled. In the yawl the mizzen is smaller, but can be useful in holding the boat's head to windward when required.

The schooner, not so often seen on the western side of the Atlantic, has also two masts, but with the smaller in front.

Boat owners, methodical as a class, are surprisingly casual about the way they describe the size of their craft. They use at least three different scales of measurement, generally without saying which is intended. They will tell you, perhaps, that a certain yacht is a 10-tonner. This could mean that when put in the water she displaces 10 tons of water; or it could mean that the yacht's net registered tonnage is ten, in which case the "tons" have been calculated by the Board of Trade to give an idea of the boat's carrying capacity after deducting the space given to stores and crew. Finally, there is tonnage T.M.; that is, Thames Measurement. This is a very vague figure indeed. It is got by subtracting the breadth of the boat from the length, multiplying the result by the breadth, and the result of that by half the breadth divided by 94. For the purposes of the T.M., the length means the length on deck and not the length on the waterline, which may be very much less. The T.M. system also takes no account of whether a boat is a frail, shallow craft floating on top of the water or a deep-chested weight-carrier of double the capacity. All the same, most people, when they say their yacht is a 10-tonner, mean T.M.

Sometimes people are equally casual when describing the length of their boat. In the case of small racing boats where the length overall is limited under class rules, the overall and load waterline length are usually the same, since for speed purposes it is best to have as long a waterline length as possible. But some racers and many large cruisers are not limited in the same way, and are designed with long overhangs which help to give the yacht increased buoyancy in a sea-way. The result is that a boat's overall length may be much greater than its waterline length. But we are not buying the boat just yet, and we may as well leave such matters of detail until we have reached that stage.

Now it is time to go sailing.

CHAPTER IV

GOING AFLOAT

THERE are different opinions about the best way of learning sailing. Some people hold that it is absolutely essential to put in some time as a crew before taking the helm yourself, others say that such advice is all nonsense and that is is far better to take the helm yourself from the start. Some helmsmen believe in books, others say that books can no more teach you to sail than they can to ride a bicycle. One school will tell you that it is far easier to learn sailing in a good medium-sized boat which gives plenty of warning of what it is going to do rather than in a small dinghy which turns and pirouettes so quickly that you cannot see what is going to happen next. Others disagree.

So let us examine these points one by one, beginning first with the question of size.

We personally believe that the arguments for starting with a small boat carry the day.

It is perfectly true that the helmsman of a small boat, particularly a small day boat, has to think more quickly than if he were sailing in a larger craft, since small boats allow but small liberties. For instance, we have known people capsize a small boat at mooring, before even the sails were up, through injudiciously stepping on to the foredeck of the boat. The extra weight forward hoisted the boat's broad stern out of the water so that she was balancing on her thin V-shaped nose, and that was too precarious. We have also seen people tip into the water when getting into a small boat because they stepped on the gunwale instead of placing their weight amidships. Certainly there are limitations to the treatment that the small boat will accept, but on the whole our advice would be to pick a 10-footer and go for one's trial trips in this rather than in something larger. The larger fixed keel boat may give you longer warning of what is going to happen than you get in a light dinghy, but can the average novice be expected to see the warning? Personally, we would not expect him to sense at once that the boat is in danger, that in certain circumstances the tide is likely to set him aground on a sand spit if he does not go about at once, or that he must alter course if he is avoid another yacht which has the right of way. Larger boats are sluggish in their actions, and once a mistake has been made it may be difficult to correct it in time. Whereas in a small boat it is a matter of a moment to alter course to avoid a collision, and if damage is done it is likely to be on a small scale.

So when the newcomer approaches the jetty for the first time we hope that it will be to enter a small boat of *moderate canvas*. We emphasize this, because even a small 12-ft. boat carrying 90 square feet of sail can be a handful to manage in anything but a light breeze. We would suggest beginning with something nearer 60 square feet for that size of boat, unless the water is very sheltered. Figure 3 illustrates the general construction of a small dinghy; figure 4 of a cutter.

The reader has by now probably wondered whether it would be better for him to take his first trip by himself or employ the services of a friend or boatman to go with him, or set out as someone else's crew. Our own opinion is that, provided the weather is suitable and provided that he will be within sight of watchful eyes on the shore, he should set out alone. By sailing the boat himself he may make some mistakes, but he will also learn quickly and gain confidence in a short time. If he takes a friend a stream of well-meant advice will only rob him of confidence in his own judgment.

No serious misfortune is likely to happen if he masters the theory of sailing first, and memorizes a few elementary precautions. From which it can be concluded that though you may not be able to learn to sail by correspondence course, you can learn how not to. Many small boats, particularly if they are raced, are fitted with wooden, metal or rubber buoyancy tanks, which are designed to keep the boat and the crew afloat even when it has been filled up with water. Small boats, such as the 12-ft. National class and the 12-ft. National Firefly class, have to undergo a buoyancy test once each season.

For this test one stands on the jetty and endeavours to fill the boat with water and to deposit in the boat iron weights

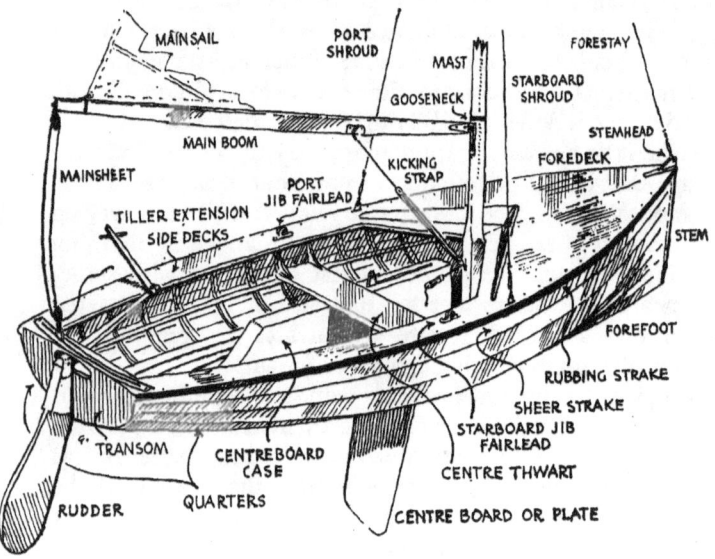

Fig. 3. Parts of a dinghy

totalling well over 200 lb. The boat, filled with water and these weights, is supposed to float for at least half an hour. There is a knack, by the way, about doing this test. To swamp the boat with water you tip the boat on to its side; therefore it is no good putting in the weights first. Why? Because if you did,

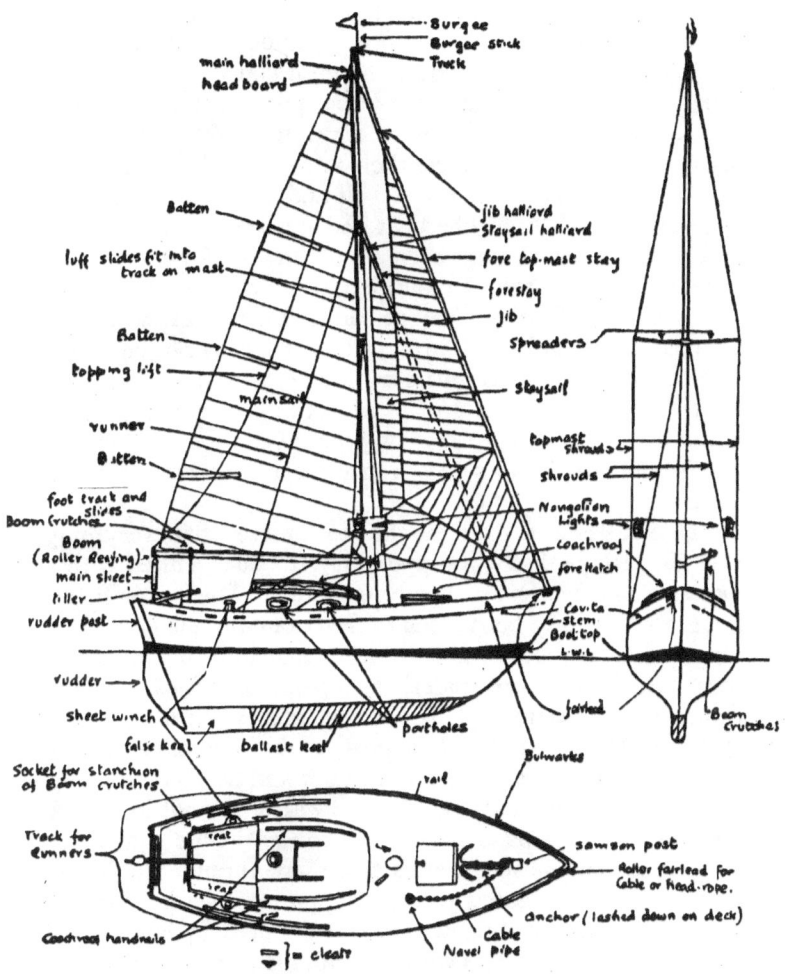

Fig. 4. PARTS OF A CUTTER
including standing and running rigging

when you turned the boat on its side to flood it, the weights would slip away from their proper positions and damage the inside of the hull. On the other hand, if you were to start the other way round and fill the boat with water, then when you stepped into the boat to deposit the iron weights the chances are that you, the weights and the boat would submerge *en bloc*. You therefore have a kind of half-and-half arrangement in which you partially fill the boat and then put in the weights, and finally, when this has been done, the rest of the water can come in over the stern. In addition, in a small broad-beamed sailing dinghy of the type which can be hired it is necessary to see that she is fairly leak-proof, which she may not be at the beginning of the season unless she has been soaked in water to allow the planks to take up. For extra confidence you can take with you one or two rubber bags or inner tubes, if you can find secure positions low down in the boat in which to instal them.

The first step is to examine the gear and see that everything is in good shape. We will suppose that the boat is fitted with a lugsail which works as already explained. The sail will, we hope, already have been laced to the boom and the yard. The after end of the boom when sailing is controlled by the mainsheet (originally called mainsheet rope), which usually passes through a block (pulley) or series of blocks attached to the transom (blunt after end of the boat) to the hand of the helmsman. The sheet must be free to run out and not in a tangle at the bottom of the boat. Coil it clockwise when not in use. A figure 8 knot (see page 70) should be tied in the end of the mainsheet to make sure it does not escape through the block. The mast of the boat is possibly supported by wire stays or shrouds, secured at the lower end of the deck by lanyards of Hambro line (cord). It is worth examining this to see that it is in good condition.

You will probably need to carry down (in addition to the oars and rowlocks) a tiller, rudder, an anchor and line, and the sail. The mast will probably have already been stepped (set in the boat), but if not you will need that, too. When the mast is set up the shrouds (stays) should be reasonably tight, but not bar tight. When pulled they should give out a deep rumbling sound rather like one of the lowest strings on a double bass.

Let us assume that all is now in order with the 10-ft. boat you have hired. (We advise hiring for a start because you may soon be graduating to something with more sail area.) Haul the boat down to the water's edge and turn her so that the bow faces directly into the wind. By doing this you will make sure that when the sail is hoisted it stays under control instead of catching the wind and straining the mast. For the purpose of giving you an easy sail we will assume that the wind is blowing off the land at an angle of 45 degrees (half a right-angle) to the line of the shore. If placed head to wind the boat will therefore have her stern and part of one side close to the water. We are now almost ready to go. The halyard must first be fixed to the yard at a point which experience shows will make the sail set properly. Possibly the yard will have a loop already fixed on it at the right spot. After hoisting the sail it will be necessary to secure the forward end of the boom, so that the luff (front edge) is properly stretched up and down and so that the boom stays close to the mast. There are several ways of doing this, the gear differing from boat to boat. A moment's examination will show you which system applies to your case.

While still ashore it is essential to make sure that the plug or drain is securely fitted into the bottom of the boat. In small boats the plug is often removed after each sail, either in order to drain out the spray or to prevent her being borrowed by small boys. It is fatal to set out without the plug. It can happen far more easily than you think, particularly if the draining holes are fitted in the transom, in which case the water will not begin to enter the boat at once.

The boat can now be hauled stern first across the water's edge and if there is enough depth the rudder can be shipped. The next thing is to check that the centre board can be lowered when you are afloat and have sufficient depth of water. On some boats the centre board is raised or lowered by means of a rope hoist and pulleys; on others it may be a wire hoist running round a drum. Other centre boards are raised or lowered simply by means of a metal bar fitted with teeth or notches rather like the teeth of a saw, which engage in the required position with a rod fitted across the top of the centre plate case. Still another type of centre board is kept in position by a friction pad. When small boats are ashore the weight of the centre plate is often taken on a pin which passes from one side of the centre board casing through the plate itself and out through the other side of the casing. This pin will have to be removed before leaving shore.

We have decided that the wind is blowing half off shore. Let us assume that as you face the land with your back to the water it is coming from a half-left direction, so that if the shore runs east-west the wind is from the north-west. To go afloat we pull the boat, stern first, in a south-east direction, and after making certain that the mainsheet is free to run out, we push the boat into the water and step aboard. The wind should then push the boat gently away from the shore, and we use this moment to ship the rudder if it has not already been done. Until the rudder has been put on and some centre plate lowered – we shall need the plate about half down for the course we are going to sail – the boat is not really under control, and if, therefore, there are any other boats moored nearby it might be better to begin instead by rowing the boat out to a mooring and making (hoisting) sail only when you get there. This may also be a good idea when sailing off a lee shore (shore on to which the wind is blowing). It will, of course, be necessary for the boat to be fitted with a good strong painter (rope attached to the stem of the boat for towing or mooring purposes). When approaching the mooring, do so against the tide, since otherwise the current will tend to sweep the boat across to the opposite side of the mooring. When you have got hold of the mooring in your hand, pass the painter through the loop

GOING AFLOAT 57

of the mooring and let out enough rope to ensure that the boat is not pinned by the nose before making fast the end to a cleat (peg) on the boat. You will thus be able to slip your mooring by remote control from the boat itself.

A word of warning is necessary here about making sail when at moorings when the wind is blowing in the opposite direction to the tide, or across the tide. Let us consider what would happen if we were unwise enough to hoist the mainsail of a boat under these conditions. The boat would originally be down tide from the mooring with her bow facing the tide. But with the hoisting of the sail the wind, coming from astern, will start her sailing and she will move up against the tide until jerked around head to wind by her mooring. Then, with the wind out of the sails, the tide will start to carry her down again to her original position, and she would begin all over again careering around violently with damage, perhaps, to herself and other nearby craft. When getting under way in these circumstances the skipper should use only a small jib, which is not let draw until he is ready to cast off the mooring. Then after the boat has been got under way she is rounded up into the wind and the mainsail hoisted. For safety, this procedure is used whenever the wind is not definitely forward of the beam (a line drawn across the boat at its broadest point).

With a small boat we need not face all these complications. The hull of the boat is flattish underneath, and when the centre board is up offers little resistance to the tide. Therefore the boat, if left to herself, when the sails are hoisted will usually face into the wind of her own accord no matter which way the tide flows. Then as soon as the mooring has been slipped, the centre board can be lowered and the boat sailed away under full control. Alternatively, if the tide and wind are opposed and the tide is very strong and the wind light, it is often possible to secure the boat to the mooring stern first to the tide with the bow pointing into the wind. In this position the tide will hold the boat safely head to wind so that she does not start sailing. The centre board in this instance should be lowered while still on the mooring in order to get the maximum effect from the tide.

Well, one gets to the stage where the boat is drifting gently off shore and you have fitted the rudder and tiller and have let down some centre plate. The gear will be neatly stowed in the bottom of the boat and the rowlocks removed from the gunwale. They should not be seen when sailing. They look slovenly and might even lead to a snarl-up if a rope got caught up on them.

The easiest point of sailing will be at about right-angles to the wind; that is to say, in this case towards the south-west (See fig. 5).

Having moved off with the sail to the port side of the boat, you will be sitting on the starboard half of the boat and on the windward side of it. As the wind is coming over the starboard side of the boat you are said to be on the starboard tack. It is important to remember whether you are on the port or starboard tack, as in certain circumstances it may decide whether you have the right of way over another boat or whether she has the right of way over you. For the time being, however, disregard the rules of traffic and concentrate on avoiding the various bits of still life in the form of boats moored nearby. If you have the choice of going either side of a moored vessel, it is better to choose the down-tide side which, in a moored keel vessel, would normally be the stern. If you go up-tide from the vessel there is always the chance that the wind will drop or the tide will be stronger than you think and you will be swept against the boat or its cable with disastrous results. Be careful, too, when passing to windward of a moored vessel, for if you are too close you may meet a sudden gust of wind and may not have enough room to spill it by letting out the boom. Nothing is more humiliating than to find yourself pinned up against the side of someone else's yacht and held there by the wind. After this happens you are likely to find your boat streaked with paint of an entirely different colour and the air will probably be streaked with the language from the owner of the other yacht.

Many owners have a habit of leaving their dinghy on a mooring with a good deal of scope, and it's easy to overlook this when passing between the mooring and a dinghy which is

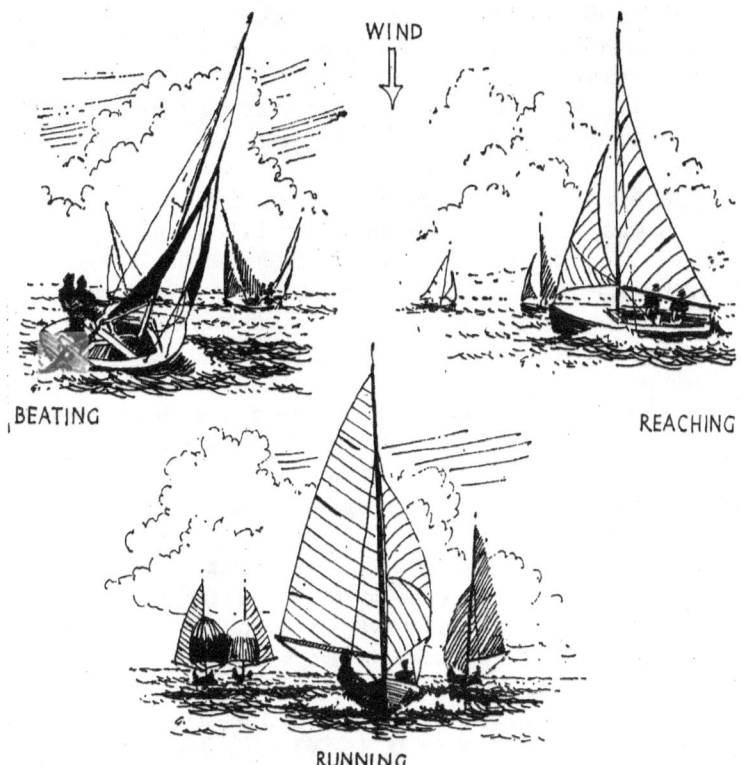

Fig. 5. BEATING, REACHING, RUNNING

attached to it. If this happens you may find that the mooring rope gets caught under your centre plate, and that if you lift the centre plate the same infernal rope will get caught round your rudder. Some rudders are of the lifting type which allows the blade of the rudder to be drawn up, but if yours is a fixed rudder you may have to do some fast work to get free. The quickest way may be to take the rudder off for the moment, but it is very much better not to get into such a jam at all.

When passing to leeward (down wind) of a moored boat or a tall building, beware of the area which is sheltered from the wind. If you are sitting on the gunwale, be prepared to move to the centre of the boat; otherwise when the wind is cut off, your boat, which has probably been heeling over, will suddenly come upright and with your weight on the gunwale it may even capsize to windward.

Let us suppose, however, that you meet with none of these difficulties, and that you are continuing on your south-westerly course. With the wind coming directly across the boat, or on the beam as we say, you are on a reach. If you were pointing a little closer to the wind (that is, a little south of a westerly course) you would be on a close reach. If you were sailing a little south of south-west with the wind abaft the beam, you would be on a broad reach. But, as already explained, you are going south-west and, after a few more minutes of this course, you should be quite a nice distance off shore. In fact, if you are in an estuary you might be approaching the opposite shore too close for your liking.

What do we do next? The answer is that we try to point nearer the wind. In order to do this we put the tiller "down" (that is, down wind and towards the sail). This turns the rudder blade to starboard and brings the boat's nose round also to starboard. Only a little bit of helm is needed, not too much. At the same time pull in the sail, which has probably been at an angle of about 45 degrees to the fore and aft line of the boat, till it is "close hauled" almost over the horse or metal bar above the transom. If you've judged things right the boat will now be sailing on the wind, i.e. as near as possible to the direction of the wind, and you will be doing what is known as a beat. This should be almost parallel to the shore. Even when travelling in open water the helmsman may find that the wind varies a good deal in strength, lightening at one moment and blowing a gust at another. During the gusts the wind will cause the boat to heel. This may look fine in pictures, but it slows up the boat for several reasons. To begin with, hulls on most small boats are designed to sail best when they are upright. If they are tilted, their under-water shape is uneven, and the boat, besides sailing slower, sails crooked and turns to one side. This in turn has to be corrected by the rudder, which acts as an additional brake. As if this were not bad enough, the boat when tilted shows less sail for the wind to act on, and the centre board, being tilted, is less efficient, so that the boat is blown to leeward off its proper course. For these reasons it is well worth trying to sail the boat "on her feet". In a small dinghy, heeling can be corrected in several ways. To begin with, the helmsman and crew can lean to windward over the side of the boat so that their weight acts as a lever in keeping the boat upright. The second method is to put the helm down (down wind) slightly, so that the boat luffs up (turns into the wind). This has the effect of presenting a smaller area of sail to the wind. The third way is for the helmsman to release some mainsheet so that the sail is not completely close hauled. This is probably the best way of correcting things. It is quicker in its effect than any leaning-out action that the helmsman can take, and it also avoids using rudder and so slowing the boat up.

If you try to point too close to the wind, closer than a half-right-angle for instance, the wind will merely slide across the surface of the sail without pushing the boat ahead. In fact, the boat will begin to drift backwards in what is called a stern board. When this happens the tiller works in reverse. Thus, to get the boat's head to port, you will have to move the tiller to port.

Sailing too close to the wind is known as "pinching".

Now, sooner or later, you have to get back to your point of departure, and it should be clear that there are two ways of getting home. One is to turn to starboard (that is, into the wind), so that the bow faces the direction of the wind. The other way would be to turn to port, so that the turn is made stern first to the wind. Consider the head-to-wind method first. It is easy to get round, but not so easy to do this turn perfectly without losing any speed. Begin by remembering that the boat, even close hauled, will not sail much nearer the wind than a half right-angle. You have to turn the boat through this half right-angle and then through another half right-angle, until it is about 45 degrees off the wind, but with the wind on the other side of the boat. In the example chosen, at the end of the manœuvre the boat should be travelling approximately north instead of west. It is important to know just where the wind is blowing, and as a rough guide it is usual to have a burgee or flag at the masthead.

Having decided when to go about (or tack, as it is called), the area being free from hazards such as pleasure launches and large waves, put the tiller down firmly but not too sharply. The rudder acts as a brake, and if it is harshly applied the boat might come to a stop and you would then find yourself in irons, pointing head to wind and unable to sail forward in any direction. You would then have to make a stern board. This is a clumsy and perhaps a risky way of going about, since the boat will be almost stationary during the manœuvre and therefore at the mercy of any really strong gust. But if, on this first tack of yours, everything goes well, the following will happen – as you put the tiller down gently the boat will turn to starboard and the mainsail will start flapping, as it always will when the boat is head to wind. As the boat continues to sail round she will pass the eye of the wind, which will then begin to blow on her port side instead of as formerly on her starboard side. As soon as this happens the block of the mainsheet will move across from the port side of the horse or similar contrivance on the transom to the starboard side. The helm should then be centralized and the boat got off as quickly as possible on the new tack. Meanwhile, the helmsman himself will not have been idle. As the boat begins to turn he moves to the centre of

GOING AFLOAT 63

the dinghy, so that as soon as the boat is on its new tack he can take up his new station on the port gunwale. The mainsheet should, generally speaking, be kept sheeted hard in during the manœuvre. Going about from port on to starboard tack is exactly the same in reverse.

It will be seen that a great deal of the trick consists of estimating how close to the wind you can sail and still have enough way on to get the boat round smoothly. The exact drill for the helmsman when going about varies from boat to boat. Large boats carry more way and need more space to go about smoothly than small craft. In most small boats the helmsman will have to face aft in order to make the most of the rather limited space between the boom, the tiller and the mast.

Now that you have got round to windward and are sailing back towards the shore, let us see what might have happened if you had turned round the other way. In this case, you remember, the boat turns round stern to wind instead of head to wind, and you were going to turn to port from your westerly course back to south-west and then to south, next to south-east and finally to east. For this manœuvre, called gybing, you will begin by putting the helm up (up wind; that is, towards you) instead of the opposite way, as you did when tacking. At the same time you gradually let out the sail, so that finally the boat is sailing a course somewhere between south and south-east. Keep it this way for a little before executing the actual turn or gybe. On your present course you are running before the wind. If you were racing, you would probably have the centre board almost right up (as opposed to half-way up on a reach and fully down on a beat). When the moment comes to gybe, the plate may be lowered about one-third. If it were right up the rudder would be of no benefit, and if it were right down there is a tendency for the boat to run up into the wind again, an event which you do not wish to happen, unless you are rounding a leeward buoy. Some experts gybe with the plate up on the theory that if the plate is up the boat will heel less. But a good deal depends on the type of boat you are sailing. Personally to start with I prefer same plate down.

When gybing a large boat, the mainsail is usually pulled in at least half-way before the gybe is executed, so that when the boom and the sail fly across the shock is taken by the mainsheet and not by the shrouds (stays supporting the mast). On a small dinghy, however, this precaution is unnecessary and even unwise in any weight of wind, for small boats cannot take big shocks of any kind. The technique is to wait until the boat is almost directly before the wind and then put the helm up a little bit more, at the same time assisting the boom and sail across at the critical moment. Let the sail go out to the FULL EXTENT REQUIRED FOR THE NEXT COURSE. Do not check it more than is absolutely necessary. Quite a small alteration of course will induce a gybe when running. The sail and boom will then travel across the boat from the port to starboard side, leaving you on the port gybe.

When running before the wind care is needed to avoid an involuntary gybe, which can happen, if the wind eddies round behind the sail, through a slight change of wind or an unnoticed change of course. In a large boat the weight of the boom and sail coming across suddenly in an unrehearsed gybe might carry away the shrouds and even break the mast. If an involuntary gybe occurs in a small boat when the helmsman is half-asleep, his next sensation will be that the water is very cold! But he may be able to correct it in time by putting the helm hard down and shifting his weight.

Suppose you are now returning to the starting-point. How is this done? The first step will be to come off the run on to a reach by putting the helm down slightly and pulling the mainsheet in, so that the sail continues to feel the full effect of the wind. (If this is not done the wind will pass straight across the sail and its effect be wasted.) On a reach in this case you will then be sailing in something like a north-easterly direction. As you near land you go about, so that the wind is once more on your starboard bow and you are travelling more or less parallel with the shore. When you have almost reached the starting-point, the helm is put down again and the boat's nose turns into the wind (which puts the brake on), so that she grounds gently with her sails under control. The centre plate should be raised at the first warning crunch underneath the boat. We have assumed that there is enough water for the rudder not to catch before the boat reaches shore. If not, it should be removed in good time and the boat steered in with the rudder loose. As soon as the boat grounds, the helmsman should get ashore and drag the boat out of the water, head to wind; otherwise under certain conditions the tide will turn her round and she will try to start sailing again.

Of course, if the wind had been blowing *on* to the shore instead of half off it, you would have followed a different procedure, for it would never do to run head on to the shore with full sail up. One way of dealing with the situation would be to round up into the wind while still some distance from shore, take down the sail and row in. Another way, requiring slightly more finesse, is to half lower the sail and let the wind do the rest. This technique is by no means fool-proof, especially if you get an unexpected gust of wind just as you are reaching the shore. A friend, who is an expert helmsman, was coming in under just these conditions with only a little sail hoisted, when a gust blew and sent her boat charging towards the shore at the same moment as another boat swung its bow around into the wind. The result was a six-inch hole through our friend's boat. On some days the force of the wind in the rigging is enough to blow a boat home without any sail showing at all.

Before closing this chapter let us list seven golden rules to be followed before going afloat:

1. Pick a day when the shipping forecast gives nothing stronger than light to moderate winds. Fresh winds will probably be too fresh for the first day's sail.
2. Wear a buoyancy jacket, which in many cases can be bought from the Government disposal surplus stores.

3. Do not wear full-length Wellington boots, which in a capsize would fill with water and prevent you from swimming. Ankle-length ones are all right provided they can be kicked off easily.
4. Crêpe rubber shoes slip and are therefore dangerous on wet decks. Wear natural rubber.
5. While still on dry land examine ropes, rigging, etc.
6. Check all gear aboard before going afloat. Rowlocks should be secured with a line in some way so that they do not fall into the bottom of the boat. The bailer should also be made fast to the thwart (cross bench) of the boat or some other suitable fixture, so that it does not fall out in a capsize – when you need it most.
7. Carry a stainless steel knife on a cord or lanyard on your belt. People have been known to get an ankle caught in a coil of mainsheet, from which only a sharp knife can rescue them. The best knives have at one end a spike which can be used for loosening stiff shackle pins. (A shackle is a link, one end of which is opened or closed by a screw pin.)

[Photo: G. L. W. Oppenheim, Amsterdam

11. A Five-O-Five planing with the trapeze in use

[Photo: Beken & S

III. Black Soo, a modern hard-chine design ocean racer with a fin-keel

CHAPTER V

KNOTS AND OTHER NOTIONS

WORKS of several hundred pages have been written on how to tie knots. They include recipes for complicated fuddles such as the wall knot, the double wall knot, the crown knot, the Matthew Walker and the Turk's Head, whose purposes are quite as much ornamental as useful. And it may be just as unwise to clutter up the mind with knowledge of useless knots as it is to put too much useless clobber into the boat.

Let us favour simplicity and a few trusted knots which will not give even under strain, but which are easily untied in a hurry. Each of them should be learnt by heart so that they can be tied, if necessary, when half-asleep – as one very often will be when turned out on deck on a pitch-black night from one's bunk in order to deal with an emergency.

Hilaire Belloc once defied anyone to describe a simple knot, such as a clove hitch, without the aid of illustrations. We do not intend to take up his challenge, but will content ourselves with describing the purposes of the most useful knots rather than the way they are tied.

ESSENTIAL KNOTS

1. *Reef knot.* The reef knot is used especially for tying reefs in sails (let us discuss this later), but also for joining any two ropes of equal thickness. For rapid untying, make it up as shown in the second illustration. (Figs. 6 and 7.)

2. *Double bend.* This is for joining ropes of different thickness. (Fig. 8.)

3. *Bowline.* The bowline forms the end of a rope into a guaranteed non-slip loop. By tying a bowline round someone in the water you can hoist him aboard, or you can moor a

Fig. 6. Reef knot

Fig. 8. Double bend

For joining ropes of different thickness; the double turn should be taken with the smaller rope

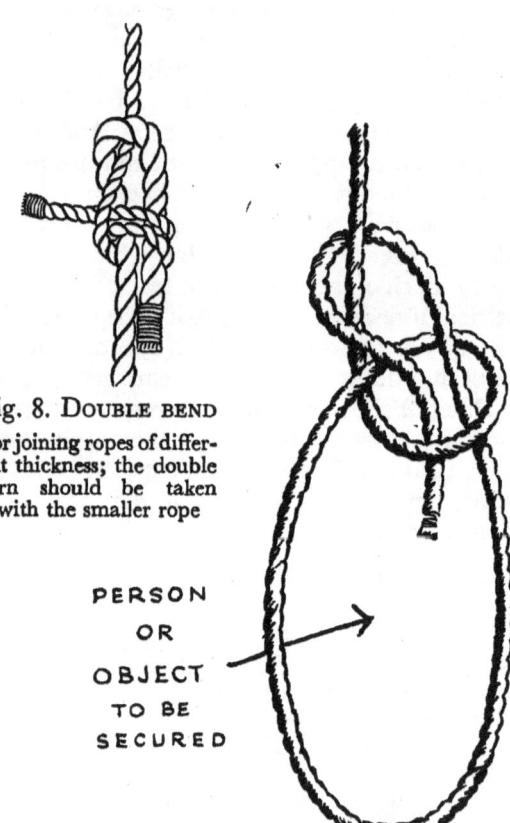

Fig. 7. Reef knot for rapid untying

PERSON OR OBJECT TO BE SECURED

Fig. 9. Bowline

boat with just the amount of scope that you want by making a loop of the right size round the mooring ring. (Fig. 9.)

4. *Clove hitch and rolling hitch.* These two knots, which are very much alike, are used for much the same purposes. With the clove hitch you can secure a rope to a pole and

Fig. 10. CLOVE HITCH

Fig. 11. ROLLING HITCH
Main strain is expected in the direction of arrow

be sure that the rope will not come off. A rolling hitch, which is a clove hitch with an extra turn, gives more confidence still. For instance, if the yard of your lugsail has not already got a special attachment for the halyard, you can use a rolling hitch with the certainty that the halyard will not slip up or down the yard. (Figs. 10 and 11.)

Fig. 12. SHEET BEND

5. *Sheet bend.* Used for attaching the sheet to the clew of sails; gives quicker release than when using a shackle. (Fig. 12.)

6. *Topsail sheet bend.* A firmer edition of the foregoing. (Fig. 13.)

7. *Figure of eight knot.* Used to prevent a rope running out through a block or fair-lead, as in the case of the main and jibsheets. (Fig. 14.)

8. *Slippery hitch.* This is a useful quick-release knot. (Fig. 15.)

Fig. 13. TOPSAIL
SHEET BEND

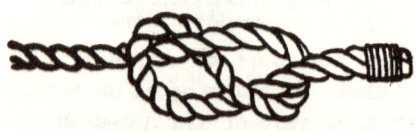

Fig. 14. FIGURE OF EIGHT KNOT
used to prevent mainsheet end from running
out through block

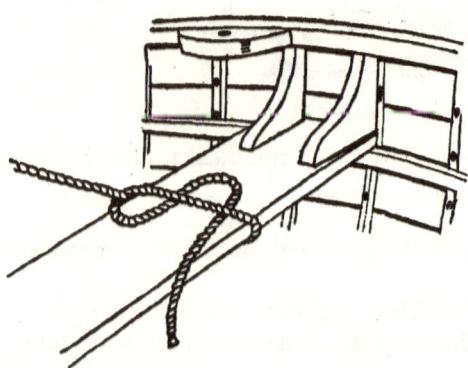

Fig. 15. A SLIPPERY HITCH
made on the thwart of a dinghy

Fig. 15a.
SLIPPERY HITCH
FOR HALYARD

KNOTS AND OTHER NOTIONS

NOT SO ESSENTIAL

1. *Fisherman's bend.* Used for attaching a rope to a mooring ring or anchor. A safe and simple knot, as the rope is double at the spot where it gets most strain. (Fig. 16.)

2. *Bowline on a bight.* An unconscious man can be safely slung on this knot, or you can hoist someone up the mast in it.

3. *Topsail halyard bend.* This can be used instead of a rolling hitch for attaching a halyard to a yard.

Fig. 16. FISHERMAN'S BEND

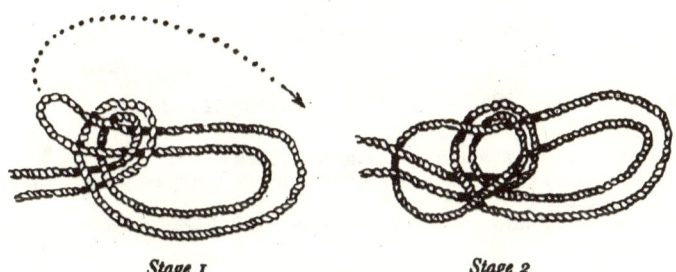

Stage 1   *Stage 2*

Fig. 17. BOWLINE ON A BIGHT

Fig. 18. TOPSAIL HALYARD BEND
for attaching halyard to yard

So much for the knots.

Every piece of rope that is cut needs to be whipped in order to stop it unravelling. There are several ways of whipping, but the two best known are those illustrated.

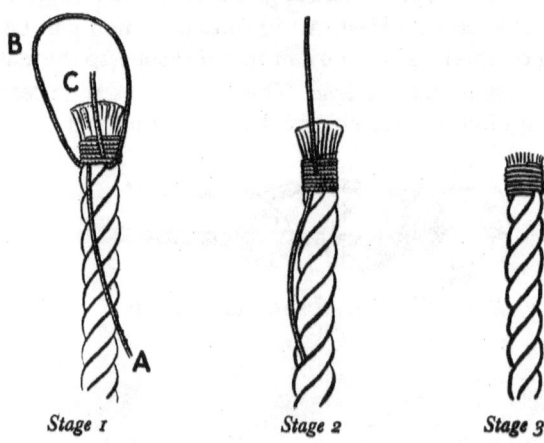

Fig. 19A. WHIPPING THE END OF A ROPE

(a) Cut off about 1 ft. of whipping twine
(b) Lay one end A along the rope and wind back over it
(c) Make a loop B and insert the other end of the whipping twine C under the last turn
(d) Continue winding the loop B round the rope till secure (stage 2)
(e) Trim up (stage 3)

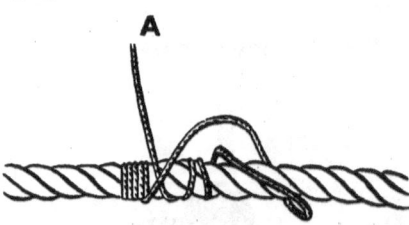

Fig. 19B. WHIPPING ROPE IN MIDDLE (WHERE AS OFTEN HAPPENS, TWINE CANNOT BE PASSED OVER ROPE'S END)

After securing one end of twine (not shown) by winding round it as in previous operation continue winding loosely. Tuck in end A and tighten up loops

KNOTS AND OTHER NOTIONS 73

The quickest piece of whipping I ever saw was carried out by an engineer friend who carries about a small contrivance favoured by electricians for putting rubber collars over the end of cables. Using this he is able to whip a rope's end in three seconds flat; it lasts perfectly. Small nylon ropes can be melted and fused by holding over a lighted match. Splicing – joining two ropes together without making a knot – may have to be done. Illustrations show short splice and an eye splice. We have purposely omitted the long splice, which is less useful than commonly believed; and remember no splice is worth doing if the rope can be joined in any other way or, better still, replaced with new. (See figs. 20 and 21.)

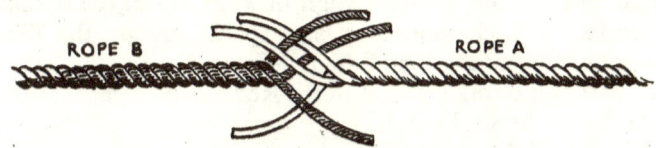

Fig. 20. SHORT SPLICE

(1) Unlay strands for distance equal to twice circumference of rope
(2) Pass each strand A against the lay (as with eye-splice) over one strand and under the next strand of B. Repeat the process with rope B
(3) Remove some of the inner yarn of each strand and repeat

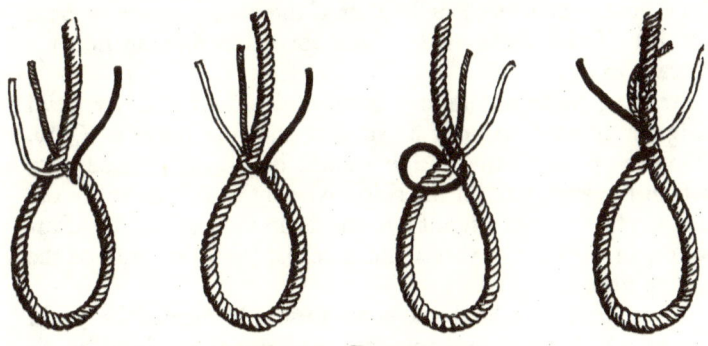

Fig. 21. EYE SPLICE

(1) Unlay strands for distance equal to 3 times circumference of rope
(2) Proceed as indicated above
(3) Repeat twice more and trim to look neat

74   HOW TO SAIL

Flags and Flag Etiquette

It can sometimes be even more embarrassing not to know about flags than not to know about knots. Apart from signals, which are dealt with in another chapter, there are six kinds of flag which are normally flown by a British yacht. The first is the Ensign, which should be worn on all occasions when it is proper to show the national colour; for instance, when entering or leaving a foreign port. (The national colours of the foreign country concerned should also be flown on these occasions.) The ensign for most of us means the Red Ensign, but certain yacht clubs have been granted the privilege of a special ensign which can be used by their members. Special ensigns include the White Ensign of H.M. Fleet, used only by the Royal Yacht Squadron as a special ensign; the Blue Ensign undefaced; the Blue Ensign defaced, bearing the badge of the yacht club concerned; and the Red Ensign defaced, with the badge of the yacht club.

The yacht flying a special ensign must be registered under the Merchant Shipping Act. The special ensign is worn under an Admiralty warrant granted to the yacht and not to the owner, who has no right to fly a special ensign elsewhere (i.e. on another boat). Nor should it be flown on the owner's yacht if the boat is chartered or lent, or if the owner ceases to be a member of the yacht club whose special ensign he holds a warrant to fly.

Breaking these regulations is expensive, and if any special ensign is hoisted without a warrant the fine may be £500. Wherever possible the ensign should be flown from its own staff in the after part of the ship. Where this is impossible the ensign is flown from a point two-thirds up the leech of the aftersail or, in the case of yawls and ketches, from the head of the mizzen mast.

If you are lent a boat you should use a burgee of the yacht club of which you are a member, and not that of the boat's owner. The burgee of a club is the second kind of flag, normally triangular, a special variation of which is usually flown by the flag officers of the club. For instance, the Commodore usually flies a broad or swallow-tailed flag; the Vice-Commodore's pennant is marked with one black sphere, the Rear-Commodore's with two. The club burgee or special flag of a flag officer is flown from the top of the mainmast or a similar prominent point.

The third kind of flag is the owner's flag, which can be anything he chooses to make it, provided that it is distinguishable from those already registered. Shipping companies, like owners, have their private flags showing the line to which the vessel belongs. They are usually rectangular in shape. The owner's flag or house flag is usually flown from the starboard upper crosstrees.

The fourth species, the racing flag, is flown instead of the burgee when racing. It indicates that the yacht in question is subject to racing rules and, as a matter of good manners, boats not racing should give way to him. The racing flag is not worn except when the boat is racing or about to take part in an event. Some racing dinghies fix a racing flag permanently at the top of the mast in order to save the wind resistance which would be caused if there were halyards to haul it up and down. But this practice should be, strictly speaking, discouraged since it claims for the smaller boats courtesies to which they are not entitled except when racing.

Fifth, there are prize flags, often miniatures of the racing flag, which are hoisted at the end of the day's racing, or at the end of the regatta, or the end of the season, according to a somewhat complicated etiquette. Second prizes are distinguished from first prizes by being hoisted below a blue flag marked with a white figure 2; a third-prize flag is hoisted below a red flag marked with a white figure 3. The prize flags can be displayed from the burgee halyards or from the masthead to the end of the boom, or back stay.

When a boat is in harbour and ready for sea, but the owner is not aboard, only the Red Ensign need be flown. It should be broken at 8 o'clock in the summer months and 9 o'clock in the winter, and hauled down at sunset. As the owner comes aboard, the club burgee or special club flag is also worn. If the owner is entitled to fly a special ensign, this will replace the Red Ensign as he comes aboard. At sea, strictly speaking, the ensign should be flown continuously by day and night but most yachts haul it down at night or when sailing or, in the open sea with no ship in sight. The same applies at sea to club burgees or to the special flag of a flag officer of a yacht club. These flags of course like special ensigns are not flown unless the owner is aboard.

Yachts are "dressed overall" on national festival days or local regattas. When a ship is dressed overall, the flags of the International Code are strung from the stem to the mast-head or mast-heads, and from there to the taffrail at the stern of the ship. The ensign should be lowered about two-thirds of its height as a salute to (i) any Royal Yacht; (ii) British or foreign warships. If sufficiently punctilious, the owner can also salute the flag officers of the club the burgee of which he is wearing, but once a day is enough if one is at home. On matters of ceremony the Royal Navy are the authorities, and the example of the senior naval officer present should be followed where appropriate.

CHAPTER VI

MANAGING MORE SAILS

AFTER you have been out once or twice in a single-sailed boat you will probably want to try your hand at something more ambitious. Not that we wish to condemn single-sail boats altogether; in fact, as we shall see, they are the best and most exacting test of SINGLE-HANDED sailing ability. Nevertheless, a boat with jib before the mainsail is more fun and, even without a crew to work it, is, for several reasons, more efficient than a boat with a mainsail only. First, as we have already noted, a boat with two sails is a better-balanced boat. The mast can be farther aft, which means that when running, the boat's bow is not unduly pressed down as sometimes happens with single-sail jobs. Secondly, when beating to windward, the jib can be kept sheeted in so that it pulls the boat along even during a gust, when the mainsail is loosed off till it flaps in order to spill out unwanted wind. These advantages are, in my view, decisive.

The jib is normally a three-cornered sail, the head being attached to the halyard and the tack to the deck near the stem of the boat. In many boats the luff of the jib is attached by spring hanks or shackles to the forestay. Sometimes these shackles or hanks are supported both by the forestay and the wire of the jib halyard, which is doubled back from its sheave on the mast down through a second pulley at the stem head to a cleat in the cockpit. These arrangements are made so that the luff of the jib can be tightly stretched – vital, if full value is to be got from the sail. A loosely hoisted jib looks as untidy as a wrinkled stocking, and apart from being slovenly slows down the boat considerably. The clew of the jib is attached to port and starboard jibsheets, each sheet usually passing through a fair lead on its own side of the deck and so to the hand of the helmsman or crew. Each jibsheet should have a figure-of-eight knot tied in the end to prevent it running out through the fairlead. Single-handed sail boats are usually provided with some form of jamming cleat for the jibsheet, so that the helmsman can get rid of it or concentrate on the mainsheet and tiller. One of the best kinds of jamming cleat consists of two toothed cams. They are shaped something like those sectors of cream cheese that you buy in round boxes. The rope is gripped between the two curved parts of two of the sectors, which turn towards one another in such a way that the harder the rope is pulled the tighter it is held. Even when jammed, the jibsheet can be freed at once from the cams by an upward pull.

The 12-ft. Firefly boats, about which I shall be saying more later, have another ingenious trick for helping the helmsman to control the jibsheet when sailing single handed. They use a single endless jibsheet, which passes through the fair leads in the ordinary way and then through a double reversible jamming cleat which can be operated by the foot.

Normally, with the boat head to wind the mainsail is hoisted first and the jib afterwards. This is because the mainsail *keeps* the boat head to wind, whereas the jib without the mainsail tends to blow the boat's head off one way or the other.

As already explained, there are occasions at a mooring when the tide and wind are in opposite directions and it is undesirable to hoist the mainsail. In such cases the jib can be hoisted first. If the wind is strong, even this may cause difficulties unless the jib is hoisted in stops (that is, secured with light stopping cotton). While in stops the jib, of course, does not catch the wind, but a sharp tug on the jib sheets will break the stops and let the sail draw. For single-handed sailing jibs are often fitted with a Wykeham-Martin furling gear, which allows the helmsman to roll them up window-blind fashion round its own luff simply by pulling a cord. This is a most convenient arrangement, but it means that the jib cannot be hanked to the forestay, and it may therefore be difficult to get it to set with a nice taut luff. When beating to windward the jib is really more important than the mainsail itself, and it will, of course, be sheeted in really hard. In that position it gives the clearest indication of whether the boat is sailing its best course. If the helmsman is pinching (that is, starving the boat of wind) by sailing too close to the direction from which the wind is coming, the centre of the luff of the jib will begin to flutter. When this occurs the helmsman will know that he is luffing up too much and that he must bear away. Similarly, when reaching on a more or less set course it is the jib which determines the position of the mainsail. The usual way to find out the correct angle of the jib is to let it out until it begins to flutter, and then draw it back until it is just short of fluttering. Then the mainsail in turn can be slacked off in the same way until the back wind from the jib makes it flutter. Of course, if when reaching the jib is hauled closer than it should be, then it will back wind the mainsail, and the mainsail in turn will not be out as far as it should be. It is nearly impossible for a helmsman sailing single handed to make these constant adjustments; which is why, as already mentioned, a single-sailed boat is perhaps a fairer test of single-handed work than a sloop-rigged craft. When running before the wind the jib plays a less important part than the spinnaker (a balloon-shaped sail) – which I shall deal with later on – but in many boats spinnakers are banned for the sake of simplicity or to save expense, and in this case the jib is used as a kind of primitive spinnaker on the opposite side of the mast to the mainsail. The jib is held in this position by a jib stick or whisker pole, one end being attached to the mast and the other to the clew of the jib. With the sails fixed this way the boat is said to be running "goose-winged".

One vital word of warning: It is fatally easy to hoist the jib upside down. Some kindly sailmakers save one from doing so by marking the corners "head" or "tack" as the case may be. If there are no marks on your jib, you may like to remedy this by tying some distinctive coloured thread through the thimble or ring at each corner.

The jib is particularly useful for handling the boat when anchoring or picking up or dropping a mooring. Let us suppose, for instance, that you are on your mooring and facing north into the tide, with the wind in the north-east. You decide that you would like to sail off on a north-west course. After both sails have been hoisted (you can do this, since the wind and tide are in more or less the same direction), you can let go the mooring and "back" the jib against the wind by pulling it to windward (starboard) with the starboard jibsheet. This will very quickly turn the boat across the tide to port, and will allow the wind to get into the mainsail so that it begins to draw. You can then let the starboard jibsheet fly and pull in the port jibsheet and be quickly under way.

A word should be said about the role of the jib when going about. When changing from one tack to another let the jib draw as long as you can, so that the boat keeps as much way on as possible. Let us suppose, for instance, that you are going about from port tack on to starboard. At the commencement of the turn the starboard jibsheet will already be pulled in hard. It should be kept that way until the jib begins to flap. Then, but not before, the starboard jibsheet can be loosened, and as soon as the wind begins to reach the starboard side of the boat the port jibsheet can be pulled in. If this is done too soon the sail will be backed, so that it may be impossible for the boat to come round on to the new tack at all. If too late, the jib will be difficult to get in. The longer the sheeting in is left the harder it will be, as the wind blows more and more on to the sail instead of across it.

One final point: It is important to see that the jibsheet you are loosening – in this case the starboard jibsheet – really is loose. If not, the jib will not come round freely to its new position and it will be hard to get in. Both jib and mainsail can be reduced in size by reefing. Jibs are, perhaps, more often reefed in small boats than in large boats, which carry an assortment of sails varying from the small storm jib carried in heavy weather, to the enormous Genoas used in light airs. Small boats have no room for such wardrobes, and therefore their jibs are often provided with some arrangement for reefing. Reefing, in the case of the jib, is usually carried on the roller-blind principle. In the case of the mainsail, the sail is reefed either by rolling it round the boom or with reef pendants. In this latter method of reefing you virtually take a tuck in the sail. (See fig. 22.)

If there is plenty of time the yacht is "hove to", so that it remains practically stationary during the reefing. For this operation the helmsman first brings the boat nearly head to wind and backs the jib (i.e. sheets it to the windward side of the boat), at the same time lashing the helm down (i.e. with the tiller to leeward). The mainsheet is close hauled – hauled in tight. In this position the effect of the jib is to blow the boat's head off to leeward, but the mainsail and rudder cancel this out and the result is that the boat sails very slowly ahead. The manœuvre should be practised under suitable conditions on the mooring. Do not wait to try it till you have to reef; each boat's behaviour is slightly different. Many small racing boats will not heave to, so that any decision to reef them should be taken before setting out.

When suitably placed for reefing, the topping lift is set up so that the boom strain is taken off the sail and when not using roller reefing, the boom is lowered into a gallows or semi-circular wooden support which keeps it steady. The halyard is then slacked off by the amount required for the reef.

For point reefing the leech (after edge) of the sail is provided with a cringle or ring sited some distance up the sail. By means of a line rove (passed) through a block, this cringle can be pulled down to the level of the clew of the sail and secured. This is the "tuck". The luff of the mainsail will have a similar ring or cringle which must also be secured. These two outer points must be attended to first, because they take the chief strain of the reef. The bunt or body of a sail to be reefed in this manner has on it a number of patches to which are sewn tapes hanging down on either side of the sail. When reefing, these tapes are

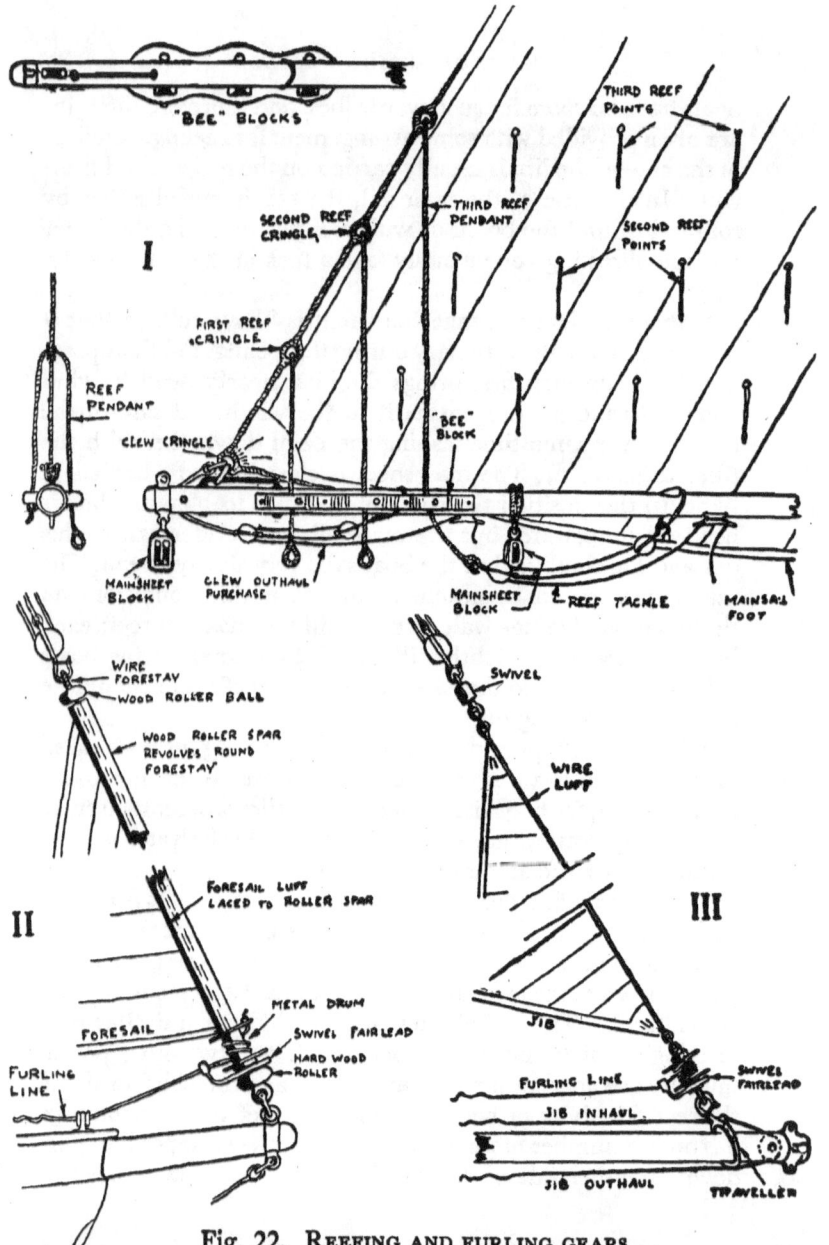

Fig. 22. REEFING AND FURLING GEARS
I. Loose foot mainsail reefing gear   II. Roller foresail gear (for small boats
III. Wykeham-Martin furling gear for jib. This gear is intended for furling not reefin

joined together with a reef knot under the foot of the sail (but please, not round the boom if you want your sail to keep its shape though sometimes I know for one reason or another this may be unavoidable).

On most sails there will be two or three sets of cringles and reef points in lines above each other, so that if one reef is not enough, two can be taken, or three. But remember, the luff and leech cringles must be secured first and released last to avoid the danger of tearing the sail. When roller reefing the mainsail, the unwanted sail is rolled round the boom like a roller blind. The boom is prevented from unrolling either by a pawl and ratchet or a worm gear, or by a line wound off the boom and made fast to a drum. Smaller boats sometimes have a simpler arrangement consisting of a square-sectioned peg attached to the forepart of the boom. This peg fits into a square swivel attached to the mast, so that the boom cannot revolve. When reefing by this method, the boom is first disengaged and then turned round by hand.

Boats fitted with roller reefing are usually provided with a claw something like a round-shaped lobster claw, so that the boom can be controlled even though it has layers of sail wound round it. This is particularly important in racing boats, where a vang or kicking strap is used to prevent the boom from rising and thus spoiling the performance of the boat when off the wind (see illustration).

When reducing sail area it is important not to destroy the balance between the sail areas of the mainsail and the jib. If the mainsail is heavily reefed down and the jib is not, then the sail area of the boat will have been moved forward, so to speak, and the boat will tend to turn away from the wind; or, as we say, to carry lee helm – a most undesirable defect. That is why, in a high wind, small-boat sailors often prefer to sail with full mainsail only rather than with reefed mainsail and full jib.

We now come to the most beautiful and the most treacherous of all sails – the spinnaker; that balloon-shaped sail used for

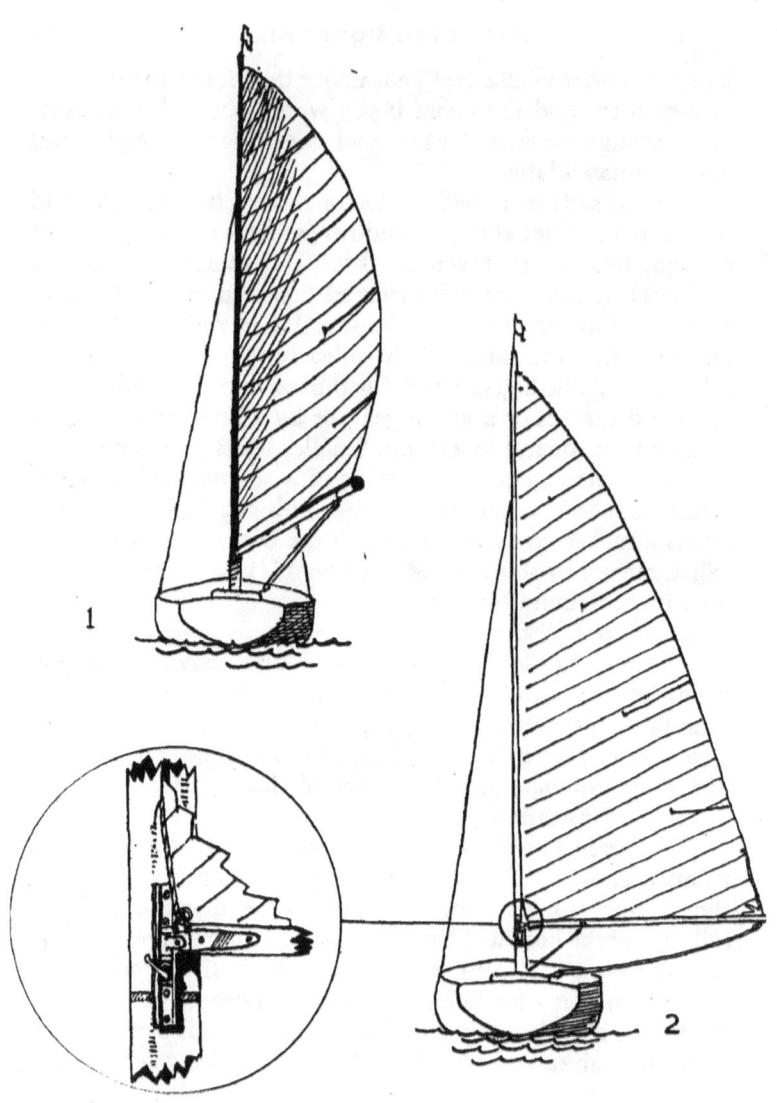

Fig. 23. USE OF KICKING STRAP AND SLIDING GOOSENECK
(1) Without kicking strap Sail is unstable and not drawing properly
(2) With kicking strap Boom is horizontal. Full Sail area presented to the wind

MANAGING MORE SAILS

running before the wind, and first carried on the racing yacht Sphinx (hence the name) in 1866. In all these years no one has succeeded in completely taming the spinnaker. With careless handling it can very quickly twist itself round the forestay. This often happens when the wind, which has been blowing from aft, suddenly comes round to the quarter (that part of the boat lying between the stern and the beam). Or a mere wave from a paddle-steamer can induce this calamity, particularly if the spinnaker hand is not extremely alert. Careless handing (lowering) of the spinnaker can lead to the spectacular situation where the sail drops into the water and acts as a scoop, so that in a few seconds nothing remains of it but a few torn shreds. With these awful warnings before one's eyes it is clearly worth taking trouble to become so familiar with the spinnaker that its use becomes second nature.

Careful preparations should be made before the sail is hoisted at all. In most cases the spinnaker will be kept in a bag, with the head or topmost of its three corners handy near the opening of the bag ready for attaching to the halyard.

Like other sails, the spinnaker should be marked with coloured thread so that the head is easily distinguishable from the other two corners. Some owners tape the edges with distinctive coloured tape, red for the port and green for the starboard side to show up unwanted twists. It also helps if the three corners are marked "Forward" and "Aft" according to the direction they will face when the sail is hoisted. When in use the spinnaker is set on its own boom, on the opposite side of the mast from the mainsail. The spinnaker boom runs from the mainmast to the tack of the spinnaker. There should be a ring permanently attached to the tack so that the guy and boom can be attached or detached separately. The clew or leeward corner of the sail is attached to the spinnaker sheet, which is led aft and controlled from there. In larger boats where there are hands enough to manage all the tackle there are other refinements. For instance, the outboard end of the spinnaker boom is attached to a fore guy which prevents its moving too far aft. It may also have a down haul and a topping lift to keep it level.

The usual procedure for hoisting is as follows: the spinnaker boom is attached to the down-haul and placed on the weather side of the mast with its future outboard end pointing to the bows of the boat. (The best type of spinnaker boom is double-ended, in which case, of course, it does not matter which end is which.) The spinnaker can be set either in stops or flying. Setting in stops is easier, but if all goes well the flying method will set the sail drawing sooner. When set flying, the spinnaker is hoisted in the lee of the mainsail unless the wind is almost dead aft, in which case it can be hoisted to weather. When set in stops, the spinnaker is hoisted to weather (i.e. on the windward side). The spinnaker halyard should have a swivel attachment for the head of the spinnaker, so that any twists can clear themselves without difficulty. Before the race the spinnaker is carefully folded and put in a bag or similar container with its three corners projecting from the bag ready for attaching. Normally the sheets and guys pass *outside* the shrouds. Remember this when getting them into position before hoisting (see fig. 24A). When preparing to hoist, the spinnaker clew is attached to the sheet, its tack to the aft guy, and its head to the halyard. The spinnaker is then gradually hoisted, being eased out if necessary under the foot of the jib. The after guy is then pulled round to the windward side of the forestay and the outboard end of the pole is then attached to both fore and aft guys and the inboard end of the boom to the mast. Next, the crew member controlling the after guy hauls the spinnaker boom aft until it is almost at right-angles to the wind as shown by the burgee. When the after guy has been secured the sail is kept trimmed by means of the sheet, which is let off as far as can be done without danger of the sail collapsing. The first signs of a collapse will be shown by the luff beginning to break. This indicates that the wind is to the side of the spinnaker rather than behind it. If the sail cannot be kept drawing by the sheet hand, it may be necessary

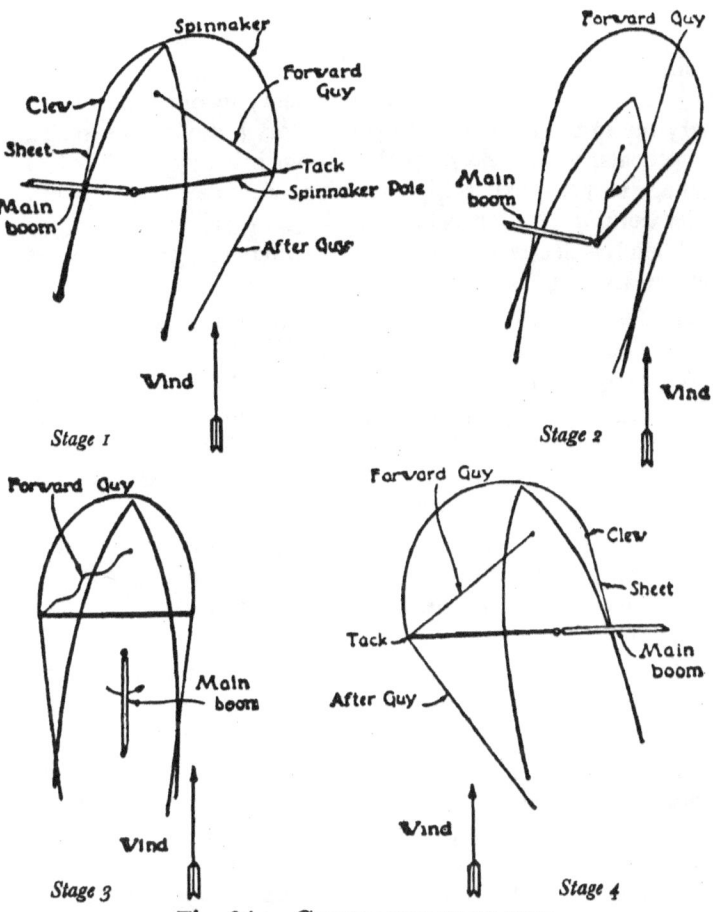

Fig. 24A. GYBING THE SPINNAKER

Stage 1. The spinnaker before the gybe
Stage 2. After-guy slacked off. Forward-guy moved to in-board end of spinnaker pole
Stage 3. In mid-gybe spinnaker attached to pole at both ends is still drawing though pole is detached from mast
Stage 4. Clew unhooked from pole spinnaker pole attached to mast and drawing on new gybe
NOTES. In a small boat (1) the helmsman probably hoists the spinnaker; (2) the gear is greatly simplified; (3) the crew should keep as far aft as possible during all spinnaker operations.

to slack off the after guy and perhaps even bear away a little for a moment. It is seldom good policy, in our opinion, to carry the spinnaker when the wind is forward of the beam. In large boats, where the spinnaker boom is heavy and hard to manage in a sea-way, skippers often prefer to set up the boom in its working position before hoisting any sail.

When it is necessary to gybe, the manœuvre is carried out as follows: (See fig. 24.)

1. Detach forward guy from the outboard end of the boom and fasten it to the inboard end.
2. Detach the spinnaker boom from the mast and snap what was the inboard end of the boom on to the former spinnaker sheet. We now have the sail attached at both ends of the boom. At this point the mainsail is hauled in and the gybe carried out.
3. The former spinnaker tack, which now becomes the clew, is detached from the spinnaker boom; and the former aft guy, which is still attached to the sail, becomes the sheet.
4. The new inboard end of the pole is then attached to the mast. A good crew can keep the spinnaker drawing throughout the whole operation.

Handing (lowering) the spinnaker presents no difficulty provided that the helmsman and crew know exactly what they are doing. It is often a help to hoist the jib and then lower the spinnaker in its lee. When the moment comes to take in the spinnaker, one of the crew slacks off the after guy while the skipper or a second hand slacks the sheet. The crew then releases the tack of the sail which then flies out to leeward, where it can easily be taken in as the halyard is lowered. If the sail falls in the water, hold it by one corner only so that it does not become a scoop.

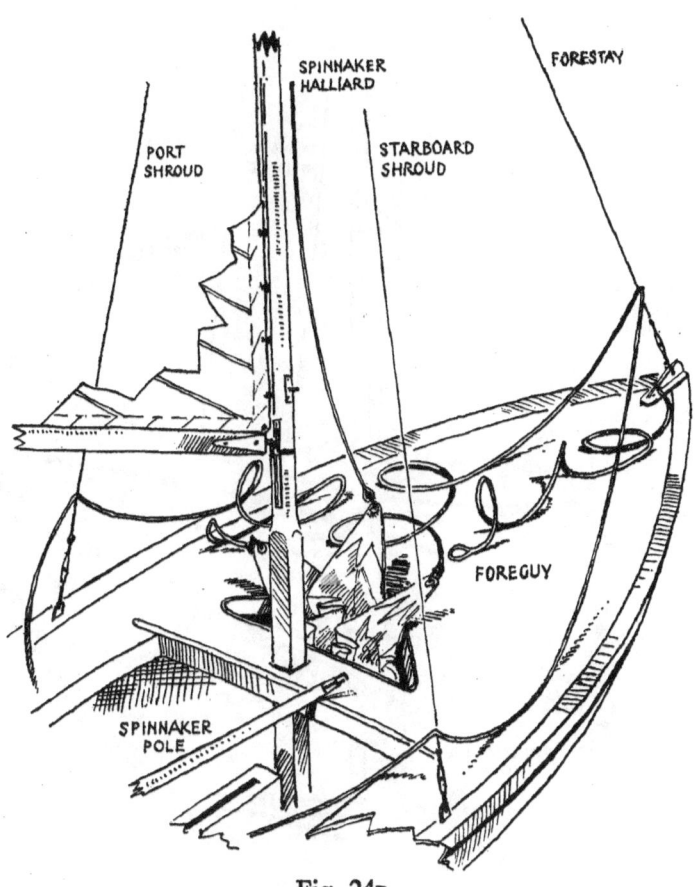

Fig. 24B.
A. Spinnaker ready for hoisting to leeward

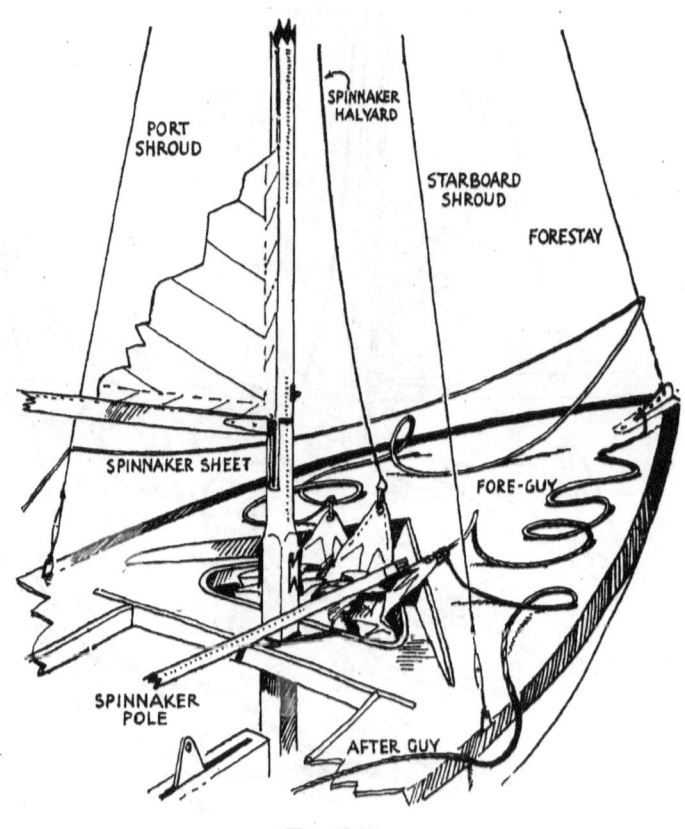

Fig. 24b.

B. Spinnaker ready for hoisting to windward

An alternative – and handier – arrangement is to attach the fore-guy directly to the spinnaker pole

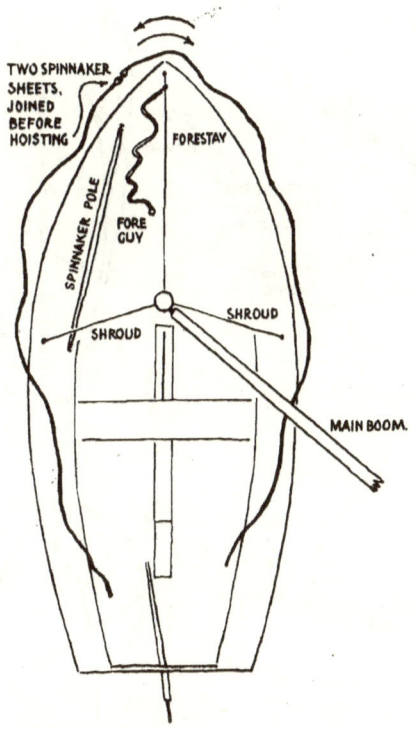

Fig. 24b.

C. Joined Spinnaker sheet can be pulled round either side of forestay for windward *or* leeward hoisting

Note.—There are two types of spinnaker halyard. One is the "double-ended" type which passes up one *side* of the mast over a sheave or pulley and down the other *side* of the mast; in this case the head of the spinnaker can be attached to either end of the halyard for hoisting on either side of the mast without previous arrangement.

The other type of spinnaker halyard passes up the inside of the hollow mast, over a fore-and-aft sheave and issues from the forward part of the mast; it is a "single-ender".

It will therefore have to be passed round to the leeward side of the forestay if the spinnaker is being hoisted to leeward, or to the other side if the spinnaker is going up to windward. In this case, therefore, the end of the spinnaker halyard should be fastened to the point at which the spinnaker sheets are joined so that it can be pulled round with them to the required side of the forestay.

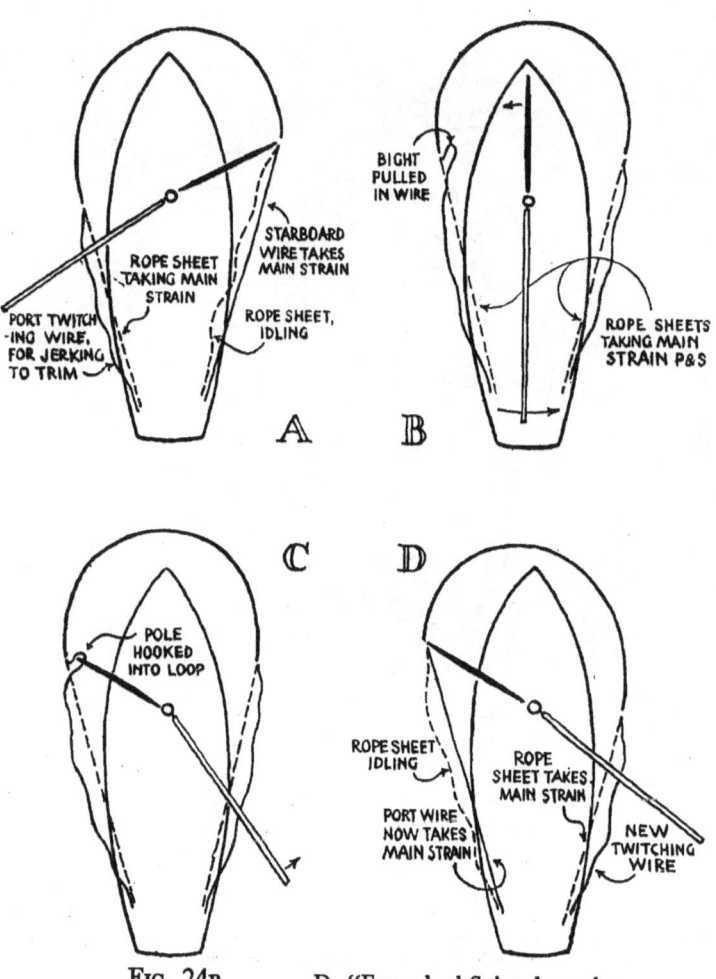

FIG. 24B. D. "Free-wheel Spinnaker gybe

Diagram shows the "free-wheel" system for gybing the spinnaker used on *Columbia*, the U.S. defender of the America Cup in 1958.

"A" Shows the spinnaker before the gybe. The wire after-guy takes the main strain from the spinnaker boom, but a rope sheet is also attached to the tack of the spinnaker.

"B" The spinnaker in mid-gybe. The starboard rope sheet takes the main strain to starboard and the port rope to port. The wire spinnaker sheet on the port side is loosed off ready for the spinnaker boom to be clipped on.

"C" Spinnaker boom is clipped on to port wire sheet.

"D" The slack on the wire port sheet is taken up by pulling it through the clip on the spinnaker boom and the gybe is now complete.

CHAPTER VII

CARE OF SAILS

MANY a man who would be ashamed to appear in baggy trousers or a smudged collar thinks nothing of stains or wrinkles which spoil the appearance of his sails. In fact, to judge by the leopard-like blotches and spots that one sees, some sails seem to have been taken for a course of mud baths instead of out sailing.

So let us attend first to the question of looks, since only a little care is needed to keep sails in mint condition. Mud, of course, is a menace. If you have gone aground and have had to go overboard in order to get the boat moving again, it is worth making a special effort to avoid bringing the mud back into the boat, where it is almost certain to attach itself to the sail when the latter is lowered. All mud should be rinsed off the sounding rod, the anchor and other gear before it is taken on board after use. Mud stains on sails may be harmless in themselves, but they give the impression that the owner in question may be lax in other and more important respects, and so take something off the sales value of the boat as well as from its appearance.

The sails are the driving "engine" of a boat, just as the motor drives a car. If the sails are distorted or pulled out of shape the boat soon gets sluggish and badly behaved, but there is this difference between a boat and a car: if a motor becomes choked with carbon it can be decarbonized, and if the cylinders become worn they can be rebored; but nothing can restore the shape of a cotton sail once it has been ruined by careless treatment. I mention cotton first because, despite the trend to Terylene, a large proportion of non-racing boats are still "clad" in cotton.

Let us suppose that a new set of cotton sails for this season has just arrived from the maker, beautifully folded and packed, fresh with a clean, tarry smell of the sailmaker's loft. These sails will have to be run in, in much the same way as a new car. When properly set they should show a fine curve. The action of the wind on the convex or outer surface of the sail helps in pulling the boat along. If a sail has been badly stretched or pulled out of shape the curve is destroyed, and the sail is left either flat or wrinkled in such a way that the flow of air is disturbed and forms back eddies which hinder rather than help progress. Clumsy handling can ruin the shape of a new sail, perhaps for ever, within a few hours.

When the time comes to stretch the new canvas, choose a fine day when the wind is light and likely to remain so. It is practically a crime to reef a brand new sail. Make sure that there are no showers about and no damp Scotch mist, which is almost as bad as rain for a new sail; in both cases the moisture will run to the bottom of the sail, where its weight will pull the fabric out of shape.

Starting with a new Bermudian mainsail, you will notice first that the canvas, both along the luff and the foot, is sewn to the ropes with a slight puckering. These puckers allow for the fact that the rope will stretch more than the canvas. The job of the first few hours' sailing should be to stretch the ropes evenly, so that the canvas takes up the shape which it originally had when the sail was cut. Stretching must be done fairly to avoid a false reshaping. Of course, the canvas itself will stretch to some extent, but not as much as the rope.

A new sail when set should be hoisted until the wrinkles on the luff just disappear, and it should be pulled out along the boom with the boom out-haul to just the same tension, i.e. to a point where wrinkles just disappear. But do not merely hoist the sail and leave it flapping in the hope that it will stretch. All that will happen is that it will wear itself out. It is far better to go for a sail and get the wind into the body of the sail. Choose for preference a place where you can go on a reach

CARE OF SAILS 95

backwards and forwards. If possible, avoid beating to windward. To do so you would have to sheet in the sail hard, and this would put a strain on the leech of the sail which, being unroped, stretches more quickly than the other sides. A gradual stretch all round is what is wanted and a reach provides the best conditions for this. After you have been sailing a little while the ropes on the foot and luff will begin to "give" and show wrinkles on the sail. When this happens, both the halyard and the boom out-haul should be tightened up again. There is no hard-and-fast rule as to how long it should take to stretch a sail; in fact, the longer the better, but we should certainly aim at eight hours' minimum. When hoisting or lowering, the boom should be supported either by the topping lift (line passing from the end of the boom to the masthead and down to the deck) or by hand to avoid stretching the sails.

Sails, particularly jibs, are sometimes supplied with wire luff ropes, in which case there is obviously no special stretching to be done as far as the luff is concerned, and the halyard can be set up fully tight. The whole sail should, however, be given every chance to stretch evenly before being put on to any hard work. Proper stretching of the jib depends largely on the correct positioning of the fair lead through which the jibsheet passes. If it is too far forward the jib will be strained downwards. If it is too far back the pull will be too horizontal to get the best from the sail.

So much for preparations. Now for maintenance. The salt left by spray should be removed from sails, particularly from the foot of the jib and mainsail, where it is apt to collect. Salt absorbs moisture and on a damp day will noticeably affect the set of a sail; it also weakens the fabric. Salt should be removed either by hosing down or by soaking the sails in cold water in the bath. Mildew, too, must be fought. It thrives on damp, poorly aired cotton sails and eats away their strength. Hence, if cotton sails are wet it is useless to put sail covers over them on the boom, since mildew is certain to start in those parts of the sail where there is no air circulating. When drying the sails remember that the reinforced parts of the sail, such as the head board, batten pockets, reef points, ropes, etc., take longer to dry. If they are all right you can be pretty sure that the rest of the sail is free from damp. Modern sails are often

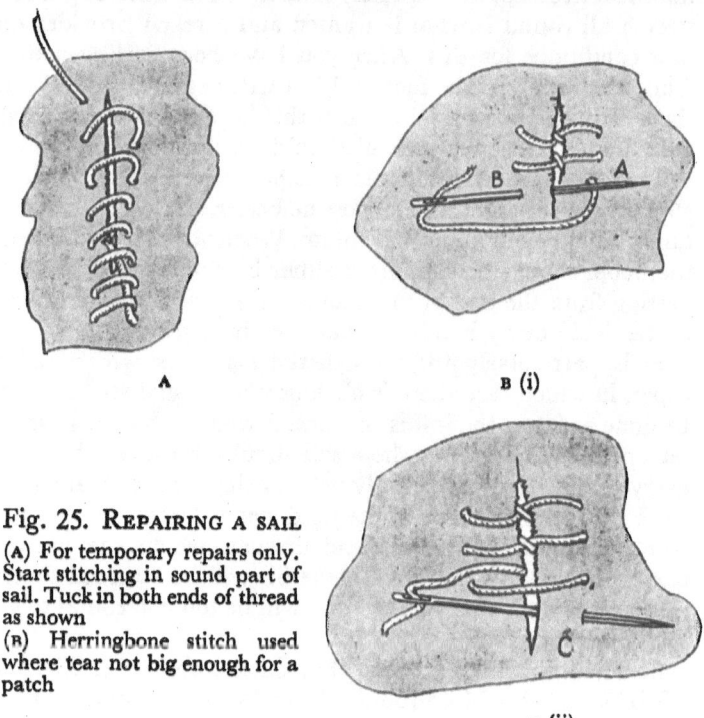

Fig. 25. REPAIRING A SAIL
(A) For temporary repairs only. Start stitching in sound part of sail. Tuck in both ends of thread as shown
(B) Herringbone stitch used where tear not big enough for a patch

treated by the manufacturers with water repellents, which turn the individual threads of canvas into a duck's back but add nothing to the weight of the sail. They can be proofed against mildew, too, though in my view it never does to rely on this lasting for ever. So much for cotton.

The change from cotton to Terylene during the last few years has come about largely because of the success of the new synthetic sails in the racing field. The material is smoother and offers less air-friction than cotton. It picks up less moisture and is therefore lighter than cotton on wet days. It does not stretch and therefore keeps its shape better. It lasts longer, is easier to wash because it drips dry; and it is not subject to rot or mildew. In addition, synthetic sails do not require as much breaking-in as cotton, though it is only sensible to avoid putting a really distorting strain on them when new.

Finally, repairs. The old proverb about the stitch in time applies particularly to sails. The end of the season is the time to make a thorough seam-by-seam survey of your sails. If this is postponed it is easy to forget little defects which one has noticed when sailing but which are fiendishly hard to find when one has the sail stretched out, perhaps in an inadequate light or on the floor of the average drawing-room. Moreover, if you send the sails to be repaired in the autumn you are giving the sailmaker a chance to do a better job than if you wait until the spring, when his best men are probably flooded with new orders or repair work from the forgetful crowd who have left things till the last minute.

If there is any doubt, it is better to have the repair done and not leave it over for the future.

In the middle of the season, in these days, it may take three or four weeks to get even a simple job carried out, and that is too long a period to be without one's sails. If the worst comes to the worst, it is possible to carry out primitive repairs at home if you have the ordinary sailmaker's tools. The repairs can be carried out as shown in the illustrations.

Very small temporary patches can normally be made with various types of adhesive tape or mending patches. But I hope you will have many years of good sailing before your sails reach this state of emergency.

CHAPTER VIII

CLASS DISTINCTIONS

CLASS boats, as distinct from ordinary craft, are built to fairly exact measurements so that they can race level against each other without handicap. Some of them are recognized as international classes by the International Yacht Racing Union. Others have a national status only, in which case in the United Kingdom they are managed by our own Royal Yachting Association. Some classes are formally "recognised" by the Royal Yachting Association without being administered by that body. Added to these are many other classes not specially recognized but controlled by private associations, in some cases by a single club only.

It is worth grasping at the outset that there are three main species of class boats, viz. one-design class boats, formula class boats and restricted class boats.

One Design boats

In the case of one-design classes, the rules provide that there shall be minor variations only between one boat and another. Often the number of sails that can be bought is limited in order to prevent the wealthier members in the class from outspending their less-well-off rivals. In some cases the number of times per season that the boat can be scrubbed and coated with anti-fouling paint (to prevent the growth of weed, barnacles, etc., which spoil the under-surface of the boat) is controlled, as well as the price to be paid for these operations.

Formula boats

Formula boats, on the other hand, can vary widely, provided that the measurements of each boat, when interpreted according to a set formula, give the same answer. For example,

[Photo: Beken & Son

Swallow Class yachts racing at Cowes. The 6-metre K47 in the background appears to have gone aground

[Photo: *Eileen Ramsay*

v. A day for a good crew—a Firefly at Whitstable

in a 6-metre boat you can choose to have an outsize sail area if you compensate for it elsewhere in your design, so that your rating when calculated from your design according to the formula still gives an answer of 6-metres.

Restricted class boats

In restricted classes, two boats can vary within certain limits both in hull design and the sail area, but you cannot overstep any one of these limits even if you compensate for it by economies elsewhere.

There is some disagreement between the supporters of one-design classes and restricted and formula class enthusiasts. The one-design man is interested chiefly in racing tactics, and his technical interest in the boat is limited almost entirely to seeing that it is well tuned. Perhaps, also, he is willing to instal one or two gadgets to improve the performance, but he is NOT interested in the problems of boat design. He does NOT wish to race in a class in which his own boat, because of its design, may be helped or handicapped by the weather. He prefers to feel that if he wins it is due to the performance of himself and his crew. He would rather be sure that if he loses it is because of his own bad sailing and not because someone else has a better-designed boat for the conditions of the day.

The restricted class enthusiast feels, on the other hand, that by redesigning his own boat he will both win more cups for himself and improve the strain of boats in general. His argument is that if you limit boats to one design only, design will stagnate. He is even prepared to argue that restricted class boats can be less expensive to the average owner than one-design boats in which alterations are banned. Rich owners, he will say, are always ready to stand the expense of trying out new improvements on boats which they later sell at reduced prices to the other members of the class. This desire to improve the breed helps to account for the appearance of many small classes of boat. Some are undoubtedly successful. Others are taken up enthusiastically for a few seasons and then wither away, being often no better than something already on the market; in which case the small production makes them expensive to build and difficult to sell.

Structurally, class boats can be roughly divided into two sections: those with centre boards and those with fixed keels. This is, perhaps, a little arbitrary, because some fixed keel boats (such as the Swallow and the Flying 15 and, of course, the International Star class) behave very much like centre board dinghies. Equally, there are centre board boats which are well ballasted, and therefore not strictly comparable with the ordinary 12- or 14-footer dinghy. Nevertheless, these are exceptions to the rule and do not blur the main differences between the two types of boat.

A class boat is, of course, more expensive than an "ordinary" boat, which does not have to conform to exact measurements or weight, but coming, we hope, from the board of a good designer, it has both a better performance and larger disposal value. The history of the class to which it belongs gives it some kind of pedigree, and its placing in regattas provides an extra character reference for the prospective buyer.

International classes (Fixed keel)

These are, as already mentioned, boats recognized as having international status by the International Yacht Racing Union, the most important international body of its kind.

The 6-metre class is the largest and most expensive of the international classes raced by this country. These fine boats have been popular for more than forty years, but had a new lease of life after the end of the Kaiser's War. No less than thirty-one of them were built between 1920 and 1923. Chosen for the Olympic Games both at Torquay (1948) and Helsinki (1952), "Sixes" have been used also in the post-war British-America Cup Race, since held at Cowes. The dimensions are controlled by formula and the waterline length of the yachts varies between 20 and 25 ft. overall, with a beam of between $5\frac{1}{4}$ and 7 ft. The sail area of the modern boats is around 460 sq. ft. The 6-metre takes a crew, including the helmsman, of four; possibly five, if a navigator is required. Competition, both national and international, is very keen, but with rising costs the future of the class seems doubtful, and it may eventually go the way of other mammoth designs such as "J" class yachts, which finally descended to handicap racing because there were too few of them for any other activity. With this danger in mind, the International Yacht Racing Union adopted the 5·5-metre class, which appeared for the first time at Cowes in 1951 and which is very much more cheaply built and is sailed with a crew of not more than three. The 5·5 is something of a compromise between the 6-metre and a very much lighter design – the international 30-square-metre boat.

As already mentioned, the names 6-metre, 5-metre, etc., do not refer to any physical part of the boat, but to the answer to a sum worked out according to a formula from the length, sail area, displacement, etc., of the boat in question. The actual sail area of the 5·5-metre is, however, not to exceed 312 sq. ft. The class has already become popular abroad, particularly in Scandinavia, and was chosen for the 1952 Olympic Games at Helsinki, and for the 1956 meeting at Melbourne where Britain won a silver medal.

Next, we come to the Dragon one-design, suitable either for racing or cruising, for which they are used extensively in Scandinavia. In this country the emphasis is on racing, and the appearance of the Royal "Bluebottle" is providing a major item of interest. Dragons were used in the 1948 Olympics and chosen for the 1952 and 1956 meetings. More than 200 of them have been built in this country since the class was first introduced in 1936. Dragons have an overall length of 29 ft. 2¼ in.; length waterline of 18 ft. 8¼ in.; a beam of 6 ft. 4 in.; and a sail area of 235½ sq. ft.

National classes (Fixed keel)

Among the national fixed-keel classes we should mention the Swallows, first introduced for the Olympic Games held at

Torquay in 1948. The Swallow is a lighter boat than the Dragon and more cheaply built. They are fast and pleasant to sail and their dimensions are: length overall 25 ft. 6 in.; length, waterline, 19 ft.; beam 5 ft. 8 in.; sail area 190 sq. ft.

International classes (Centreboard)

A number of international centre board classes also deserve mention. The first of these is the International 14-ft. class which furnishes, perhaps, the finest example of the modern planing dinghy. Open boats with large sail area, these "14s" demand a high standard from both helmsman and crew. They are restricted class boats with no limitation on the method of construction; it may be carvel or clinker or even metal. Many of the newer models are moulded boats. There are no limits on what an owner may spend in order to reach perfection. International 14s are raced in the U.S.A., Canada and New Zealand as well as in the United Kingdom, where the principal event is the Prince of Wales Cup, presented by His Royal Highness the Prince of Wales in 1927. (A more rugged partially decked version of the 14 ft., known as the National Redwing, is sailed in the open sea, particularly in the West of England.)

The Flying Dutchman, chosen for the Olympic Games of 1960 is an extremely fast boat (19 ft. 10 in. long, 190 sq. ft. sail area) for two men. (They have to be Super-men.) In a breeze the crew hangs out on a trapeze. (See plate 2.)

The Five-O-Five is a fast, agreeable and good-looking boat of 16 ft. 6 in. length, also sailed with a trapeze. It has also been given international status and was considered for the Olympic Games.

The Finn, repeatedly chosen for the single-handed event in the Olympic Games, is one more interesting class. This 14 ft. 9 in. long, single-sail boat has no rigging whatever on the mast, and the forward end of the boom is slotted into the mast so that a kicking strap is theoretically unnecessary. The beam is 4 ft. $11\frac{1}{2}$ in. and the sail area 107·6 sq. ft. The Finn is a

CLASS DISTINCTIONS 103

pleasant boat to sail and a lively performer, but has yet to become popular in the United Kingdom. The International 10-sq. Metre canoe is also used for single-handed sailing, though not in the Olympic Games. In the 15-ft. range the chief boat not already described is the Snipe, which is definitely the largest one-design class in the world. The Snipe is a chine boat 15 ft. 6 in. overall length, with a beam of 5 ft. and a modest sail area of 100 sq. ft. More than half the several thousand Snipes in the class have been built by amateurs. World Snipe championships are regularly held on both sides of the Atlantic.

The Yachting World Cadet, designed specially for young people, is now also an international class. They can be raced under class rules and by those aged under 18. The Cadet is a square-nosed, hard chine plywood boat, and because the angles of the chine are constant is easily built at home. Cadets have mainsail and foresail, plus a small spinnaker which helps to train the crew in the very important job of off-the-wind sailing. The dimensions are: overall length 10 ft. 6 in.; waterline 9 ft. 3 in.; beam 4 ft. 2 in.; total sail area $55\frac{1}{2}$ sq. ft.

More than two thousand Cadets were built and registered in the first ten years after the class was launched in 1947. The rigging is extremely simple and the boat light enough to be lifted easily. Sidedecking is broad enough to prevent the boat from filling when she is over on her side. Like the Duckling, the Cadet can be sailed by two light-weights, helmsman and crew.

National classes (Centreboard)

We now come to the national centre board classes, administered by the Royal Yachting Association, which means that such things as alterations in price, rigging, etc., have to be approved by the Dinghy Committee of the Royal Yachting Association. The largest of these classes (numerically) is the National 12-ft. restricted class, of which more than 1,000 had been built at the beginning of 1953. National "12's" were first introduced in 1936 for those who wanted to race but who could not afford an International 14-footer. They are clinker-built, mostly with fore- and side-decking and have a sail area of 90 sq. ft. Many of the earlier models were built to a special design by Uffa Fox, which was published in the magazine *The Yachting World*. Ian Proctor designs have had many successes in the last few years.

The national Firefly 12-ft. class has, at the time of writing, overtaken the National 12-ft. in numbers. It is a moulded boat with the same sail area as the National 12, but slightly more beam. The cross-sections are also slightly fuller, giving a more stable and easily controlled craft in hard weather. In other respects there is little to choose in the performance of the two boats. Both plane in the right conditions, though not as easily as the International 14-footer.

At least two national classes of centreboarder can be sailed three up. They are the national Swordfish 15-ft. one-design, and National 18-ft. restricted class. The National 18-footer, clinker-built, is a good sea-boat and superior in performance to most other 18-ft. classes found round our shores. Its main drawback is that it is not easily loaded on to a trailer, and the national championship is therefore organized regionally instead of at one single centre. The Swordfish, in contrast to the National 18-ft., is a moulded boat with a length of 15 ft., beam 5 ft.; sail area 130 sq. ft.; designed with a rather low-aspect ratio. It is a fairly stable boat and suitable for the middle-aged club member who likes to feel something solid under his feet, with a little more room for ducking under the boom than he gets in a 12- or 14-footer. The Swordfish is heavier to lift than the 14-footer, and I would say that they would do best at river clubs, where they are easily launched without the tidal difficulties met with in an estuary. It is, however, possible to leave the Swordfish on sheltered moorings, since it takes a wind of about forty miles an hour to blow one over even where there is a tidal stream through the moorings. In the right conditions a Swordfish will plane very fast.

CLASS DISTINCTIONS 105

Another of the national classes is the Merlin-Rocket 14-ft. class, which is the result of a merger between a family design (the Rocket) and a racing type (the Merlin). The latter was a very speedy but highly sensitive craft, which had been decked in in such a way that there was very little chance of any water getting into it even when it was capsized on its side. Also, however, there was very little room for the crew. The less-uncompromising design finally adopted is therefore all to the good. The national Merlin-Rocket is a restricted class, though the rules are designed to prevent the oldest boats from being outclassed. It continues to increase in numbers.

Other classes are recognized as National by the R.Y.A. but are not administered by that body. One of these, the British Moth, is designed for single-handed sailing, and is one of the smallest one-design boats in the world. It has a mainsail only, of 63 sq. ft.; length overall 11 ft.; waterline only 8 ft. 6 in.; beam 4 ft. 3 in. The Thames is the main stronghold of the Moth class. It is "recognized" by the R.Y.A.

Another small plywood boat, designed for family use, is the hard chine plywood Yachting World Heron dinghy. It can take four people sailing with ease under normal conditions.

The "Yachting World" General Purpose 14-footer is used in many clubs for racing and is easily built at home.

The Yachting World Hornet (length 16 ft.) is another extremely lively class. The beam is only 4 ft. 7 in., which makes the boat fast and able to plane easily. Under the right conditions the Hornet will "get up" and plane even when the wind is forward of the beam. The most interesting feature of the Hornet is the sliding seat or plank, which allows the crew to sit with his weight right outside the boat and only his feet in the gunwale. This, of course, helps to compensate for the narrow beam. The Hornet is one of the few boats in which the crew's job is quite as interesting as that of the helmsman. The boat is hard-chine plywood and can be built at home.

The "Enterprise" (length 13 ft. 3 in.), the "Graduate" (length 12 ft. 6 in.) and the Fleetwind (length 12 ft. $1\frac{1}{2}$ in.)

are all excellent inexpensive hard chine designs recognized by the Royal Yachting Association.

The Flying 15, designed by Uffa Fox, is another keel boat which behaves like a dinghy, but it is a good deal more sedate than the international Star. In essence, the Flying 15 is a version of the International 14-footer modified to take a fixed keel. It draws only 2 ft. 6 in. The Flying 15 is an extremely lively though sometimes wet boat. The class is sufficiently well established to take part in Cowes Week, though conditions in the Solent on a rough day often prove a severe test of the boat's capabilities. The Flying 15 is well decked in, but carries a number of buoyancy tanks in case of emergency.

Other classes

Among unrecognized centre board classes, the Duckling moulded 9-footer built by Fairey Marine Ltd. is of some interest. The method of construction allows it to have an almost semi-circular bow, which takes more bodies and gear than other boats converted and of the same size. Like other moulded boats, Ducklings stand up very well to tropical conditions. The sailing models are fitted with a gunter rig designed so that the whole mast can be stored in the boat itself. There is a jib as well as mainsail. Curiously enough, the international Star class, which was picked for both the 1948 and 1952 Olympic Games, is not recognized by the I.Y.R.U., though it is now to be found all over Europe as well as in the U.S.A., Latin America and the Far East, and has been flourishing for more than forty years. The boat has a hard-chine hull and a fin keel carrying 890 lb. It measures 22 ft. 9 in. overall and has a length (waterline) of 15 ft. 6 in.; a beam of 5 ft. 9 in.; is sailed by a helmsman and one crew. Its sail area of 281 sq. ft. is large for the size of the boat, and even in comparatively light airs much of the time of the helmsman and crew is spent clinging on to the side of the boat in an effort to keep her upright. This is the most probable reason why the class has not become more popular in this country.

While I am about it, I should mention three other classes which normally sail at Cowes. The first of these is the present Redwing class, which was completely redesigned after a fire had destroyed the original master-plans in 1938. The modern Redwing, easily distinguishable by its red sails, is a very clean-looking boat with a waterline of 20 ft. and sail area of 200 sq. ft. The rule bars spinnakers. The Victory class also race at Cowes. They have 2 ft. 6 in. draught; 16 ft. 6 in. length (waterline); and sail area of 195 sq. ft. They were, like the Redwing, designed by Mr. Nicholson and modified by Mr. S. N. Graham. The letter "Z" on the sail is the distinguishing mark. Almost next door in the alphabet is the X class one-design, numbering over seventy boats widely distributed over the Solent and Chichester Harbour area. They have a length overall of 20 ft. 8 in.; waterline 17 ft.; and sail area of 210 sq. ft. They stand up to rough weather very well.

Both the Victory and the X class boats have light draughts which make them suitable for shoal sailing, and there is no difficulty – alas for the crew! – in jumping overboard to push the boat when it has grounded.

We do not propose to review the many other classes of local keel boats to be found around our coasts. There are several reasons for this. The first reason is that experimenting with keel boats is an expensive business, consequently most of them follow conventional lines and do not warrant special descriptions. Moreover, keel boat classes are in many cases long lived and many have become old-fashioned. They survive because there is nothing to replace them. Many of them offer very good sport and are well suited to the local conditions under which they are sailed. Often these are the very reasons which prevent them from being more widely adopted throughout the country.

The rules on page 108, printed by courtesy of the Royal Yachting Association, illustrate the care taken to ensure fair racing between boats in the same class.

ROYAL YACHTING ASSOCIATION

ALL INTERNATIONAL CLASSES

Material of sails shall be confined to woven fibre cloth except that one unwoven transparent panel not exceeding 3 sq. ft. (.279 sq. m.) – or such other area as the class rules prescribe – may be permitted below half height in any sail. Sails shall be capable of being stowed in sail bags of conventional dimensions.

RULES OF INTERNATIONAL 14-FT. DINGHY CLASS

HULL AND CENTRE BOARD

1. *Boats to be open.* Boats are to be entirely open, i.e. undecked, and nothing which in any way alters this characteristic is allowed.

2. The following clauses give general guidance in amplification of Rule 1:

   (a) No surfaces within the hull may be arranged so that they will divert water overboard or into the centre-board box.

   (b) Bulkheads which could contain a significant amount of water in any given part of the boat are not allowed, but this restriction does not apply to buoyancy apparatus provided the latter is disposed in accordance with Rule 23, nor to the centre-board box provided the extensions before and abaft this are not so constructed as to contain a substantial weight of water in one half of the boat.

   (c) Open lockers to provide stowage for small gear may be fitted at or below buoyancy apparatus level. They must comply with (a) and (b) above.

   (d) The mast thwart, if fitted, may be braced in such a manner as is structurally necessary. It shall not exceed 6 in. in width.

   (e) In addition to the mast thwart one other thwart which may not exceed 6 in. in width, or two other thwarts neither of which may exceed 4 in. in width, may be fitted.

   (f) The centre-board box may be covered in over all or part of its length, but such covering is not to exceed 8 in. in width.

3. *Construction.* (a) Boats may be built of any material or construction, but the shell or planking of the hull must be of uniform material and thickness throughout. No projections other than the gunwale, foresail and spinnaker fairlead assemblies, bilge keels, suction balers, stem-band, keel-band and rudder fittings are allowed to extend beyond the surface of the skin. Foresail and spinnaker fairlead assemblies may not project beyond the outside edge of the gunwale, except that mounting plates, if used, may be wrapped round the gunwale.

(*b*) Metal forefoot fittings, outside channels, outriggers, sliding seats and all similar contrivances, bilge boards, double rudders and inside ballast are prohibited.

4. *Length overall.* Not to exceed 14 ft., excluding normal rudder fittings.

5. *Beam.* The beam is to be measured overall.
   (*a*) At the widest point not to be less than 4 ft. 8 in., nor more than 5 ft. 6 in. (in boats registered after 1st November 1953).
   (*b*) At mid-length 8 in. above underside of keel-band not to be less than 4 ft. (*Note.* This applies only to boats completed since 1st January 1937.)

6. *Depth.* Inside the shell of hull at mid-length not to be less than 1 ft. 9 in. measured vertically from a horizontal line joining the upper surfaces on the gunwales to the planking 6 in. from the fore and aft centre line of the boat.

7. *Weight.* When weighed the boat must be in dry condition, which is defined as having been out of the water, dried out, and in a dry place for a period of four weeks or longer. New boats must be weighed before they are put into the water for the first time. The weight shall not be less than 225 lb. including keel-band, essential fixed metal work and buoyancy apparatus (whether movable or fixed) but stripped otherwise of all gear, sails, spars, rudder, removable bottom boards and centre board. If boats, when new, are found to be under weight owing to any error in building, correctors, not exceeding 10 lb., may be added above the waterline. Correctors are not to be removed or altered without the boat being officially re-weighed by a measurer.

8. *Sheer.* The sheer of the boat must be a fair continuous concave curve.

9. *Flare and tumble-home.* A taut tape containing any vertical cross-section of the hull (including the gunwale assembly) shall not anywhere outside the hull pass at a greater distance from the nearest point of the outside skin of the hull than 2½ in. The sum of the tumble-home of the topsides shall not exceed one twenty-fourth of the greatest beam.

10. *Gunwale assembly.* The total width of the gunwale assembly, including inwale(s) skin, outwale(s) and rubber, shall not exceed 3 in. In timbered boats, the thickness of conventional timbers, if these are extended to the top of the gunwale assembly, and provided that the spaces between them are not filled in, shall not count in measuring the total width of the gunwale assembly. Normal breasthook not extending more than 9 in. aft of the stem, and quarterknees not extending more than 9 in. forward of the after part of the transom, may be fitted, giving additional width.

11. *Metal keel-band.* A metal keel-band, which is not to be let into

the keel, must be fitted over the whole length of the boat from transom to stem, around the forefoot, and for a minimum distance of 6 in. up the stem. This band is to be of metal not less than $\frac{1}{32}$ in. nor more than $\frac{1}{4}$ in. in thickness, and is to be of a cross-sectional area not greater than $\frac{1}{12}$ sq. in. except near entries to centre-plate slot, where the width may be increased as required to effect continuity between the single strips forward and aft and the dual strip in way of centre-plate slot. The metal keel-band is to be adequate to protect the bottom of the boat when on an even keel, and, when the boat is ashore on a level surface, must bear in conjunction with either one of the two bilge keels.

12. *Bilge keels.* To be fitted one on each bilge so that the boat will bear on the main and one bilge keel when ashore on a level surface. The sectional area of these to be not less than $\frac{3}{8}$ of a sq. in. for a minimum length of 4 ft. with a maximum width of $2\frac{1}{2}$ in. The material is to be wood or the same as that of the skin of the hull.

13. *Centre board.* The width of the inside of the centre-board box and the opening in the keel for the centre board shall not exceed $1\frac{3}{8}$ in. No device shall be used to alter the plane of the centre board. The maximum weight of a composite centre board shall be 60 lb., but if of uniform material, except for a protective coating such as galvanizing or paint, it may be of any weight. No portion of the centre board when housed shall extend above the gunwale line or below the keel line of the boat. Unless the centre board is positively buoyant it must be arranged to lift out. Only one centre board may be fitted.

14. *Automatic bailing and draining apparatus.* Automatic bailing apparatus of the pilot-head or suction types, not exceeding a total effective cross-sectional area of 1 sq. in., is permitted. It may operate through one or more holes in the bottom of the boat or in the centre-board box. In addition, one or more holes, not exceeding a total effective cross-sectional area of 2 sq. in., are permitted in the transom to act as a gravity drain.

Pumps and mechanical baling devices other than the above are not allowed.

15. *Distinguishing mark on hull.* (Applicable only to boats requiring a British Certificate and first registered after 6th September 1950.)

The boats of this class must bear the class number cut upon the transom or hog piece in figures not less than 1 in. in height.

SAILS, SAIL AREA, SPARS AND RIGGING

16. *Sail measurement.* (a) FORE TRIANGLE. The height I is to be measured from a horizontal line gunwale to gunwale at the fore side of the mast to where the line of the luff of the headsail, when extended,

cuts the mast. If the sheave of the spinnaker halliard is above the luff-line as defined above, then I is to be measured to the top of the spinnaker sheave. The apex of the fore triangle is to be indicated by a distinctive mark on the mast.

The base J is to be measured along a horizontal line from the fore side of the mast to the point where the line of the luff of the headsail, when extended, cuts the gunwale line. The mast must never be stepped so that the certified measurement of J is exceeded.

(*b*) MAINSAIL (if bermudian). The luff A is to be measured between the upper edge of a lower black band on the mast, and the lower edge of an upper black band on the mast. The upper edge of the lower black band is to mark the lowest position where the line of the top of the boom when at right angles to the mast cuts the mast. No part of the headboard of the sail shall exceed in height the lower edge of the upper black band.

The foot B is to be measured from the inner edge of a black band at the outer end of the boom, along the top of the boom, to the after side of the mast excluding the track; but if there is a groove in the mast for the sail, the measurement is to be to the fore side of the groove.

The measurements I, J, A and B above are to be entered on the measurement form by the measurer.

(*c*) The width at half height shall never exceed $\frac{B}{2}+2.50$ ft. and at three-quarter height shall never exceed $\frac{B}{4}+2.20$ ft.

(*d*) The half height measurement shall be taken along the line of the fold which is formed when the top forward corner of the headboard is placed on the bottom forward corner of the tack, with the two halves of the luff coinciding and the sail smoothed out.

(*e*) The three-quarter height measurement shall be taken along the line of the fold which is formed when the top forward corner of the headboard is placed on the mid-point of the luff, with the two upper quarters of the luff coinciding and the sail smoothed out.

(*f*) When these measurements are taken, the sail is to be smoothed out in dry condition on a flat floor. All measurements are to be taken over the full width including roping, and any hollows in the leach are to be bridged by straight lines.

(*g*) MAINSAIL (if not bermudian). If the mainsail is other than bermudian its area is to be measured in full, except that the leach is to be taken as straight, the necessary dimensions and the total area, together with such diagrams as are required, being entered upon the measurement form. A black band is to be painted on the gaff or yard, near its upper extremity, to mark the upper limit of the peak and also on the boom to mark the outer limit of the clew.

17. *Sail plan.* (a) The sail plan shall in no case exceed 22 ft. 6 in. above the gunwale line.

A gunwale line black band is to be painted on the mast, and no part of this band may protrude above the gunwale line.

In boats which are bermudian rigged the distance between the upper edge of the gunwale line black band and the lower edge of the uppermost black band on the mast (see Rule 16 (b)) shall not exceed 22 ft. 6 in.

In boats which are gunter or gaff rigged the 22 ft. 6 in. measurement is to be taken from the upper edge of the gunwale line black band to the lower edge of the black band on the head spar (see Rule 16 (c)), with this spar set up in a straight line in extension of the mast. With these rigs a further black band is to be painted on the mast to mark the position above which the throat cringle may not be hoisted.

In all cases where the mast is stepped on or above the gunwale line the 22 ft. 6 in. measurement is to be taken from the gunwale line in way of the mast. If a mast jack is used in such cases, the measurement must be taken with this fully extended.

(b) The height of the foretriangle I shall not exceed 14 ft.

18. *Sail area.* The maximum sail area is 125 sq. ft. measured according to the formula $\frac{A \times B}{2}$ as to a bermudian mainsail, or the full area (see Rule 16 (c)) of a mainsail other than bermudian, plus 85% of $\frac{I \times J}{2}$ as to fore triangle.

The headboard of the mainsail must not exceed 4 in. in width measured at right-angles to the mast.

The maximum dimension of the spinnaker headboard must not exceed 4 in. Otherwise no restrictions are placed on the size or shape of the spinnaker.

The overall length of the spinnaker boom must not exceed the dimension J (base of the fore triangle).

19. *Battens.* The number of battens in the mainsail shall be four, each spaced within 5 in. above or below the respective points on the leech of the sail which divide the leech into five equal parts. The maximum length of the uppermost and lowest battens is 2 ft. 6 in. and that of the two intermediate battens 3 ft. 4 in.

20. *Distinguishing marks on sail.* On each side of the mainsail shall be the number "14", and beneath that number the national letter

and class number of the boat as stated upon this form thus:

$$\frac{14}{\text{K 616}}$$

The figures shall be 12 in. in height, and shall be disposed in accordance with I.Y.R.U. Rule 12.

21. *Boom.* The boom must be capable of being passed through a circle 4 in. in diameter.

22. *The following are not allowed.* Mast or boom designed or built with a permanent bend, rotating mast, bowsprit, bumpkin, double luffed sails.

BUOYANCY

23. *Buoyancy apparatus.* Not less than three tanks or other approved buoyancy apparatus must be fitted so that the buoyancy of the boat, in the condition in Rule 24, and when full of water, exceeds her weight by not less than 200 lb. Not less than 80 lb. of the buoyancy must act within 5 ft. of the stem, and not less than 120 lb. must act abaft of amidships. In boats built after 1st January 1936 no buoyancy apparatus which is within 9 ft. of the stem shall be placed less than 6 in. below or, alternatively, less than 6 in. away from the gunwale. Buoyancy apparatus placed in the after 5 ft. of the boat may be faired off evenly from a minimum of 6 in. below the gunwale at 5 ft. from the stern to a minimum of 3 in. below the gunwale level at the stern. The horizontal surface, actual or projected, of the buoyancy apparatus shall not exceed 23 sq. ft. provided that any such area in excess of 15 sq. ft. is within 5 ft. of the stern.

24. *Initial test.* Before a certificate can be obtained all boats must pass the following test of buoyancy: with sails, boom, rudder, tiller and all loose gear removed from the boat, but with the centreplate and mast in position, weights of cast iron or denser material totalling at least 234 lb. are to be placed in the hull and disposed as to at least 94 lb. (absolute buoyancy 80 lb.) within 5 ft. of the stem, and at least 140 lb. (absolute buoyancy 120 lb.) abaft of midships. In this condition the boat, after being filled with water, must float for thirty minutes with its gunwales clear of the water throughout their length. The measurer must be satisfied that the buoyancy apparatus is reasonably watertight.

25. *Annual re-test.* The certificate of registration is valid for twelve months from the date of the original buoyancy test, or any subsequent re-test, provided that it is endorsed with the date of the buoyancy test, and signed by a club official. For annual re-test only, and provided that no alteration of the buoyancy apparatus or of its position in the boat has been made, the weights specified in Rule 24 may be

replaced by persons of minimum combined weight of 280 lb., not immersed above the knee.

Any alteration to the buoyancy apparatus involves re-measurement and re-test as stipulated in Rules 23 and 24.

MISCELLANEOUS

26. *Crew.* Two, including helmsman.

If a member of the crew during the course of a race leaves the boat voluntarily, he shall be deemed to have been lost overboard within the meaning of Rule 19, para. 4 of the I.Y.R.U. racing rules.

27. *Support for crew prohibited.* The use of any apparatus or contrivance outboard or extending outboard and attached to the hull, spars, rigging or crew, the purpose or effect of which is or may be to support or assist in supporting a member of the crew outboard or partially outboard is prohibited.

28. *Time allowances.* There is no time allowance in this class.

29. *Anchors.* It is not compulsory to carry anchor or grapnel in this class.

CERTIFICATE

30. *Certificate.* A certificate issued by a national authority to a boat numbered in the class shall remain valid so long as the boat continues to comply with these rules, provided that there is a current buoyancy endorsement (see Rule 25).

The owner of the boat is responsible that the certificate shall not be rendered invalid from any cause.

(In the case of British certificates, issued by the R.Y.A., a change of ownership necessitates re-registration.)

I am saying little in this book about what it costs to buy a boat – a tantalizing but inevitable exclusion. For prices of new and second-hand craft vary not only from year to year, but from country to country. At the time of writing, for instance, prices in the United States are much above those in Britain which, in turn, are higher than those in Scandinavia.

It follows that no catalogue can be more than the haziest of guides – subject to revision without notice. The following prices were those generally ruling in Great Britain in the late fifties:

10-ft. second-hand knock about sailing
dinghy . . . . £35 upwards
ditto (new) . . . . £60–£90

12-ft. second-hand class racing boat	£80 upwards
ditto (new).	£130–£170
14-ft. class racing boat (new)	£140–£350
2-berth cruiser (no auxiliary motor)	£600 plus
4-berth cruiser (no auxiliary motor)	£900 plus
4-berth cruiser (with auxiliary motor)	£1,200–£2,750

CHAPTER IX

CAN I BUILD HER?

THERE are two kinds of people who build their own boats. The first are those who like carpentering for carpentering's sake, and the second are those who take up a hammer and chisel only because there is no other way they can afford a boat. Our sympathies are with the second group. The idea of giving up anything more than a couple of months in the winter to building a boat is repugnant to me. I shall not quarrel with any reader who disagrees, but simply suggest that he puts down this book and buys something of a far more technical nature which will show him how to build anything from a speed-boat to a schooner. It will doubtless include chapters on plank boats and we are content to leave it at that; for while it is quite possible for an unskilled amateur to build a plank boat, my view is that he is unlikely to be able to do so economically without help from a trained carpenter or boat-builder.

Surveying the limited field open to someone who has had but little carpentering experience, and who wishes to go ahead on his own, I see that there are two small-boat possibilities. The amateur can decide (1) to buy a ready-moulded veneer hull for completion, or (2) put together a plywood hull, using sheets of ply and "pre-fabricated" timber parts. Course (1) offers the easier line of country, since a pre-shaped hull takes most of the difficulty out of the job and all the amateur builder need do is to instal various ready-made units, such as centre board housing, buoyancy tanks and one-piece deck, to have the completed boat. This method, however, limits the choice of the owner to those firms who happen to be supplying moulded hulls at the time when he wants to order a boat. The second course – that of assembling the boat at home with sheets of plywood and pre-shaped, pre-sawn kits of parts – offers a wide range of designs, particularly on the hard-chine field. Professional yards, both at home and abroad, admit that it is quicker and cheaper to assemble boats from ready-made parts supplied to them than to do the whole job themselves. The saving obtained by building yourself often amounts to as much as one-third of the finished market selling price. Let us examine a typical kit of parts supplied for the amateur builder and see what we get.

First, there is the framework or ribs of the boat. A well-built plywood class boat of, say, 11 ft. in length will have five or more frames (which in this case means pairs of ribs), the ends of the ribs being close together at the bow and stern and farther apart in the middle, where the boat is wider. These ribs are supplied planed square and shaped according to their position in the boat. By having the frames longer than you need you can build the boat upside down, and during construction it will be raised off the floor and supported by the ends of the frames. When the boat is finished the ends of the frames on which it has been standing are cut off level. This procedure avoids the expense of making special stocks to hold up the boat. Instructions supplied with the kit tell you the method of procedure. If the parts have to be stored before using it is best to varnish them for protection and lay them on a shelf out of the sun to prevent possible warping.

When assembling, the ribs, known professionally as timbers, are first attached to the hog (which runs above the keel along the bottom of the well), to the gunwales (forming the outer edge of the deck), and to the chines. The chines, hog and gunwales are attached by various methods to the stem and transom, according to instructions also supplied. On to this skeleton the sheets of plywood are laid, glued and screwed.

In a pre-fabricated kit such as we have described you will receive a set of frames planed square and shaped according to their position in the boat, with recesses into which the gunwales and hog are to fit. The deck beams which support the decking are shaped in advance to the right curve, and you will find a housing or space cut to receive the king plank – the centre plank in the decking which supports the two halves of the deck.

All this does not mean, however, that you will be able to build a boat without doing any work. Before you have finished you will probably have used several different kinds of screwdriver, a paring chisel, mallet and hammer, drill and bits, 2-in. adjustable plane and finally a spokeshave, which helps to plane in spots which could not otherwise be reached. The design of plywood boats is simple in the extreme, but they are by no means as slab-sided as one would think at first sight. In fact, there are more curved surfaces than straight ones. For instance, the bottom of the boat, as seen in profile from the side, is not flat but rocker-shape; and the two chines, though they start parallel, curve in to meet at the stem. How are we to fit the curving hog, chine and gunwale to the rectangular timbers over which they pass? The answer is by bevelling away the rectangular corners of the timber so that the curved member fits in snugly. When building it is important that the gunwales should be fitted well home in the frames, so that the plywood skin of the boat can be properly secured to the frame itself. (See fig. 26(a).)

A fine springy batten can easily be tacked on and used as a "pathfinder" to show how much bevel is needed. A few G screw clamps are extremely useful for holding these curved members temporarily in place for a final check up. Sometimes it is necessary to steam the chines, and perhaps the gunwales, so that they can be bent to the right position. A kettle of boiling water poured over the wood in question may serve. Keep pouring for as long as possible with a small stream of water moving over the whole of the timber continuously. If the boiling water does not do the trick you may have to construct a homemade steamer. For this purpose you will need a rain-water pipe long enough to take part of the timber to be steamed. Plug one end of the pipe with a piece of wood 1 in. thick, held in position by three or four screws bored through the pipe. Then bore a hole in the plug to take the kettle spout. Pack the open end lightly with a cloth or sacking while steaming. Steaming time should be about one hour per inch of light timber, plus an extra half an hour. Thus if the timber is $\frac{3}{4}$ in. $\times$ $1\frac{1}{2}$ in., three-quarters of an hour plus half an hour is plenty. It is probably worth making a wooden prong for twisting the chine or gunwale into position.

The above "recipe" and much of the information in this chapter has been provided by the Bell Woodworking Company of Leicester, the leading specialists in this field of pre-fabricated kits. Their treatise, *Home Boat-Building Made Easy*, is well worth special study. The marine plywood to be used for the skin of the boat (it should be stamped BSS. 1088 WBP) is almost ideal for amateur builders. It is put together under high pressure, and can stand temperatures near to boiling or freezing point without coming apart. It has the same strength as timber planking, with little over half of the thickness. Using plywood, your joints are fewer than with planks, and they can be sealed with glue to give a permanent closure which never dries out or needs special treatment such as caulking. The plywood is both glued and screwed into position on to the boat. The procedure is first to make a trial fitting, and then, if this is satisfactory, to hold the panel in position with a few pathfinder screws or nails, and mark round it so that it is easy to replace it in the same place when ready for gluing. Mark it on the under side with the outlines of the ribs to which it is to be fastened. Take off the panel, mark the pathfinder screw holes in the framework of the boat so that when gluing you can replace the panel in the same spot. Then, turning the panel upside down, drill holes at the points shown by the outlines of the members you have just drawn. The holes should be drilled so that the shank of the screw (the smooth part above the thread) fits tightly. Allowance will have to be made so that the head of the screw can be got down flush with the surface of the skin or deck. The screws should vary from $1\frac{1}{2}$ in. to 4 in. and nails from $1\frac{1}{2}$ in. to $2\frac{1}{2}$ in., according to the amount of tension to be overcome.

It is worth having several sizes of screwdriver. When screwing into hardwood, bore for the shank of the screw and counter-bore (bore again but with a finer drill) for the thread of the screw, using the bits shown here as a guide.

Gauge	4	5	6	7	8	10	12	14
Bore	$\frac{1}{8}$	$\frac{1}{8}$	$\frac{5}{32}$	$\frac{3}{32}$	$\frac{3}{16}$	$\frac{7}{32}$	$\frac{1}{4}$	$\frac{1}{4}$
C'bore		Bradawl			$\frac{3}{32}$	$\frac{1}{8}$	$\frac{1}{8}$	$\frac{5}{32}$

Here is a good way of knowing when to stop boring for the shank and to begin counter-boring for the thread. Measure off a piece of wood dowelling, drill through and beyond it so that the amount of drill projecting equals length of shank. The wood will then act as a stop when you have bored deep enough for the shank. Vaseline or similar grease will help to get smooth work, particularly in the case of the larger screws. It may even save the screw from breaking. Gluing the plywood is a very simple process. The glue is applied to only one of the surfaces to be joined, and a liquid known as hardener to the other. The glue can best be spread with a piece of wood, and the hardener with a brush. Aerolite 300 glue with hardener is one of the best combinations for the purpose.

When assembling it is essential for the hardener-covered surface to be wet or at least damp when the joint is closed, and it is therefore recommended that the glue be spread first and the hardener brushed on just before making the assembly. Do not move the surfaces once they have been brought together unless this is unavoidable. Three different hardeners are supplied with Aerolite 300, namely, Fast setting, GBQ.X.; Medium setting, BBP.X.; Slow setting, GBM.X.

For all practical boat-building work the slow-setting hardener (GBM.X.) is the most convenient; it will set sufficiently for the joint to be worked on after four to five hours. Using the fastest hardener (GBQ.X.), the clamping time under the same conditions (say, 60–70°F.) would be only about two hours. The time allowed for adjusting the assembly after the surfaces have been brought together is much less when using the fast hardener (GBQ.X.) than with the slow hardener (GBM.X.). In fact, at a temperature of, say, 70°F. the permitted time, known as the closed assembly time, is:

5 minutes for the fast-setting hardener (GBQ.X.);
10 minutes for the medium-setting hardener (GBP.X.);
20 minutes for the slow-setting hardener (GBM.X.).

The permissible shuffling times for the slow hardener (GBM.X.) over a range of temperatures are as follows:

Temperature	50° F.	60° F.	70° F.	80° F.
Time in minutes	60–70	40	20	10

Large panels should be given a trial fitting dry as mentioned previously, and the glue and hardener applied later. The panel is then replaced and located in position by means of the pilot screws used on the previous fitting. The screwing or nailing is then completed as quickly as possible. In general, the hardeners supplied are colourless, so that glue lines at the joints are also clear. For certain work, however, a coloured hardener is an advantage, since it shows at a glance whether the part concerned has been fully covered. Different hardeners have each a distinguishing colour, namely GBQ. (brown), GBP. (green), GBM. (purple). When ordering a coloured hardener you merely omit the suffix "X". Therefore if the slow hardener (GBM.X.) is required in coloured form it should be ordered as GBM.

When using Aerolite 300 it is not essential to have close-fitting joints, as the glue itself will take up a considerable gap. In fact, too much pressure will often force the glue out and cause a weak joint through glue starvation. To get the best results make sure that the surfaces are clean and free from oil, grease and grit.

Aerolite can be bought as a powder (known as Aerolite 306) for mixing with water to produce the liquid glue (Aerolite 300).

Powder has the advantage of keeping for at least two years

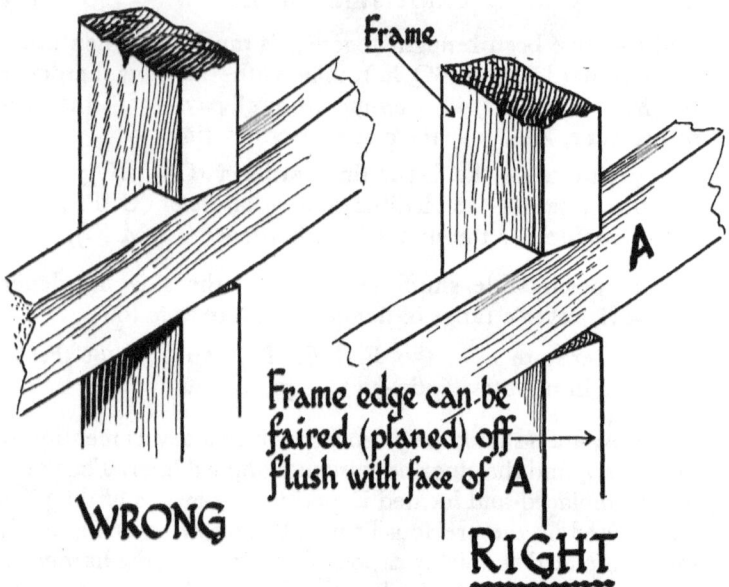

(a) Fitting the curved gunwale to rectangular frame

(b) Fitting plywood panel to the hog

Fig. 26 (a) & (b). BUILDING AT HOME

(c) King plank rebated to take decking flush

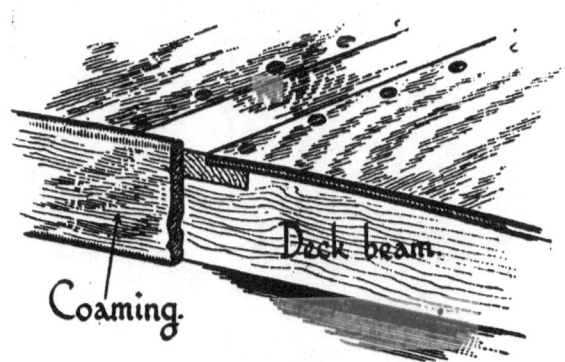

(d) Glued coamings improve the boat's appearance

Fig. 26 (c) & (d). BUILDING AT HOME (*continued*)

(e) A simple way of joining the deck beam to the gunwale

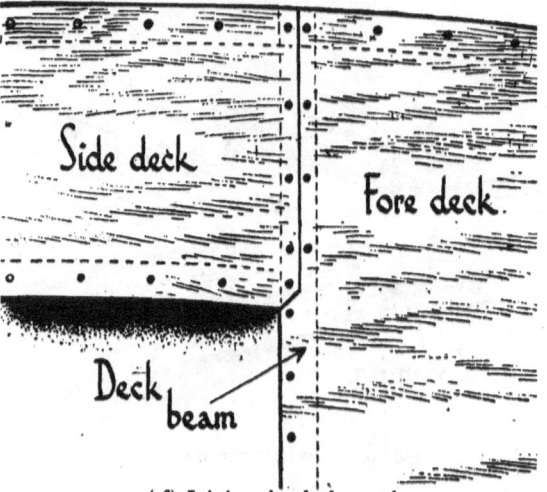

(f) Joining the deck panels

Fig. 26 (e) & (f). BUILDING AT HOME (*continued*)

without deteriorating, as compared with liquid glue's life of three to four months. When building the hull it will probably be necessary to make several joins in the plywood sheeting. This is carried out by means of a backing strip laid into the framework of the boat. In other words, a section of framework equal to the thickness of the plywood strip is cut away and a backing strip is fitted flush with the cut-out area. A $2\frac{1}{4}$-in. wide backing strip is broad enough. When making the joint the first panel is glued and nailed into position and joined to the backing strip with two staggered rows of copper nails, the points of which are cut off to about $\frac{3}{8}$ in. of the skin and clenched over. Wipe the surface glue from the backing strip so that this is clean to receive the second panel when required.

When fitting a plywood panel to the hog, cut the plywood roughly to the required shape (see fig. 26(b)); clamp this into position, getting the panel to touch the side of the hog where possible. Then, using a small block of wood about the thickness of the widest gap between the panel and the hog, run the block along the side of the hog marking the plywood with a pencil held against the block. This allows the plywood to be cut exactly to shape. If the plywood has to be twisted, make a trial fitting with a brown paper pattern and get from this the exact size of plywood.

It is important to see that the centre board casing of your boat fits tightly enough to prevent leaks. Here is a procedure which the Bell Woodworking Company has found to work extremely well:

(i) Plane the bottom of the centre board case, so that it fits into the curve of the hog to within $\frac{1}{16}$ in. at least.

(ii) Mark round the case in that position as a guide, so that you can take it out and replace it later in the same position.

(iii) Drill holes and counter-bore for six screws at not more than $2\frac{1}{2}$ in. apart. These six screws will hold the case in place while the holes for the remaining screws are bored and counter-bored.

(iv) Unscrew the six screws, take off casing and brush clean.
(v) Cover the area of the joint with Prestik leak-stopping tape.
(vi) Replace the centre board case in the same position by means of the six screws already used and put in the permanent screws. All screws should be retightened after two days and given a further tightening after another two days.

Finally, the decking. When fixing the decks, glue and nail or screw round the outside edges only, otherwise there is a danger, under certain weather conditions, that the decks will corrugate. Decks should be nailed rather than screwed, except where a king plank is rebated (cut into) to take the plywood flush. Here it is advisable to use small screws, since in small boats at least the king planks are not usually heavy enough or solid enough to be nailed. Where possible, finish the screws with the slots of the screw heads in line, as this is more pleasing to the eye and is better for cleaning and rubbing down. Illustration shows a king plank with rebate to take plywood decking (fig. 26(*c*)).

Cockpit coamings (see fig. 26(*d*)) add greatly to the appearance of any small boat, and the timber being very thin costs little extra. The small additional weight can often be compensated for by substituting softwood deck beams for hardwood ones, since these will not be seen when coamings are fitted.

If you have the time and four or five G-clamps at your disposal, coamings can be glued on bit by bit at night and morning.

The advantage of gluing coamings is that this does away with screw heads which can otherwise damage clothing, etc. You can prevent the clamp from marking the face of the wood by placing a bit of scrap timber under the clamp heads.

Deck beams are normally dovetailed into gunwales, but in

small dinghies with plywood decking this operation can be considerably simplified, as shown in fig. 26(*e*).

The shallowest possible vertical and horizontal trenches are cut in gunwales to take the square shoulder of the deck beam. In some cases a slight bevel on the shoulder will be needed to suit the curve of the gunwale, but this is far simpler than the alternative – a compound-bevelled dovetail which, unless skilfully carried out, distorts the curve of the gunwale. If the simpler method is used and the outside 2 in. of deck beam is glued when gluing decks to gunwale, a perfectly satisfactory job will result.

For deck panels: If the dinghy is to be fully decked, add forward panels first, side panels next, and aft panels (if any) last.

A simple mitre joint, as shown in fig. 26(*f*), is the neatest way of joining panels.

If deck beams are too thin for this purpose, screw and glue a "plant" piece to the side of beam to increase width where required.

We have dealt here mainly with hard chine boats, but a system has recently been devised whereby the amateur can build a round bilge boat from plywood without the complexities of moulding. Uffa Fox has designed the 14-ft. Pegasus specially for building from kits by this method.

A boat carefully made and put together in this way can be equal in every way to the professional product.

Questions of painting and finishing are dealt with in the next chapter.

CHAPTER X

LONG LIFE TO THE BOAT

THERE is no golden rule for maintaining a boat. Your plans, for instance, are bound to be influenced by the size of your yacht, your own talents as a handy man, by the amount of your bank balance, by the capacity and reliability of the boat yard, by the amount of time you can spare during the winter, and, not least of all, by whether you live near to your boat or far away from it.

At one extreme you have the owner who leaves everything to the yard and has a complete fit-out before the beginning of each season. At the other end of the scale there is the man who has to do everything for himself, even if it means waiting for a month for suitable weather for that last coat of paint. Often he has to work throughout the season to avoid getting behind. But both rich and poor should be well acquainted with a list of items that need regular examination if a boat is to remain seaworthy. It is largely a matter of common sense.

Fitting out should be begun at the end of the last season rather than at the beginning of the new one. The work comes under five main headings:

  (i) The hull structure;
  (ii) Hull and deck painting;
  (iii) Interior cleaning up and repainting;
  (iv) The rigging and equipment;
  (v) The engine, where used.

A list of the main jobs to be done should be prepared towards the end of each season and materials ordered. The amount of work that you do yourself will have to be arranged with the shipyard. Some yards have no objection to your doing all maintenance jobs yourself; others may object to this one-sided arrangement, which provides no employment for their hands. It is a matter for negotiation, as the diplomats say. In any case, there are a number of jobs, such as caulking (filling up gaps between the planks with cotton or similar wadding), which an amateur would be wise not to tackle for the first time without help from the professional.

Perhaps the best way would be for us to go over the boat together and see what needs to be done. You can then decide which jobs you may tackle yourself and which will be left to the yard. We will assume that you have just taken over the boat at the start of a new season and wish to make your own check, starting from scratch.

The first operation will be to remove the boat's cover and store it away, if it is not wanted. The cover should be marked with the boat's name and labelled showing which end is which, so that it can be easily replaced on the boat at the end of the season.

The hull should first be carefully inspected to see that the wood is sound, particularly in spots where the air does not circulate freely. Any leaks should have been marked the previous year. It is worth searching for new leaks which could possibly develop. The rudder fastenings will need looking at, and also the keel bolts. Examine the centre board case, where worms often start their work of destruction. If you have bought the boat, much of this inspection work will have been done by your surveyor before purchase. When it comes to painting the hull or the deck you can drag in those friends who promised to help. If the paint is peeling only in spots it can be scraped and then built up for repainting with trowel cement or putty. If it is badly cracked the paint must be scraped off to the wood either with paint remover or blow-torch (but not both, as most paint removers are inflammable). Any surface to be painted or varnished must be clean and dry. To re-paint the bare hull, coat first with priming, then with stopping for making good major hollows, then with trowel cement for minor depressions, rub down with sandpaper, then give a second coat of priming followed by two undercoats and a finishing coat. Different undercoatings and finishes are used for wood above and below the waterline. Varnish if in fair condition may be sanded down or given a wash with a wet cloth and pumice powder before revarnishing. Here, again, the surface must be clean and dry before the new coat is applied. If varnish has to be removed, this must be done with chemical stripper. Varnish cannot be safely burnt off. After varnish has been stripped, the woodwork should be cleaned off with white spirit; before using varnish, fill in any cracks with transparent grain filler. Then give several coats of varnish, sanded down between each coat. Do not sand against the grain when preparing to varnish. Painting and varnishing should be carried out on a dry, windless (non-dusty) non-frosty day before dew-fall. The thicker the paint is put on, the sooner it will start to crumble away. Varnish on the other hand should be flowed on with a good full coat – it does not matter how full so long as there are no runs. If paint has been standing in a tin mix it in four stages: (1) **pour off** the top third into a clean tin after removing any skin; (2) **stir** the remainder to an even consistency; (3) pour the remainder into the clean tin while stirring; (4) strain through **clean wire** gauze. One should paint from right to left if **right-handed** and from the top downwards, so that drops will not spoil the completed work. Stir paint regularly; but not varnish, in which stirring simply produces air bubbles. Add thinners (the right ones) if these are called for. Get advice from an expert **before** using paint different from what has been used before. Some old paints underneath will affect new paints on top. Get advice about your brushes and their treatment. Never stand them on end. A rub down with wet-or-dry (waterproof) is given between each coat. Do not worry if bare wood shows through again after your first rub down. You will have filled up most of the grain – an important step forward. Wash off the particles with water so that the surface is quite clean. Finishing coats of paint may be applied with the spray gun, but priming and anti-fouling must be put on with a brush.

The decks will also probably need attention if you want to assure yourself of a leak-proof season. Small leaks can often be stopped with composition, sold for the purpose. Other leaks will have to be caulked. Much depends on the kind of deck you have. I am not in favour of leaving decks bare; bare decks have to be sluiced regularly with water to keep them tight. Varnished or painted decks are less affected by extremes of heat or moisture and therefore keep tighter. It may be as well to apply non-slip paint or varnish to them if you are renewing. Canvas-covered decks are still better protected, and if the canvas is properly painted will last for years. Old canvas that has to be repainted must be scraped clean or replaced.

When cleaning brushes, wash first in turpentine or turpentine substitute and then in soap and water. If you can get a lather this means that the brush is clean.

Spars should be checked for cracks. Cracks *across* the spar are serious and will mean a replacement. Longitudinal cracks along the spar can be filled with a putty-like mixture. One recommended mixture is made up as follows on the stove: Dissolve ½ pint linseed oil in 1 lb. resin. Add 4 oz. beeswax and 3 oz. turpentine.

Ordinary putty will not do as it sets hard, and therefore under certain conditions will widen the crack.

Careful examination needs to be made of cupboards and any other areas where air does not circulate freely and where there might be rot. Any rotted wood must be cut away ruthlessly and a bit extra for safety. The chances of rot will be less if hatches, drawers and cupboards have been left open during the winter.

A rather messy internal job in larger boats is to remove the ballast so that the bilges can be properly cleaned. Each pig (piece) of ballast must be marked with its position in the boat before removal. When de-ballasting it is worth while protecting your woodwork with plenty of old sacking, so that the wood does not get scratched. It may be possible to haul the pigs out by a rope attached to the boom, which can be raised by means of a halyard. There is less risk of strain when lifting ballast if you stand with your legs together. When the ballast is out the bilges should be cleaned out, and the limber holes (holes which allow the bilge water to run from one part of the boat to the other) cleared out. Often a loose chain is fitted which needs only to be pulled to and fro several times to clear the limber hole. When the bilge is dry and sweet it should be painted with red lead or bitumastic. The ballast will probably require cleaning before being replaced. In the case of iron ballast, the worst of the rust can be chipped off with a hammer and chipper. After cleaning, iron ballast should be coated with red oxide, but lead ballast needs no paint.

The rest of the interior will have to be cleaned with soap and water plus a small amount of ammonia. It is well worth applying anti-mildew spray in spots where there seems a chance of its developing.

The fittings, such as fuel and water tanks, need careful examination, and all fastenings should be rechecked. Toilet and water pumps may require new washers or strainers. The bilge pump should be tested. It is worth painting the plumbing outlets with anti-fouling paint. Electric light installations need careful watching to detect corrosion.

Standing rigging for the mast, etc., needs a thorough examination. It should be scrapped if there are any signs of rust corrosion, fraying or roughened wire. Trouble often occurs at the wire splices, and the covering should be removed from these for a thorough "look-see". Weaknesses can often be detected by bending the wire up to a right-angle several times. Wire rigging trouble can often be postponed if not avoided by giving it a winter bath of boiled linseed oil warmed to blood heat. The wire should be left in the bath at this temperature for an hour.

Blocks and shackles, bolts and winches should be gone over and preferably taken apart and oiled to see that the pins are sound. It is vital that the anchor chain and warps should be in good shape and that there should be ample safety equipment, including fire extinguishers, life preservers, medicine chest, repair outfit and spares. Ropes should be opened up by twisting against the lay. If the heart is discoloured you need a new rope. Check all navigation lights. Before launching see that all plugs and sea cocks are closed and that the insurance policy is working. Verify that documents such as certificates of register are up to date; make a note of the number of binoculars, sextant, etc., to help recovery in case of theft. Are your charts in order? Is the yacht's name and port of registration painted on the dinghy? How about the racing flags and burgees? Check the compass.

If the boat is to be left on moorings, the bottom will need anti-fouling paint. It is quite possible for the owner to do this himself, but since with most anti-fouling paints the boat must be immersed in the water within twelve hours of application, arrangements may have to be made with the yard in advance to see that this is done. The type of anti-fouling to be used will probably depend on local conditions and whether the growth of barnacles, etc., is heavy or light.

Above all, get advice from a paint expert. Different paints are needed for wood in various parts of the boat – and painting metal is a technique on its own.

The engine should be overhauled by an experienced mechanic according to the maker's instructions.

CHAPTER XI

GOING RACING?

RACING in Britain is supervised by the Royal Yachting Association under rules agreed by all countries belonging to the International Yacht Racing Union. Those who go yacht racing must know their rights and obligations under these rules, so that they can compete without unfairness to themselves or to the other yachts. Furthermore, if when racing you damage another yacht through disregarding the International Yacht Racing Union rules, you may be legally liable for damage in just the same way as if you had disregarded the international laws of the sea described in Chapter XVI. This point was decided in 1894 when a yacht, the Satanita, ran into the Valkyrie on the Clyde during a race and sank her. In the legal case which followed, one side held that at the time of the collision the two yachts were bound by the racing rules which they had agreed to observe. The other side argued that the two vessels were bound by the Board of Trade rules and had no right to change to a private code of their own. After the case had been tried in three courts, the House of Lords upheld the legality of the racing rules.

The main difference between commercial and racing rules is that in commerce no risk whatever is theoretically run, whereas during racing the boats may be within arm's length of each other and under certain conditions, when they are going in the same direction, are legally allowed to obstruct one another.

The principles of racing rules are easy enough to understand, but not always so easy to apply in the heat of the moment or even in the club-room afterwards. By a decision agreed in November 1958, The International Yacht Racing Union rules have been changed and brought closely into line with those used by the North American Yacht Racing Union. The changes fundamentally affect British racing so that a great many otherwise excellent books published in Britain on racing and tactics have become out of date. So if you buy a book devoted to the rules – as I would advise doing this as we shall be dealing here only with general principles – make sure that it has been written with the new rule in mind and not with the old one.

One of the main principles of the new rule concerns the measures which a boat can take to prevent another boat on the same tack from passing her either to windward or to leeward.

Let us take first the boat that is trying to pass to windward of the boat which she is overtaking. Officially these boats do not affect one another until one overlaps the other, and the two yachts are within two overall lengths of the longer of them.

Once within this distance, one yacht overlaps another when any part of her hull, spars or sails is forward of an imaginary line projected abeam from the aftermost point of the other's hull and spars.

Under these conditions, assuming the starting line has been crossed and cleared, a yacht may luff a windward yacht as sharply as she pleases, and head to wind if she likes to prevent the latter passing, until the helmsman of the windward yacht, when sighting abeam from his normal station and sailing no higher than the leeward yacht, comes abreast of the mainmast of the leeward yacht. Thereafter the leeward yacht may not sail above her proper course while that overlap continues to exist.

When there is doubt, the helmsman of the leeward yacht can assume that he has the right to luff unless the helmsman of the windward yacht has shouted "Mast Abeam" or words to that effect. The leeward yacht must always respond to this warning, but she can protest after responding if she thinks that it has been wrongly called.

Thus we see that everything depends on the relative positions of the two boats when the overlap was made. If the helmsman of the windward boat was abreast or in front of the mast of the leeward boat when the overlap began then the leeward boat can only continue on her proper course and cannot luff, as long as that overlap continues.

For the purpose of this rule, an overlap which exists between two yachts when the leading yacht crosses the starting line, or when one or both of them completes a tack or a gybe, shall be regarded as beginning at that time.

(Before the starting line is crossed a leeward yacht helmsman may not luff unless his mast is ahead of the windward helmsman, and, even then, only gently.)

What about the case of a yacht overtaking another to leeward? In this instance the windward yacht is not entitled to bear away to leeward of her proper course (to prevent the other passing) when she is clearly within three of her overall lengths of the overtaking boat. In turn the overtaking boat must not "crowd" the other and, when establishing an overlap to leeward, must allow the windward yacht plenty of room to fulfil her newly acquired obligation to keep clear of the leeward yacht.

If the two yachts are on different tacks or gybes the rules are different too. The main principle is that the starboard boat (which means the boat receiving its wind from starboard and consequently with her boom to port) has the right of way on almost every occasion.

The only exceptions to this are:

1. When a starboard yacht crosses the starting line before the starting signal, in which case she has no rights over a port tack yacht which has started correctly.

2. When a port tack yacht has correctly made an overlap inside a starboard yacht at a mark ending the downwind leg of the course. In this case the outer yacht, though otherwise holding right of way, must follow the

general principle of allowing the other enough room to round the mark.

3. At night when it may be impossible to see whether a yacht is racing and subject to these rules. In this case the normal non-racing international rule of the road is followed, which gives a yacht close hauled on port the right of way over a yacht running free on starboard.

Most of the other rules are common-sense ones. For instance, you may not tack or gybe if it means getting in the way of another yacht. If a yacht tacks into a position which will subsequently give her right of way, she must do so far enough away from a yacht to enable the latter to hold her course until the tack or gybe is completed and, at that point, there must still be enough room for her to keep clear. The burden of proof in this case rests on the yacht making the tack or gybe. If two yachts tack or gybe at the same time, the one on the other's port side shall keep clear.

Later we will discuss one or two of the rules in detail. Even when you have the right of way, you are not entitled to put another boat in danger either by running her into an obstruction or ashore. In such a case you must give way; and, if you think fit, make a protest.

Protests play an important part in seeing that the rules of yacht racing are properly observed. During a race there is no refereeing, and if a difference of opinion arises between two of the competitors it can be settled only afterwards by the aggrieved helmsman lodging a protest. And there is nothing unfair or unsporting about making such a protest. Indeed, when there is a difference of opinion it is far better to have it looked into than to leave one skipper to criticize another without the latter having the chance to state his side of the matter. Protests are heard first by the sailing committee of the club concerned, with the right of appeal to the Royal Yachting Association; and from a study of the cases which are published each year by the Royal Yachting Association it is clear that the protests serve a valuable purpose, and have led in the past to considerable improvements in the rules.

Having mastered the main principles of racing rules, the next thing is to lay some plans for winning the race, preferably while still ashore. The first step is to get the boat in first-rate order. The finish on the bottom is particularly important, because skin friction is one of the chief factors in preventing a boat from getting its maximum speed. Old roughened paint surface will not only act as a brake, but will encourage weed and barnacles. Club rules sometimes limit the number of times that the boat can be scrubbed and repainted during the season. This is all the more reason for starting in A1 condition. Later, if the boat cannot be hauled out of the water, the bottom can be scrubbed with a long-handled scrubbing brush from the dinghy. Small boats that are lifted out of the water after each race should be hosed down with freshwater to remove mud, grains of salt, etc., and so preserve the surface of the varnish.

Any pre-race tuning will include an inspection of the rigging to see that the mast is evenly stayed.

It is also worth while hoisting the sails and having someone else sail the boat around a little. Few skippers ever see what their sails look like. The rigging should be kept as simple as possible and fittings kept to a minimum. But it will be a great deal easier to tune your boat's mainsail if the mast is fitted with a sliding gooseneck which allows the tension on the sail to be varied by raising or lowering the boom. (See fig. 23, p. 84.) Too many gadgets betray the novice. "Tuning" also includes adjustments to the way the sheets, etc., are led, the way they are secured and released, and dozens of other details that get noticed only when one sails the boat constantly.

After the boat has been properly prepared the skipper can tackle the crewing problems. If a crew of only one is carried it will be easy enough to determine his duties, but if two or three are carried several practice sails will probably be necessary to sort out who does what. The crew should know the boat well enough to help get her ready and sailing. In many cases a member of the crew will be responsible for setting his watch or stop-watch to agree with the chronometer from which the starting guns are timed.

Both helmsman and crew should pay particular attention to the weather reports, tide conditions and the course to be sailed. These may influence the choice of sails to be carried as well as tactics during the race. Sailing instructions for the race should be read, marked and learnt. They include the names and re-call numbers (displayed if the yacht crosses the starting line before the starting gun has been fired) of the yachts entered; the class or race flag to be used by the officer of the day, the time of the start; starting line; the course to be sailed; and the marks, with directions on which hand they are to be passed. Sailing instructions should also mention any special directions given if the course is shortened, and the method by which competitors will be notified of any change of course. A shortened course may or may not mean a variation in the finishing arrangements. Sailing instructions should state any time limit within which the race is to be finished and the method of dealing with protests.

Any change in sailing instructions should be given by a signal or in writing to each yacht affected at least fifteen minutes before the starting signal is made. Word-of-mouth instructions are not sufficient. Apart from the sailing instructions, both helmsman and crew should make themselves familiar with the signal for cancellation of the race (made by hoisting the letter "N" of the International Code over the class* or race signal), and the abandonment signal ("N" flag with three sound signals). For a postponement, the signal is usually the answering pennant of the International Code hoisted over the class or race signal as follows:

(*a*) For a fifteen-minute postponement the answering pennant alone with the class or race signal. This fifteen-minute postponement can be extended indefinitely at fifteen-minute

* If the signal is to apply to the *whole* day's racing programme, no class signals need be shown.

intervals by lowering and raising the answering pennant.

(*b*) For a thirty-minute postponement the answering pennant over a single ball or shape. This thirty-minute postponement can be extended at thirty-minute intervals by adding one ball or shape for every thirty minutes.

Postponements are reckoned from the advertised time of starting the race, and not from the time the postponement is made. If the course is shortened the letter "S" of the International Code is usually hoisted, together with the class signals of those races affected.

Races are normally started as follows:

Ten minutes before the start the flag of the class or race concerned is broken out. Five minutes before the start of the race the "P" flag of the International Code is broken out. At the start both of these flags are lowered. Attention is drawn to these signals by the ten-minute gun, five-minute gun and starting gun respectively. If any part of the yacht is past the starting line when the starting signal is made, her recall number is displayed and attention drawn to it with a sound signal unless the sailing instructions prescribe other arrangements. The recall number should be kept displayed until the yacht has recrossed the starting line. Until she has done so, she must keep out of the way of others which are starting, or which have already started, correctly.

The main class racing flags used in Britain are as follows: *International:* "D" Dragon class, "J" Finn class, "K" Flying Dutchman, "L" Twelve Sq. Metre Sharpie, "M" International 14-ft. class, "W" International 5-0-5 class, "Y" International Cadet class. *National:* "B" Swallow class, "F" Firefly class, "O" Merlin-Rocket class, "R" 18-ft. National class, "T" 12-ft. National class, "U" Swordfish class, "V" National Redwing class. *Recognized Classes:* "A" Flying Fifteen, Albacore, G.P. 14-ft.; "E" Enterprise, British Moth; "G" Graduate; "H" Heron; "Q" Fleetwind; "V" Osprey; "W" 17-ft. Dolphin; "Z" 18-ft. Jollyboat; 3rd Sub-Flag Y.W. Hornet class. These are the shore signals and not the distinctive marks on the sail.

We next have to consider the relationship between the helmsman and crew. It may be quite different afloat from what it is ashore. Some skippers who are ordinarily light-hearted and cheerful become tense and grim under the trying conditions of the race. THEY FREQUENTLY SHOUT AT THEIR CREW. The latter should provide himself with a double thickness of skin and an outsize sense of humour. The better sort of skipper will try to give his crew an idea of the tactics which he proposes to adopt during the race, but even if the crew is being kept in the dark he should obey all orders without question. There must be only one skipper on the boat. This should not prevent the crew from giving information (as distinct from advice) to his skipper. It is his duty to warn the skipper of right-of-way boats which may be hidden from the skipper by the sail. Equally, the crew should warn the skipper if the boat seems to be in danger of running aground. The crew should also note how other boats are doing, whether they are getting better slants of wind, etc., by sailing a different course. The crew should keep on the look-out for the marks of the course, and tell the skipper as soon as he sees them. He should not point unless he wants to give free information to his rivals.

No beautiful friendship between helmsman and crew will survive unless both are well informed about the principles which make a boat sail fast. Without such knowledge they are apt to become accustomed during a race to the sound of distant gunfire as others win, instead of hearing the winning gun as they themselves lead the fleet over the finishing line. So let us see what is supposed to happen as between the wind, the sails, hull and water in a sailing boat (Fig. 27).

In brief – for theories are dull – the scientists have submitted that the effects of the wind on a boat are twofold. The boat is partly pushed and partly pulled by the force of the wind on the sails, though it is hard to be certain what is happening at any particular moment unless you have a wind tunnel handy

142   HOW TO SAIL

for testing. The pushing effect is shown in the following diagram. In this, AB represents the sail and CD the direction of the force of the wind meeting the sail at D. Now, as we are

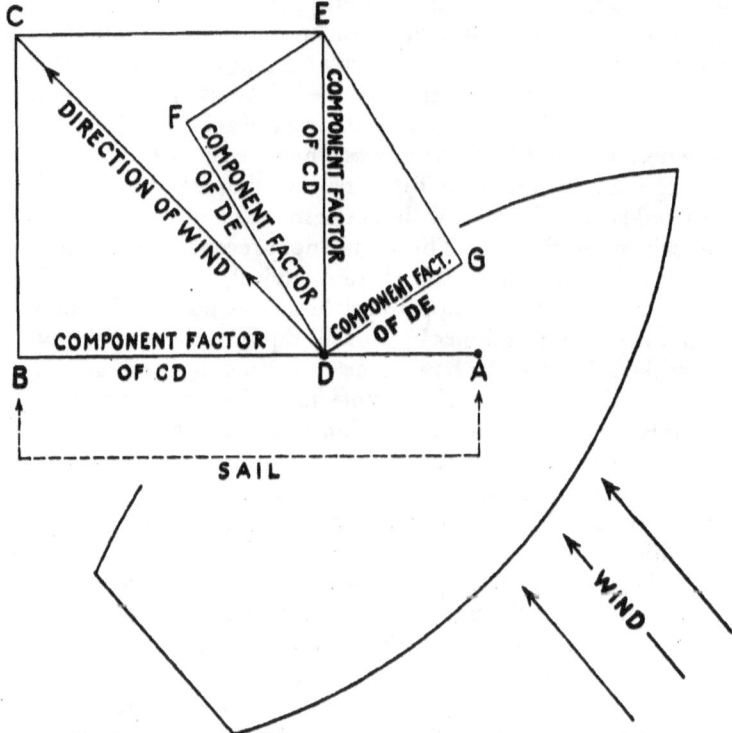

Fig. 27. SHOWING THEORETICAL ACTION OF WIND ON SAILS
AB = sails; CD = wind; DG = forces propelling boat forwards

supposed to have learnt at school, this force CD is the equivalent of two component forces acting at right-angles to each other. These component forces are represented by the lines DB and DE. Now, DB runs parallel to the sail and therefore has little effect on the movements of the boat. In fact, we can disregard it; but the other force represented by DE is important. It, too, can be split up into two forces acting at right-angles to each other, i.e. DG impelling the boat forwards and DF impelling the boat sideways. This sideways motion is resisted by the shape of the hull, and the main result is to move the boat forward. Not all experts agree with this explanation, but it is widely accepted.

A similar diagram can be prepared to show the effect of wind suction forwards from the leading edge of the sail. Scientists picture this suction being produced in much the same way as it is on the upper surface of an aeroplane wing, when the current flowing over the convex upper surface of the wing forms a partial vacuum which lifts the plane upwards. In the same way the wind passing round the leeward curved surface of the mainsail "lifts" the sail forward.

The suction effect varies, of course, according to the boat's course. It is least when running and greatest when going to windward. It will be affected by the cut of the mainsail and the positioning of the jib.

Another refinement must be added to the foregoing theory in order to complete the picture of our sailing boat. This refinement is the apparent wind. Imagine a steam train standing in a station with the wind blowing along the tops of the carriages from the guard's van towards the engine. Which way will the smoke go? Forwards, of course. But now picture the train in motion. When it gets beyond a speed of ten miles an hour, which way will the smoke go now? Why, backwards. In other words, the real wind which we got in the station has been replaced by the apparent wind caused by the movement of the train forwards.

Similarly, if when the train had been standing in the station the wind had been blowing across the track instead of along it, then, when the train began to move, the smoke would have changed direction and would have started to blow diagonally away from instead of at right-angles to the line of the carriages.

The same change of direction occurs when a boat moves through the water. For example, when going to windward the apparent wind will be farther ahead than the true wind and slightly stronger. In gusts, when the speed of the wind increases faster than the speed of the boat, the effect will be to free the wind, so that it appears to blow less from forward and more abeam. But when the boat picks up speed the apparent wind will swing forward again. When running, the apparent wind will be lighter than the true wind because of the motion of the boat down wind. This helps to explain why reaching rather than running is the fastest point of sailing; when reaching the boat does not move away from the wind. Similarly, if the tide is carrying the boat to windward, the apparent wind increases; and if the tide is taking the boat to leeward, this will make the apparent wind weaker. The direction of the apparent wind, and not the true wind, is shown by the burgee or racing flag at the masthead.

The next piece of theory – we are nearly through the wood – concerns the work done by the keel and centre plate, both of which, as already explained, help to stop the boat from skidding sideways. The theory of the thing is simple. A round metal disc is easily pulled through the water, thin edge first. But an attempt to move it sideways meets with what boat designers call lateral resistance. The centre of this lateral resistance is at the centre of the disc. If you made a hole in the centre of the disc and put through a piece of string knotted at one end and pulled the string sideways, the effect would be the same as if you had pulled the whole disc sideways.

It is just the same with a boat. The boat moves fairly easily ahead through the water, thin edge foremost, but offers lateral resistance to being moved to one side. Like the disc, the boat has *its* centre of lateral resistance at the point where, if you pulled it sideways, the effect would be the same as if you pulled the whole boat sideways. Boats have to be designed so that when they are in motion the centre of lateral resistance comes neither too much ahead of, nor too far behind, the theoretical centre of the sail area. If the centre of lateral resistance is too far aft, then the boat will tend to turn more and more off the wind as the pressure increases on the sails. This might lead to a dangerous situation in a squall, especially if there is difficulty in spilling wind from the sails. A boat with this fault is said to carry lee helm.

In the same way, if the centre of lateral resistance of a boat is too far forward the boat will gripe or try to turn to windward at the slightest provocation, and you will spend your time wrenching the tiller towards you to get the boat on her proper course. When a boat behaves in this way she is said to carry weather helm.

As in the case of the wind there is an apparent centre of lateral resistance as well as a true one, and this apparent centre varies its position according to the speed of the boat through the water.

The centre of lateral resistance in a centre board can be altered to suit the particular course which is to be sailed. Putting the centre plate fully down advances the centre of lateral resistance, so that the boat sails closer to the wind; hence the centre board is usually fully down when beating to windward. Raising the centre board moves the centre of lateral resistance aft. That is why, when reaching, the plate is partly raised. When reaching, you do not want the boat, whenever there is a puff, to turn into the wind, for this would have to be corrected with the rudder with a corresponding loss of speed. Therefore the plate is raised, perhaps, as much as half-way up on a reach. While on this subject we should mention that at most times a boat does not travel on a straight course but obliquely through the water, for the centre board does not entirely eliminate side slip or lee way. On an oblique course even the fin-like centre board offers some resistance, and the farther it can be raised when reaching the better, provided that it does not increase lee way. When running before the wind, lee way is a negligible factor, and the plate can usually be fully raised unless required for use in conjunction with the rudder. Some helmsmen believe in lowering some plate when running if the boat develops a roll either through the clumsiness of the crew or because of an unfavourable wave formation. Rolling on a run can also be checked to some extent by pulling in the sail and luffing slightly.

Having found the boat, and mastered the theory of its motion through the water, it remains to put the knowledge into practice. Apart from strategy and tactics which we shall discuss in the next chapter, most races are won by a combination of small errors made by other boats. Probably the winner makes errors, too, but not quite so many. Even on a short race there may be as many as dozens of tacks and roundings of buoys. The helmsman who can make half a length on each of these operations stands a very good chance of being ahead at the finishing line. A good deal of place-changing takes place during the windward leg of the course when the boats are on the beat. The reason is clear – on the beat it is not the course which you steer in relation to the next mark which is important, but your course relative to the wind. It takes an experienced helmsman to know automatically how close he can point to the wind without pinching, and how far off the wind he can sail without dropping away to leeward behind the other boats. Apart from the start of the race and the finish – if you are in the lead – the beat is probably the most exciting part of any race.

A somewhat different technique is required off the wind, where you are steering rather more on a fixed course, and where your sails, instead of being close hauled, are out as far as they will go without fluttering. This kind of sailing needs far more patience than beating to windward, and often more concentration.

And now, if the reader is still undaunted, we can proceed to discuss the tactics and strategy by which races are often won.

CHAPTER XII

WINNING MOVES

We shall divide this chapter into two sections; the first will deal with general tactics useful in any kind of weather, and the second with tactics used in special circumstances, e.g. on the wind, off the wind, or in light and heavy weather.

General tactics

What moves can the yachtsman legitimately use to put his rival at a disadvantage? We have already explained how one boat is entitled to luff another in order to prevent the latter from passing to windward, and you can, of course, blanket him if you succeed in overtaking to windward. In order to blanket you will have to allow for the fact that your wind shadow will probably be farther aft than you think it is. This is because your sail must be between that boat and the direction of the apparent wind, not the true wind. If you cannot manage to take your opponent's wind you can give him your own. This you will do if you are slightly ahead and to leeward of him, under which conditions the wind coming from your own sails will backwind his.

It is perfectly legitimate to hamper a boat by crossing her path when you are on starboard tack and she on port, but you must never tack in another boat's water in order to do this.

This rule may often be used to advantage. For instance, you can often carry a rival boat out into the centre of a strong tide out of which she would have tacked had she been clear of you.

The question of what you may or may not do when reaching a mark or obstruction is an interesting one and we shall now examine in greater detail the new racing rule on this point.

First we must distinguish between marks and obstructions, because in certain cases they are treated differently. Marks in the course are the objects which the sailing instructions require a yacht to pass between or on the required side. A mark begins to have a required side only when a yacht starts or when it begins, bounds or ends the leg of the course on which she is sailing. If a yacht fouls any part of the mark itself (excluding the cable to which it is attached) she must be disqualified.

Obstructions to sea room are craft under way (including another yacht holding right of way), craft at anchor, aground or capsized, wrecks, the shore, pier structures, fish weirs or traps, and shoals over which the yacht in question may not be safely navigated.

If two yachts on the same tack overlap when one of them reaches either a mark which they are about to pass on the required side or an obstruction to sea room, the outside yacht must give the other room to pass or round it.

The same applies to two yachts on opposite tacks when, with the wind aft, they are about to pass on the required side of a mark or an obstruction to sea room on the same side.

It does not apply under any other circumstances – for example, to yachts close hauled on opposite tacks or to cases where the overlap was not made until after the leading yacht had got so close to the mark or obstruction that she could no longer choose which side of it she will pass. It does not apply either at the start of a race.

At the start, there is usually a great deal of competition at that end of the line which allows the boats to go off on starboard tack. There is also a great temptation for boats to try and barge there at the last minute by reaching down to it and blanketing boats which are starting in the normal way.

In order to discourage this particular manoeuvre, the rule contains an "anti-barging" law, the provisions of which are as follows.

Before the starting line has been crossed the normal rule of "windward boat keep clear" applies, except that only gentle luffing is allowed.

When approaching the starting line to start, however, a leeward yacht is not obliged to give room to any windward yacht on the same tack to enable that yacht to pass to leeward of a mark of the starting line which is surrounded by navigable water.

This means that until the starting signal has been made a windward boat can be forced to steer for the wrong side of the mark, although she has an overlap and although the leeward boat presumably has no intention of going the wrong side of the mark with her.

This is intended to discourage boats from barging in from the windward side of the mark and so causing congestion.

After the starting signal has been made, the leeward yacht can no longer deprive a windward yacht of room at the mark either by heading above her proper course for the first mark if the wind is free or by luffing above a close-hauled course if on a wind.

But this still squeezes out any boat which, at the start, is to windward of a close-hauled course from the starting mark to the next mark if the start is a beat, or is to windward of her proper course for the first mark if the wind is free.

There is one other important rule which applies to certain obstructions only and not to marks.

If two yachts are standing close-hauled on the same tack towards an obstruction to sea room which requires the yacht to leeward to alter her course to clear it and if she is unable to tack without colliding with the yacht to windward, she may hail the yacht to windward for room to tack. After being hailed, the yacht to windward must immediately allow the yacht to leeward room to tack.

But if the obstruction is named in the sailing instructions as a mark in the course, or is a right-of-way yacht on the opposite tack, the yacht to leeward has not the right to hail for room if the boat to windward can fetch the object in question.

If the leeward yacht chooses to clear the obstruction by bearing away she shall allow the windward yacht to do so too if she wants to.

The start is probably the most important single incident in any race. If you cross the line "with" the gun (that is, a split second after it has been fired) and ahead of the rest of the fleet, you have gained something far more than mere distance. For if, as often happens, the first leg is a beat to windward, you have a clear wind *and* smooth water; whereas a poor start gets you a storm of dirty wind and waves from the leading boats, a handicap which few helmsmen can afford to give away.

To make a good start it is important to get out on the water in good time. Make a time-table of how long it takes to collect your gear, your crew and, if necessary, the dinghy which takes you out to your boat. Then allow some minutes for making sail and getting off the mooring. Allow another ten minutes for emergencies. Then you should be all right. Aim to get the boat sailing at least a quarter of an hour before your race starts. More than that, on a blowy day, may take the freshness off you and your crew. At most clubs races are started at ten-minute intervals, and as you first go afloat the class before yours will still be manœuvring near the starting line. Do unto them as you would like them to do unto you – keep out of their way, but be ready to make your first timing run as soon as they have started. You must, in any case, be off your mooring or away from the jetty by the time your five-minute gun is fired.

Make sure just where the starting line is; don't count on being able to see the marks used by the starter. Often as the gun is about to go the true line may be obscured by sails of other boats or of your own. While the coast is still clear, find a boat or a mooring on the line and near to the end of the line you plan to use for the start. Or two objects in line on shore (two on each shore if you are racing on a river or estuary) may be useful if not too distant. It is much harder to line up with remote marks than with near ones.

Your tactics on the start will depend partly on the weather conditions on the day of the race and partly on the kind of boat you are racing. Small boats can, if necessary, "loiter with intent" close to the line before the gun goes, because they need only a little time to pick up the necessary speed for the start. With larger boats it is less important to cross the line with the gun than it is to cross at good speed even if you are a few seconds late. But in either case it is no good being first over the line if you have failed to pick up the necessary speed.

The state of the tide may affect your judgment, too. If there is a fair tide and a fresh breeze, both sweeping down the course, it may be fatal to be over the starting line even before the gun. At Cowes one year we watched a well-known racing boat battle for over forty minutes to get back over a line she had crossed a moment or two before the race started. That was one race she never won. Equally, with a light breeze and a foul tide (i.e. the tide against you) it may be fatal to stand back too far from the line. In such conditions it may pay you even to drop your kedge overboard to prevent being carried away, but do it quietly in case others haven't thought of it. It may take several minutes before they realize that they are drifting backwards and you are not. If you drop your kedge it must be on the start side of the line (not on the course side) or you will be deemed to be over when the starting gun goes. You must recover your kedge yourself.

If you are early at the start it is quite legitimate to "jill" about the line, spilling wind out of your sails in order not to cross before the gun is fired, provided you observe the other rules of the road. It is not legitimate to check your way with a bailer or any other device apart from the afore-mentioned kedge.

When preparing for the start it is worth making several test runs to the line from the same point, timed by stop-watch. Remember, though, that as the time of the start draws near there will be more and more boats manœuvring for position. They may slow you down either by interfering with your wind or by creating stopping waves. Furthermore, if you are a windward boat or on port tack, you may have to give way to them just at the moment you have started on your final run. You must allow for this.

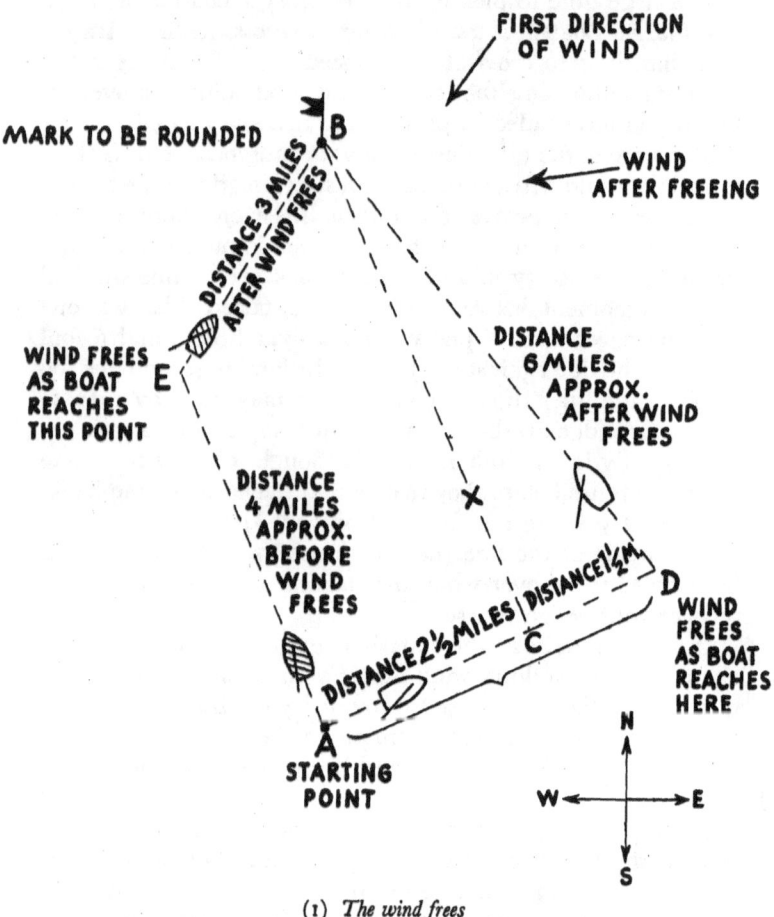

(1) *The wind frees*

Fig. 28. (A) CHOOSING THE RIGHT TACK

When the wind frees, shaded boat at E is able to lay the mark. White boat at D has overstood and must sail extra distance. In any case white boat should have tacked at C since D is farther from mark than C, but even if white boat tacks at C she gains nothing from wind change

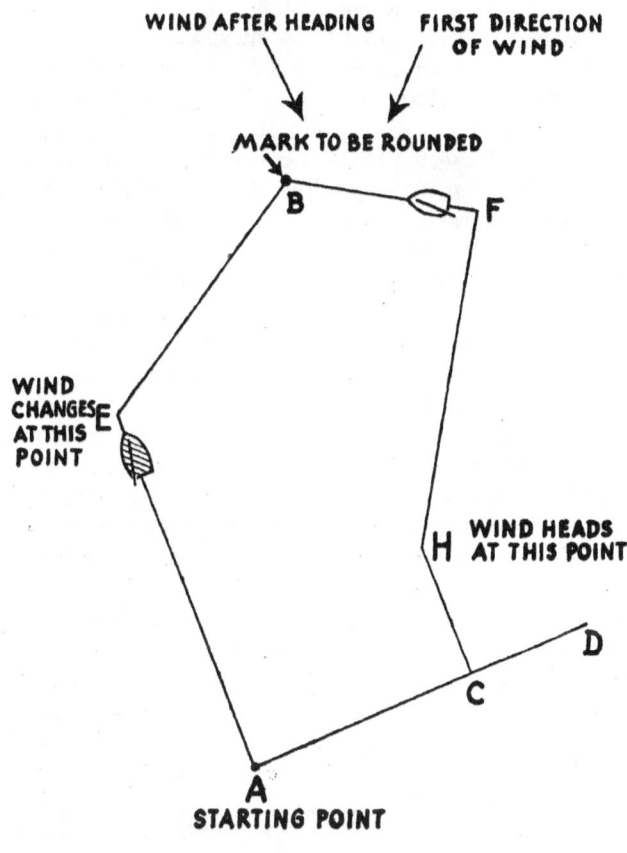

(2) *The wind heads*

Fig. 28. (B) CHOOSING THE RIGHT TACK (*continued*)
This time the white boat duly tacks at C instead of D thus saving some distance. But she is still at a disadvantage when the wind changes, the course E B being shorter than H F B

Much will depend on which end of the line you decide to cross. If you habitually make good starts, then it will be all right to choose the same end of the line as everyone else. But if you cannot be certain of pulling out of the ruck, then it may be better to be sure of a clear wind at the freer end of the line.

Some days the windward end of the line will have advantages. Other days the set of the tide is more important. If the tide is fair (helping you), you may decide to start at neither end of the line but in the middle. A study of the early starts of the day may give a clue as to the best side to choose.

Your approach to the first mark of the course must be carefully thought out. It may be useless to go for the windward end of the line, for instance, if it means you have to bear away on a dead run later in order to reach the mark. The boats which started to leeward will reach up to the mark and, travelling faster, might round before you.

You have also to consider what course you are going to take after rounding. At certain states of the tide and wind it may pay to round a buoy closely. On other days it may pay to keep along a shore at all costs, and on such occasions, though you will pass the buoy on the correct side, your best course may be fifty yards from it.

On days when you have failed to make a good start, a shift of wind can help to bring you up among the leaders again if you sail on the right tack. Let us suppose, for instance, that your next mark is due north and that the wind is north-north-east. You have the choice of making your first tack either ENE. or NNW. The latter is the longer leg and will take you nearer your mark. It should be chosen, because if the wind heads you, you will be at less of a disadvantage, and if the wind frees you may be able to fetch the mark with a single tack or none at all (figs. 28(A) and 28(B)).

But look what happens if you take your short leg first. If the wind changes northwards to become a header you may, when this happens, be little closer to the mark than you were at the start, and yet if it moves round to the east you may even overstand (sail farther than you need to reach the mark). Many racing skippers are apt to overstand even if the wind is steady. This is not justifiable except as insurance against having to put in an extra tack.

If, when beating for the mark, you expect a change of wind and there is little or no difference in the length of the two legs (e.g. if your course and the wind are both dead north), then choose the leg pointing most directly in the direction of the expected wind, the one that isn't blowing yet. Then, if headed, you may be able to go about and fetch the mark without any further tacking. Often on a warm day the new wind will be an on shore breeze from the sea, induced by rising temperatures on land. If the new wind is to blow in the opposite direction to the original breeze, there may be a period of calm while one wind kills the other.

Weather reports frequently give a clue on wind behaviour, as we shall see later.

You can profit from a change in the strength of wind as well as from a change in its direction. Thus if a light wind is strengthening it may pay to edge over towards it, so that you get the extra strength before the rest of the fleet. If the wind is dropping, you must allow for the fact that the tide will become a more and more important factor as the race goes on. You must, in fact, get well up-tide of the course.

Tactics in special circumstances

It is often possible to pick up several places while rounding the mark. This does not necessarily mean turning round the mark and cutting your corners in the shortest possible circle. To do so in anything but a small boat would probably mean a violent use of the rudder, which would cut the boat's speed severely. As with tacking, the aim should be to carry out the whole manœuvre smoothly without losing way.

At the same time you should try to get the inside berth at the buoy, provided that this does not involve cutting in on leading boats. A leading boat is not bound to give an inside boat room to round the mark unless she has made an overlap before the leader has reached the buoy and has maintained it up to the buoy.

Cutting in can be dangerous as well as unsportsmanlike. Sailing too far to windward in order to get the inside position at the buoy is often poor tactics, for it may involve approaching the buoy on a run at a time when the other boats are coming up on a reach.

It is highly satisfactory to come up to the buoy on starboard with all the other boats on port, but this manœuvre succeeds perfectly only if your course is "bang on" to the buoy

If there is a gap of, say, fifty feet between you and the buoy, then the other boats may be able to fake going about and then pass under your stern, and so round the buoy ahead of you. If you had left no room they would inevitably have had to tack and go outside of you.

Finally, you have to consider what is to happen *after* you have rounded the buoy. For instance, if you are coming on to a beat you will want to edge up to windward as soon as possible after rounding. In these conditions it may pay to start your turn a little wide of the mark, otherwise you may find that by the time you have turned and close hauled your sails you are quite a way down to leeward, and that boats that took the mark wide to begin with have ended up to windward of you.

Places can be gained during the leeward leg of the course, though less easily, perhaps, than when on the wind. The simplest manœuvre is that of covering the leading boats (that is, taking their wind and so creeping up on them).

Your wind shadow, of course, will be thrown by the apparent wind and not the true wind, which means that a boat directly to leeward of you may not be blanketed. Because of the boat's movement your wind shadow will fall farther aft than it would if the boats were stationary. Often a leading boat, in order to avoid being blanketed from behind, will edge up too far to windward, giving you the chance of passing her on a reach while she is running.

In light and medium breezes some ground can be gained on a broad reach or near run by bearing away down wind during the puffs and reaching back during the lulls. By bearing away you will stay longer in the puff, and then, when the wind lightens, you can make a better use of it on a reach than you could have done on your original course; and, as you may have to get a little above course, you will be nearer the source of the next puff.

On a dead run it often pays to cross tack down wind sailing first on one gybe and then on the other, because, as already explained, boats reach faster than they run.

Finally, there is the effect of the tide, which wins races again and again for the helmsman who knows how to make use of it. The general principles are simple. The tide tends to run fastest in the centre of any channel (that is, in the part where the water is deepest). Its speed is slowed down in the shallows on either side of the channel by the friction of the ground. It follows that when sailing with the tide you keep out in midstream, and when sailing against the tide you keep close to the shore. The main exception to this rule is that the tide moves faster round a spit or point at the side of the channel or over an isolated shoal which obstructs the flow of the current. Apart from this, it is worth making a careful study of the local tide conditions. Sometimes a tide will take longer to flood than to ebb. This fact should be allowed for in your racing plan of action. Also, the strength of the tide varies according to the height of the tide on any particular day. Sometimes the direction of the currents will change before high- or low-tide has been reached. The highest rate of flow often occurs half-way between high-water and low-water, and there are periods of slack water both when the tide has finished flooding and when it has finished ebbing.

In any race it is well worth knowing just how far in shore you can go. If close enough in you can often pick up an eddy (that is, a current of water going in the opposite direction to the tide). Obviously, this can be a tremendous advantage. It sometimes pays to go a long way off course in order to pick up an eddy. The speed of the tide is affected by the breadth of the channel. It will be fastest in the narrows and most sluggish where the channel is wider. This gives you a chance to plan your tacks, so that, for instance, when sailing into the tide you spend the shortest possible time in that part of the course where the tide runs strongest. If your tack takes you almost head on into the current you may be able, by pinching slightly, to lee bow (i.e. allow the tide to press on your lee bow) and so be pushed up to windward. When running with the wind and tide, tacking down wind (that is, sailing first on one gybe and then on the other) is particularly effective. The boat, being sideways to the tide, will be carried faster than she would be if on a dead run, and the apparent wind which might otherwise be practically nil when running on a light day is stepped up. Do not allow yourself to get too far to windward with a fair tide, for under these conditions it is far harder to get back on course. With the tide against you, tacking down wind on a run is less effective, because the current forces the boat farther off course than is the case with a fair tide. Moreover, a foul tide automatically increases the speed of the apparent wind when running, and it is therefore less necessary to go on a reach with the object of picking up extra apparent wind. When running, the plus or minus effect of the tide is less than when the wind is forward of the beam. When beating, for instance, a fair tide not only carries the boat along but increases the apparent strength of the wind; a foul tide, on the other hand, not only holds the boat back but decreases the effect of the wind. Hence, when on a beat be doubly careful to get your tide exactly right.

We have yet to deal with that irritating kind of day when there is little wind, or none at all. On such occasions it pays to use new sails which still have plenty of curve in them. Your older canvas, if it is cotton, will probably have been stretched flat. The new sail pays, because often a light breeze which is not strong enough to blow out an old sail will act if the sail is already disposed in a youthful and shapely curve. It is important not to disturb this curve either by clumsy movements in the boat itself or by a sharp pull on the sheet. On a light day movements must be cat-like, and the helmsmanship extremely gentle. It pays to use lighter tackle in light winds and, since little purchase will be required for holding the mainsheet, to dispense with some of the blocks through which it normally travels. It then requires far less labour to push out the boom as required to its best angle. Often on such a day it will be impossible to pick a pre-determined course. Any fixed plan of campaign worked out on the assumption that the wind you have got will remain steady, or that by sailing a certain course you can pick up a steady breeze, may have to be thrown overboard. It may be useless to do anything more than profit from whatever puff happens to be blowing at the moment in an effort to sail towards the mark. It may be fatal to use a short-lived puff to sail off in the hope of finding a new slant. Often on a fluky day it may seem as though the other boats are getting all the breaks; yet it may be unwise to try and sail over to them each time you see they have a puff, for it may have died out before you get there, and in the meantime you will have taken an oblique course and may have missed a puff which you would have got if you had stayed where you were. Fluky weather may none the less favour the boats which are behind and which can profit from the mistakes of their leaders.

CHAPTER XIII

YOU ARE OFFICER OF THE DAY

EVERY spring a small printed postcard reaches the writer from the secretary of his sailing club which reads: "This is to notify you that you are Officer of the Day on Saturday, the 30th May" (or whatever date has been chosen) "and that if you do not attend yourself you are responsible for finding a substitute." Such a summons makes the victim appreciate what others do for him during the rest of the season.

Strictly speaking, races at any yacht club under Royal Yachting Association Rules are controlled by the Sailing Committee under whose auspices the races are being sailed. The Committee is responsible for the organization of the races, their cancellation or postponement, the alteration of courses, and the observance of the rules; but it is the Officer of the Day, poor fellow, who is frequently appointed to represent the Sailing Committee. Without him there can be no properly conducted races. Perhaps this is some consolation to him as he puts on his smartly creased trousers and peaked yachting cap – a permissible form of dress on these occasions. Of course, if it is raining and the platform is not sheltered, any waterproof clothing goes.

On arriving at the club – at least an hour before the start of the first race – the Officer should collect his equipment, which will include the chronometer, the starting gun and sufficient blank cartridges (remembering that extra rounds may be required if yachts are over the line at the start and have to be recalled, and if courses are shortened). Certain flags will be required for hoisting, notably the Blue Peter (which is flown five minutes before the start of each race) and the class flags of the classes which are racing, the flags for postponement and for cancellation or shortening of course. In addition, the Officer

YOU ARE OFFICER OF THE DAY

will need a starting sheet for recording the names of the boats and helmsmen, their sail numbers and recall numbers, their time of finishing and other remarks. Finally, the sheet should contain a column for the declaration to be made by each helmsman at the conclusion of the race to the effect that he has observed the rules during the race. The recall numbers – a series of metal plates with numbers 0–9 painted, one on each plate – should be ready to hand, so that they can be displayed at once to helmsmen who have crossed the line before the starting gun and who must consequently return. In addition, the Officer will need binoculars, megaphone and a whistle used for notifying the non-winning boats that they have duly crossed the finishing line. The loud-hailing equipment, if any, should be tested. Care should be taken, if rain is likely, to keep the ammunition dry and to protect the starting sheet. The flag signals to be made are hoisted in advance properly furled, so that they can be broken out at the correct moment by pulling on the hoist.

If possible choose a starting line one end of which is no more favourable than the other, as this avoids bunching at either end. Bunching will be avoided if the following rules are observed:

(i) Ideally, the first leg of the course should be directly to windward with the starting line at right-angles to the first leg of the course. But because most people prefer to start on the starboard tack which gives right of way over other boats, Race Committees usually favour the port tack end of the line in big races by shortening the distance from it to the mark. The bigger the race, the stronger should be the advantage given to the port tack end.

(ii) If the course to the first mark is a close fetch, the starting line should be laid at right-angles to the direction of the wind. In this way, although one end of the line is nearer in distance, both will require the same amount of sailing.

(iii) If, on the other hand, the start has to be a run, the starting line can be laid at right-angles to the direction of the course without unduly favouring either end of the line.

¶ The starting line should be equal at least to the sum of the overall length of the competing boats plus 25 per cent. The finishing line should, if possible, be at right-angles to the last leg of the course.

In general, the faster classes should be started first if they are going round the same course. It is also important to avoid a situation where the classes are likely to finish at, or about, the same time. Above all, avoid setting courses in which boats of different classes are likely to be rounding the same mark at the same time, but in different directions.

Soon after arrival the Officer of the Day should agree on courses, possibly after consultation with the captain of the class concerned. In heavy weather, when deciding on the course, the Officer of the Day should arrange, if possible, for yachts to tack round marks rather than gybe. Sailing instructions must be clear. When the Sailing Committee prepares for a race, it is bound to supply every yacht entered with written or printed sailing instructions containing all the information likely to be needed by the competitors. All the marks in the course should be properly named and described. Often a sailing club will print in advance the courses to be sailed and will display as sailing instructions merely "Sunbeam Class, Course No. ——", or a visible indication of which courses are to be used. This is quite all right, but if there is any change in these original sailing instructions it must be communicated in the way provided by the sailing instructions. It is not necessarily sufficient to put a notice on the club board or to announce the fact by loudspeaker to the boats concerned. The course should be displayed at least thirty minutes before the start of the race concerned.

I have found it convenient, when acting as Officer of the

[Photo: Group Captain Haylock, R.A.F. (retd.)

VI. Yachting World Cadet Class in action

VII. Shearwater Catamaran [Photo: Eileen Ramsay]

Day, to prepare in advance a time-sheet set out in five columns as under:

Time	Sound signal	Flag signal up	Flag signal down	Notes
10-20				Display 14-ft. course
10-30				Display Sunbeam course
10-40	10-minute gun for 14-ft. class	14-ft. class flag		
10-45	5-minute gun for 14-ft. class	Blue Peter		
10-50	Starting gun 14-ft. class. Also 10-minute gun for Sunbeam class	Sunbeam class flag	14-ft. classs flag and Blue Peter	

and so on.

If the Officer of the Day considers, after the course has been posted, that it has become unsuitable in view of changed weather conditions, it is up to him to say so. He can, if he likes, postpone the race or cancel it before the start, which is why he should arrive in good time; or he can abandon a race while it is in progress. He will also need to organize his team, for it is impossible for one man to do everything. A good plan for the start is to have one man to call the time in minutes and seconds up to the gun; a second man to help note in advance which boats are likely to go over prematurely, so that the recall signals are ready for display; and a third man to watch the line to see who is actually over. The second man can also check that boats are afloat and off their moorings before the five-minute gun, and make a note of all the starters. (One of the main duties of the Officer of the Day is to account for all starters at the end of the race.) A fourth man should be in charge of the gun itself, and a fifth in control of the flags. During the racing the Officer of the Day should keep watch for any protest flags or infringements of racing rules which take place during the race.

At the end of a level class, remember that if your boats arrive bunched together and you are short-handed, it is more important to get the order of finishing than to get the time of the finish. In handicap races it is essential to get both the order and the time. It is worth jotting down the sail numbers and times of the returning boats on a piece of paper from which they can be copied later on to the proper starting sheet. To record the finishing order straight on to the starting sheet often means a certain amount of searching, so that before you have recorded one boat's arrival the next is over the line.

So far, we have assumed that everything runs smoothly. In practice, you may consider yourself extremely lucky if it does. There have been occasions when the gun has failed to fire – which makes it all the more important to break out the flag smartly. There have been occasions when the gun has fired but the five-minute Blue Peter has failed to break out. The Royal Yachting Association Council have taken the view that these do not wipe out the start, but they certainly can be disconcerting to the helmsmen. If there are a number of unidentified premature starters, or an error in starting procedure, the Officer of the Day can sound a general recall consisting of two sound signals and a postponement.

The Officer of the Day must do everything possible to make clear signals if he wishes the course to be shortened. If possible, the finishing arrangements (i.e. the direction of approach to the finishing line) should be the same in a shortened course. The shortening signal should be given by hoisting the class signal under the letter "S" as a signal for the race to finish with the round about to be completed, or in such other way as the Sailing Committee may decide.

The hearing of protests made by one yacht against another is a study in itself, and every Officer of the Day should make

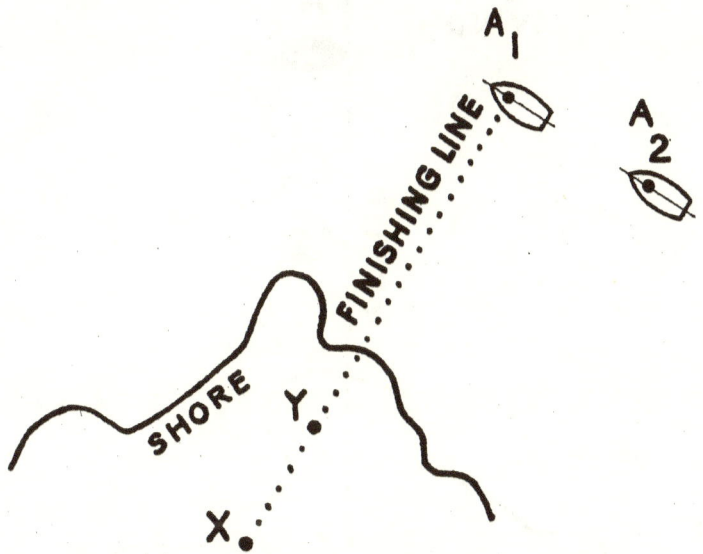

Fig. 29. A MARK BOAT DRIFTS OUT OF POSITION
Mark boat has drifted from position A1 to position A2. Competitors uncertain of their finishing line

himself familiar with the proper procedure as laid down in the Royal Yachting Association Rules. If the Sailing Committee see an infringement of the rules, or have reasonable grounds for supposing that a competitor has in any way infringed the rules, they shall act on their own initiative as if a protest had been made. But they are not entitled to disqualify a boat for what may be considered a breach of the rules under their own observation without giving the offending helmsman a chance to

166   HOW TO SAIL

defend himself except where the yacht in question has failed to cross the starting or finishing line correctly.

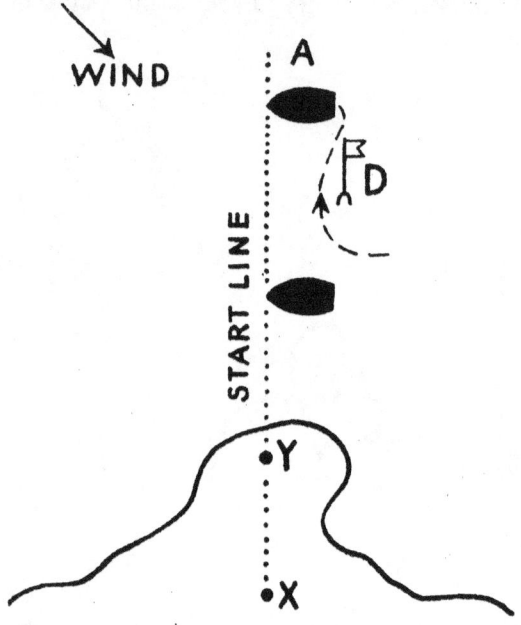

Fig. 30. STARTING MARKS POORLY ARRANGED
Distance mark D should be on course side of starting line, not on 'start' line

A most perplexing situation for the Officer of the Day occurs when one of the marks named as a mark in the course shifts or even disappears, as has happened before now. If any mark is missing or has moved from the vicinity of its stated position, the Sailing Committee must, if possible, replace it in its proper place or substitute a new mark. But if it is impossible to do this in time for the competitors to round or pass it, the race may be resailed or declared void at the discretion of the Sailing Committee. If, as sometimes happens in a strong tide, the mark disappears temporarily and then reappears later so that the leading boats failed to round it correctly, then it would obviously be unfair for the following yachts to profit by this accident.

Another ticklish situation may develop if either the starting or finishing distance mark drifts at all. The sailing instructions should make clear exactly what the finishing line is. In the diagram on page 165, for instance, the mark boat has drifted from position 1 to position 2, and unless the sailing instructions are clear the helmsmen may be puzzled to know whether the finishing line is a prolongation of the line XY or a line between X and the mark boat's present position, or between Y and the mark boat's present position, or a continuation of these lines on the off shore side of the mark boat.

Similarly, at the start, if there is a mark boat on the starting line which because of the tide and wind cannot be kept strictly in line with two points on shore which mark the shoreward end of the starting line, then the mark boat should be placed on the course side of the starting line and NOT on the side where the boats will be before the start. The diagram (p. 166) will show why this is so. Boat A, by tacking round the distance mark D before reaching the starting line, has been able to gain a special advantage over the other competitors who approached the starting line direct. Had the distance mark been on the course side of the starting line this could not have happened. Also, if the mark is on the start side it may be difficult to control whether boats have in fact rounded it on the correct side before crossing the line, and this may lead to protests.

Nowadays, with large national classes of small boats, the inter-club meetings call for a good deal of organization. In this connection the suggestions prepared by the Royal Yachting Association are particularly helpful. These suggestions give a number of useful reminders of things which might otherwise be forgotten, as follows:

General
   (*a*) A.A. signs on approaches to dinghy park.
   (*b*) Provision near the dinghy park for:
      (i) storage and drying of sails and gear;
      (ii) changing rooms and lavatory accommodation for competitors (especially ladies).
   (*c*) Where possible arrangements should be made with local boat yards for stocks of spares and arrangements for repairs, etc.
   (*d*) Where residential accommodation is limited or remote from the club, arrangements for lunches, teas, etc., should be made.

Dinghy park
   (*a*) No overhead wires between park and launching place.
   (*b*) Enough space for boats to be rolled over to get at their bottoms.
   (*c*) Berths marked out for each boat preferably diagonally, so as to allow masts to clear next boat when rolled over. It is suggested that berths should be allocated in the order of receipt of entries.
   (*d*) Launching trolleys – some can be borrowed from other clubs.
   (*e*) Dinghy marshal and handling party in charge of launching.
   (*f*) Night watchman.
   (*g*) Hay bags (for propping boats when ashore).
   (*h*) Freshwater for washing down.
   (*i*) Mooring trot of hauling-off lines, so that boats can make sail clear of the launching jetty.

Publicity
   (*a*) Press (local and national) – hand-out of results each day after racing.
   (*b*) B.B.C. – result of principal event.
   (*c*) Photographs.

CHAPTER XIV

TIDES AND TIDAL STREAMS

TIDES offer a free hitch-hike twice a day to mariners in most parts of the coast. Playing the tide can lift your boat from the turtle into the dolphin class. It can add two or three knots to a boat's speed or cut it to nil if the wind is light. The result is that by working your tides you can cut down tremendously the time it takes to sail from one place to another. This is the reason why you read so often in sailing sagas of boats getting under way at about three or four in the morning. The skipper knows that the hardship of rising three hours earlier may lead to a saving of ten to twelve hours' sailing through catching a favourable tide.

Moreover, unless you know your tides you are never certain whether it is safe to get across a swatch way or whether you must keep to the main channel. When you have spent a hot summer day heeled right over on the mud at an angle of 45 degrees you will realize that in this case ignorance is not bliss.

Years of study are necessary in order to know exactly how tides work. We shall have to content ourselves with general principles only. Briefly, the tides are essentially tidal waves raised up from the sea by the attraction of the sun and moon. One of these tidal waves, the lunar-tide, is on the part of the earth nearest to the moon; and the other, the anti-lunar-tide is, broadly speaking, on the opposite side of the globe. As the earth revolves each day, the waves move across the earth. The attraction of the sun is also sufficient to raise two smaller tidal waves – one nearest, one farthest away from the sun. When there is a full moon or a new moon, both the sun and the moon are in a position where they act on the same part of the oceans at the same time. The result is that the tidal waves at that time are larger and we have spring-tides. But when the moon is not full or new, then the effect of the moon's pull is no longer increased by that of the sun, so that we have smaller tides known as neaps. Spring-tides thus occur twice during each lunar month of twenty-nine days, during which the moon will have circled completely round the earth. One series of spring-tides occur at full moon when the moon is on the same side of the earth as the sun; and one at new moon when the moon is on the opposite side of the earth from the sun. In between these times, when the tides are increasing in height from neaps to springs, they are said to be coming up; and when they are decreasing from springs to neaps they are taking off. The distance between the moon and the earth varies. When the moon is nearest to the earth the tides are bigger. Sometimes this occurs at spring tides but not always, and never at two springs running.

Owing to the shape of the earth the effect of the full or new moon and its tidal wave is not felt in Britain for two or three tides after, but high-water will always occur at a more or less constant interval after the arrival of the new and full moon. That is, in each lunar month the first high-tide will occur at roughly the same number of hours and minutes after the moon's passage over the meridian of that place. This interval is called the establishment of the port in question. Because of the earth's movement the moon takes nearly twenty-five hours to reappear over the same spot and so the lunar-tide will be about fifty minutes later each day than on the previous day, and in theory the time between two successive high-waters is therefore twelve hours twenty-five minutes. Often, however, the interval varies. When it is decreasing the tides are said to be priming; and when it is increasing they are said to be lagging. In many areas the land causes variations. There may be two tides a day, or the tide may flood for seven hours and ebb at increased speed for five with various periods of slack water in between; and, as already stated, the tidal currents sometimes turn not at high-tide or low-tide, but at times in between. It all boils down to

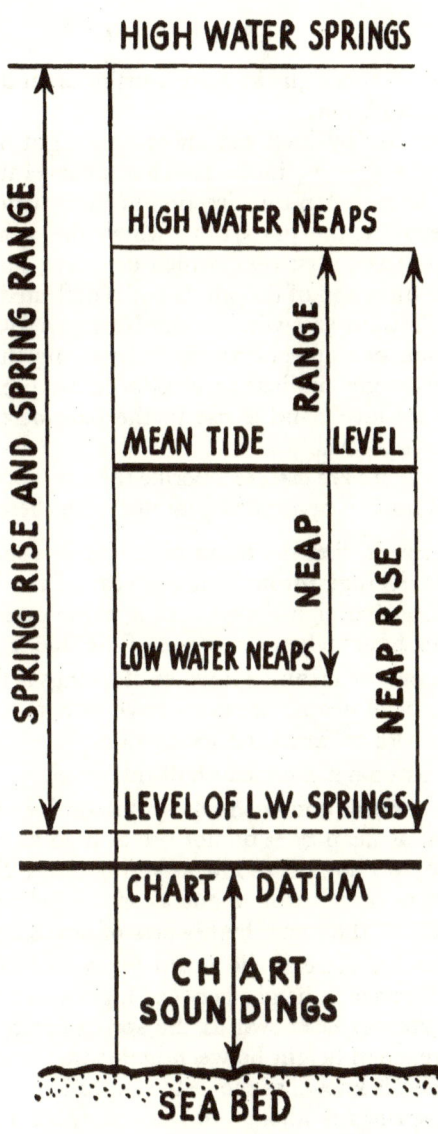

Fig. 31. TIDE LEVEL DIAGRAM

the fact that although tides are worthy of study they are not easy to get to know.

The weather by itself can affect the height of the tide. For instance, if a strong wind is blowing for several days, the sea-level will be raised in the direction towards which it is blowing and lowered in the parts from which the wind comes. The wind also causes a current, which does not, however, exactly follow the direction of the wind, but is deflected by the earth's motion. Thus an east wind in the Northern Hemisphere normally produces a current running slightly north of west. A fall in the barometer, indicating a reduced air pressure, tends to raise the sea-level; and a rise in the barometer pressure depresses the sea-level.

Various terms are used to describe the levels of tide, and it will be as well now to become acquainted with these. (See fig. 31.)

(a) There is, first the mean high-water of springs, which is the average throughout the year of the highest of two successive high-waters during those periods of twenty-four hours when the range of the tide is greatest.

(b) Below the mean high-water of springs is the mean high-water of neaps, for, as we have seen, the neap-tide does not rise so far as the spring-tide.

(c) Next comes the mean half-tide level.

(d) Below this comes the mean low-water of neaps. Now, just as neap-tides do not rise as high as spring-tides, so they do not fall so low as spring-tides. The mean low-water of neaps is about as much below the half-tide level as the mean high-water of neaps is above.

(e) Finally, there is the mean low-water of springs. The difference in height between high-water and low-water of springs is known as the spring range, and the difference in height between high-water and low-water of neaps is known as the neap range. The mean low-water of springs is about the same distance below half-tide level as the mean high-water of springs is above high-

TIDES AND TIDAL STREAMS 173

tide level. The chart datum level used in Admiralty charts is usually slightly below the mean low-water of springs.

Now that we know what we are talking about, we can get an idea of how to work the tide-tables. As already mentioned, the time at which high-tide occurs varies from place to place. It would obviously not be worth while to calculate advance figures each day for every small place around the coast, and therefore the Admiralty give in their tide-tables published each year the predictions of high- and low-water and the height for every day in the year for a number of standard ports only. From these standard ports it is possible to calculate conditions in the less-important places nearby. The time and height differences between the standard ports and these secondary ports vary by different amounts at various stages of the moon and because of local irregularities in the coast, but the Admiralty Tide-Tables take account of those times and heights of high- and low-water at the standard port when the variations are greatest and least, so that it is always possible to get a close estimate. That is the background to the system for finding the time of the high-tide and low-tide, and the levels above chart datum of high-tide and low-tide.

We now need some method of discovering how much water there will be at a given time between low-tide and high-tide, for in general the tide does not ebb or flow at the same rate during its rise or fall. As a very rough guide it may be said that if the tide is to rise 12 ft. in 6 hours, it will rise 1 ft. in the first hour, 2 ft. in the next hour, 6 ft. in the next 2 hours, 2 ft. during the fifth hour, and 1 ft. in the final hour. This rough guide is not, however, accurate enough for Admiralty purposes. For example, if a tidal wave enters a bay, the water-level there will rise and the wave will decrease until a common level has been found. But this will not necessarily occur at predicted high-tide. In the Admiralty Tide-Tables there is a series of very full tables by which it is possible both to find the height of the tide at times between high- and low-water, and to find the time at which any tide will reach a certain level. These Admiralty tables take into consideration not only the exact time taken by the tide to rise or fall on that particular day, which is called the duration, but also the exact range of the tide. General tables of this kind cannot be used in certain areas between Swanage and Selsey or in the Firth of Forth, where local conditions produce pronounced divergencies from the normal; for these areas special tables are given.

Compared with tide-tables, a tidal stream atlas which shows the currents is easy. Most atlases show the direction and speed of the current for each hour after high-tide. In British atlases the high-tide chosen is that of Dover, or some other convenient standard port. Charts, as distinct from atlases, often show arrows feathered on one side to represent flood streams thus ⪢, and plain arrows ⟶ for ebb. Sometimes the rate of flow at half tide is given, too; but this is not so useful as when the time after high or low-water is shown, too, because, as we have seen, tidal streams often turn before or after high- or low-water. The following arrow shows both time and rate, and indicates that the speed of flood is $2\frac{1}{2}$ knots 3 hours after low-water of LOCAL TIDE ⪢. Ebb-tidal streams are shown in the same way without feathering, and the time shown is the number of hours after local high-water.

Thus ⟶ indicates that the tidal current at that point at springs runs at 1 knot 2 hours after local high-water.

A single arrow of this kind will not, however, tell you how long the tidal stream is going to last, nor necessarily whether the speed given is at springs or neaps.

Such information is given for various positions on Admiralty charts, in tables showing the direction and rate of the tidal current for each hour before and after high-water at Dover both at springs and neaps.

Not so picturesque as arrows in an atlas, but, where available, more practical I think.

CHAPTER XV

MEET THE WEATHER MAN

THE yachtsman who knows but a few nursery rhymes about red skies and rings around the moon is an extravagant and perhaps a dangerous sailing companion. When in estuaries his errors in weather forecasting may lead to nothing more serious than a needlessly uncomfortable bucketing through going out over-canvased. But off shore, picking the wrong weather may lead to the loss not only of canvas and gear, but in extreme cases to that of the ship herself.

You will sometimes hear people say: "I don't know very much about the weather. What the B.B.C. and other experts say is good enough for me." But this is glib talk which simply does not fit the facts. Official weather experts do not claim to give more than general inferences and forecasts. Their forecasts for the British Isles or anywhere else are based on what the weather is in the surrounding areas and on the probable direction of movement and development of that weather. But they cannot always be right. If, for instance, after their forecast has been published, the movement of, let us say, a depression speeds up, or a ridge of high pressure unexpectedly collapses, what happens to our fine friend who prides himself on being no expert? Obviously, he is flummoxed.

In any one area there are local peculiarities – mountains in particular – which affect the weather in ways to which the forecaster, because of the limited scope allowed him, cannot refer. But the yachtsman who has some knowledge of cloud, wind and pressure systems can interpret official weather forecasts in terms of local conditions to get accurate results.

Amateur, as opposed to professional, weather knowledge pays off bigger dividends in Britain than in most other countries. This is because, as we know to our cost, our weather is almost always changeable. Not for us the regular monsoons, the desert dryness of the Sahara or the snows of Nova Zembla. Instead, always something new, maybe something the experts were not expecting. Britain stands in a kind of no-man's-land between two weather "empires". The northerly of these empires is the cold-air region around the North Pole. The southerly empire is the warm-weather system from the tropics. These two realms permanently fight a new battle of Britain. This fight has never been won or lost.

A second reason why it is unsafe to leave everything to the experts is that most of our weather comes to us from across the Atlantic, where it is hard to discover and track as it approaches our shores. Hence the scope for the well-informed amateur to make his own predictions.

We shall most easily understand the often unprintable British weather if we first take a look at the world system of winds and pressure, systems of which the British Isles forms a part; for winds seeking to correct inequalities of pressure are the main factors in weather.

As can be imagined, there is a hot belt around the Equator. The Equatorial air when it is heated expands and rises and cold air flows in from farther north and farther south to take its place. If the earth were stationary, this circulation of air to and from the Equator would probably be in a due north and south direction, the Equatorial air moving due northwards over the polar air coming south. Owing, however, to the daily rotation of the earth the winds are distorted, those in the Northern Hemisphere blowing to the right and those in the Southern Hemisphere to the left. Thus the cooler surface air currents which replace the Equatorial air approach the Equator from north-east and south-east respectively instead of from north and south. We thus have the famous north-east and south-east trades one meets in almost every sea saga. The rise of hot air at the Equator results in a belt of low pressure there. The Equatorial air eventually piles up in two areas about 35 degrees N. and 35 degrees S. of the Equator, creating a belt of high pressure which, we shall see directly, affects our own climate. There, in a nutshell, are the main wind and pressure factors of the world's weather.

These conditions might be permanently unchanged if the earth were a regular sphere and if there were no variation in the seasons. Unfortunately, this is not the case. The seasons do change. The earth's axis is not perpendicular to its course round the sun. During half the year our Northern Hemisphere is inclined towards the sun and we get summer, and during the other half of the year the Southern Hemisphere has its summer. This alone is enough to extend some high-pressure regions and diminish others.

The position of land and sea masses adds to the complexity of the set-up. In summer the land becomes hotter than the sea, and in winter colder. High-pressure areas therefore form over the continents in winter and over the oceans in summer. Low pressures occur over the oceans in winter and over the continents in summer. Thus in winter there is a marked Siberian "high" which disappears in summer. Most summers the area of high pressure normally found in the Atlantic over the Azores spreads until it reaches almost to the British Isles.

Taking a closer look at Britain's weather, we see that it comes to us from several different directions. First, there is so-called "polar" air from the north.

This may approach either over the sea (in which case it is called maritime polar air), or from the north-east (in which case it will be continental polar air). Maritime polar air usually brings with it cool, showery weather and good visibility. It has picked up moisture while crossing the sea. Continental polar air, unlike maritime polar air, picks up no moisture *en route* and brings, as in our spring easterlies, a dry and cold blast. Being dry it carries no clouds to act as a blanket at night; consequently, we often get heavy frost associated with continental polar air stream. North-easterlies, however, pick up some moisture from the North Sea and are both cold and cloudy.

A good supply of tropical air also comes to Britain. Because of the slant given it by the earth's rotation it usually approaches us from the south-west across the Atlantic Ocean. Because it is warm it can and does soak up a great quantity of water – far more than the polar maritime air – and when it encounters a polar front it has to shed some of its water. When cooled it cannot hold as much water as when hot. That is how we get most of our rain.

The westward flow of air towards this country is fairly constant because of the area of high pressure around the Azores, i.e. about 35 degrees N. Here we may draw attention to one of the most important weather rules: *that winds blow clockwise around an area of high pressure in the Northern Hemisphere and counter-clockwise in the Southern Hemisphere.* They blow counter-clockwise around a depression in the Northern Hemisphere and clockwise in the Southern. Being close to the northern edge of the Azores (Northern Hemisphere) high, we get the westerly part of the clockwise winds. Occasionally, too, but less often, we get hot winds from the Sahara.

That is the general picture of Britain's weather. We shall now go more carefully into the question of how to observe and interpret it. Of all the weather instruments in use, the barometer remains the most useful. It records the pressure of the atmosphere. The vast quantities of air around and above us exercise a pressure which is something in the nature of 15 lb. per sq. in. That is, if we took and weighed the column of air rising vertically upwards from an area of ground measuring 1 sq. in., the answer should be 15 lb. But this pressure is not constant and its variations are the surest clue to the weather to come.

The earliest barometers were operated with mercury. They were made according to the following recipe: Take a straight glass tube, not less than 33 in. long, hermetically sealed at one end and open at the other. Fill to the brim with mercury. Keeping a finger over the open end, turn the tube upside down and submerge the open end in a bowl of mercury. The liquid will fall slightly, leaving a vacuum at the top of the tube, but the pressure of the air will keep the remainder of the column from running out of the tube. The height of the column varies with atmospheric pressure, and can be measured. It is normally around 30 in. This contraption – the ancestor of the mercury barometer – would, of course, be useless for taking measurements in a pitching boat, and at sea a different type of instrument is used. This is the aneroid barometer, which records the effect of air pressure on a metal box from which as much air as possible has been exhausted. The variations in pressure are recorded on a dial.

Modern barometers register pressure as millibars; 1,000 millibars, the normal pressure at sea-level, equalling 15 lb. per sq. in. (approximately).

There are good reasons why the mariner pays particular attention to his barometer. Nature abhors a vacuum and where there is an area of low pressure, winds will rush in to fill it up. So a drop in pressure often means winds to follow. Further, we already know these winds can be depended on to blow in certain directions because, as we have seen, in the Northern Hemisphere they blow not directly towards the centre of a depression, but counter-clockwise around it (all winds in the Northern Hemisphere being deflected to the right); and in the Southern Hemisphere the winds blow clockwise around a depression (all winds are deflected to the left). Thus the barometer gives us a clue as to where the weather is coming from as well as what it will be.

In order to get a clear picture, weather experts prepare charts (such as we see in the paper) to show which areas have depressions, areas of low pressure and which have anticyclones, or areas of high pressure. For this purpose in such maps you will see that places having the same barometric pressure are joined by lines known as isobars. Isobars are generally shown for every four millibars. Where the isobars run close together differences in pressure are clearly "steep". It follows that the winds here will be stronger than at other points where the gradient of pressure is more gradual. The "ideal" depression is, of course, a series of oval isobars inside each other, each smaller oval indicating a drop in pressure.

Let us now consider in greater detail how a depression is formed, why the barometer falls, and the reason for the bad weather that follows. We shall look at the situation first as it would seem to an observer overhead. We shall have to imagine that he could distinguish at sight between warm air masses and cold. A depression is formed when two air masses of widely different characteristics meet together. In the Atlantic, polar air from the north and tropical air from the south can be visualized as flowing almost parallel to each other in opposite directions, meeting on what is known as the polar front. The polar front is not a cliff-like vertical wall but a sloping one, the gradient of which moves upwards from the base of the warm air mass across the cold air mass. When this front is disturbed, a depression begins to form. Looking from above we see a tongue of southern warm air invade the northern cold air mass. A wave-like bulge forms and the barometric pressure under the bulge begins to fall. This is because warm air, volume for volume, is lighter than cold; and, if it can, it rises, relieving pressure below. This fall in pressure sets the winds in motion counter-clockwise, as we have seen, in the Northern Hemisphere, clockwise in the Southern. The forward boundary of the invading warm air at ground-level is known as the warm front, and the rear boundary between the two masses at the root of the tongue of warm air is known as the cold front. The area between the two is the warm sector.

The centre of the depression lies at the tip of the warm sector, and the pressure is lowest there. As we reach the area of the cold front we find the barometer rising again as the atmosphere fills with cold heavy air. As the process continues the tongue of warm air presses on and up into the cold air mass. This, of course, cools it, so that it cannot hold its moisture and eventually rain falls – in advance of the arrival of the warm front at ground-level.

In the later stages of an average depression the cold air, being heavier, undercuts the warm air completely and lifts it off the ground, producing a second douche of rain sometimes called clearing showers. When the warm air has been finally undercut the depression is said to be occluded or shut off. Many depressions arrive off Britain's shores in this advanced state of decay. Their presence is reflected in the barometer, the winds or the rainfall, but there may be no pronounced warm or cold front.

We have dealt here with a typical depression. There are variations on this theme, such as the small secondary depression which travels with the main depression, frequently to the south of it; but we have no time to pay them attention, and for those who have there are many admirable books on the subject. What we can say is that in most depressions there is a definite sequence of events which become apparent to an observer on the ground. Before describing this fully we shall make a diversion and speak of clouds. These are excellent weather guides and well worth distinguishing.

To-day's names for clouds are based on a classification sketched in 1803 by Luke Howard, a London chemist and the father of British meteorology. He noticed the wispy clouds, which he named "cirrus" because they reminded him of a lock of hair; he distinguished the cumulus or "heap cloud", the stratus or "sheet" cloud, and the nimbus – the undistinguished-looking cloud which carries the rain. These terms are still used to-day, although refinements have crept in, in view of the different heights of various types of cloud.

The cirrus clouds are on the highest level—in fact at 20,000 ft. or over.

They come in three varieties:

1. *Cirrus*. These are detached clouds of delicate-tufted, plumed or fibrous appearance, usually all white. These clouds occur at high levels where the cold is so intense that water vapour turns to crystals. Cirrus clouds indicate warm air pushed upwards into a cold area. Often

they mark the very top of the slope of the warm front of a depression moving towards the observer, and are therefore a sign of trouble to come.

2. *Cirrocumulus*. These clouds – the mackerel sky of weather rhymes – resemble ordinary cirrus clouds arranged in wavelets or ripples without shadows. Often they are the next stage in the approach of a depression – a little farther down the slope towards the warm sector of a depression.

3. *Cirrostratus* is a sheet-like form of cirrus. Just thick enough to give the sun and moon "haloes", but not enough to blur their outlines. A kind of milky veil.

We next come down in the sky to two more kinds of cloud in the area between 20,000 ft. at the upper level and about 6,500 ft. at the lower level. Here the clouds are composed of water droplets rather than ice crystals, and are thicker and therefore greyer in colour. There are two main varieties:

4. *Altocumulus*. Layers or patches of cloudlets very much larger and rounder than cirrocumulus, arranged in groups, lines or waves, sometimes with shading. They have no special weather significance.

5. *Altostratus*. Like a thickened cirrostratus. The sun shows through these clouds faintly, as through ground glass. This watery-looking cloud is a bad-weather warning.

We next come to clouds stretching from 6,500 ft. almost to the ground. There are three of these:

6. *Stratocumulus*. A formation consisting of layers or patches of roundish masses, or rolls of soft and grey cloud with darker parts. A rather purposeless cloud which often persists, especially in winter, for days at a time. Has no special weather significance.

7. *Stratus*. This is technically known as "a uniform layer of cloud resembling fog but not resting on the ground". The broken variety is "fracto stratus". As a low cloud, stratus is the special enemy of the aviator.

8. *Nimbostratus.* This is a low-lying, formless, rainy cloud, dark grey and nearly uniform. It often seems to be feebly illuminated from inside. Usually, but not always, produces continuous rain or snow.

The above classes have all been clouds haunting their own particular levels of the sky. The next two, however, are fine, towering masses stretching from perhaps 1,600 ft. often up into the cirrus regions.

9. *Cumulus.* Thick, puffy, cauliflower clouds which look white unless viewed directly against the sun. The base is horizontal and well defined, the upper surface dome-shaped with rounded projections. Cumulus is usually part of a column of air rapidly rising upwards because of the heat of the sun. It is thus a fair-weather cloud. When the heat of the sun is cut off the cumulus vapours sink down again until the sun reappears the next day.
10. *Cumulonimbus.* The tenth and final cloud in our gallery, cumulonimbus (the thunder cloud), is the most interesting of any in the collection. Officially it consists of "heavy masses of cloud with great vertical development whose cumuliform summits rise in the form of mountains or towers, the upper parts having a fibrous texture and often spreading out in the shape of an anvil". The base is similar to that of nimbo stratus and there is often a trail of precipitation (virga) with a layer of ragged cloud below. Heavy rain, lightning and thunder can all be produced by cumulonimbus.

Thunder clouds are produced by strong ascending currents of damp air. Sometimes the heat of the sun on the land can bring this about. Similar instability occurs when a cold current abruptly overrides or undercuts a warm air mass. Thunder clouds often appear to approach the observer against the wind. This is because in thundery weather the wind in the upper air which brings the thunder cloud may well be blowing in a different direction to the surface wind.

As the damp air rises its water vapour condenses to raindrops; some of these drops fall from the body of the cloud as thundery showers, so beloved of forecasters. Others are carried farther up into the snow level. They are frozen into ice pellets and when the vertical currents can no longer carry them upwards they fall, carrying with them a layer of snow. In the nether regions of the cloud this layer of snow soaks up a new supply of water.

Then if the hailstone is again blown upward, as happens in a well developed thunder cloud, this outer layer of the rain pellet becomes solid ice. This, if repeated sufficiently, often produces hailstones "as large as pigeons' eggs".

What, then, of the thunder?

The noise is, of course, the resistance of the air breaking down under the power of the electric flash between the thunder cloud and the earth, or between one cloud and another. Sometimes the lightning falls in a single flash directly to the ground, in which case we hear a clap of thunder. Sometimes the flash does not go straight to the ground or there may be several flashes at the same time. In this case we hear not one clap, but a rumble of thunder, because the flashes have been at various distances from us and the sound of them does not reach us at the same time. If the discharge is between one cloud and another, the sound may be almost completely muffled and all that the observer sees is the reflection of the flash in the form of sheet lightning. Roughly, sound-waves travel at about 1,000 ft., or one-fifth of a mile, per second. The length of flash from cloud to ground is usually about one mile. Lightning injures its victims both by blasting them with the shock wave of heated air or through a direct shock leading to violent contraction of the muscles.

The most commonly accepted explanation of lightning is that during the churning that goes on within the thunder cloud drops of rain are continuously split up, and that this process produces a separation of positive and negative electricity. The drops keep their positive charge and the air becomes negatively charged. The air, moving more freely than the water, tends to pass to the rear of the cloud. Electrical discharge subsequently takes place between the positively charged part of the cloud and the ground or a negatively charged area of cloud.

The thunder cloud, like any other disturbance, affects the barometer. As the storm approaches with the wind blowing towards it, the barometer falls slowly. When the storm arrives overhead the wind begins to change its direction, blowing outwards (forwards) from the storm. At this point the barometer rises. Heavy, positively charged rain or hail begins to fall at this point, and the barometer begins to steady usually at a level slightly above what it was before the storm. The rain continues for a considerable time. As the cloud moves farther on, rain falling on the observer will consist of drops which have passed through the negative air at the rear of the cloud. They will not be as large as those in the front of the cloud.

The thunder cloud is thus a minor depression in itself and may soon pass when the conditions giving rise to it no longer apply.

We can now return to the problem of the normal depression and its progress. (See fig. 32.)

Let us first see what happens when a depression passes north of an observer, and then what occurs if it goes to the south. The effects are different.

The southern observer will see first the warning cirrus clouds, then in all probability cirrostratus. On the approach of the depression the wind begins to back against the sun, perhaps from north-west through west to south or even south-east. The glass will begin to fall, and so will the rain – some distance in advance of the arrival of the warm front, first as drizzle and then steadily. At the same time the wind increases to strong or perhaps gale force. The rain is often the heaviest near the line of the warm front. There is further intermittent rain throughout the warm sector and, at sea, this is the part of the depression in which fog is most likely to occur.

The first sign of a lift is very probably a change in the wind, which begins to veer round from south-east to south then to west and finally to north-west, by which time the cold front should be approaching. When it does so, one may look for the "clearing showers" that occur when the final remnants of the warm air are scooped onwards. And then comes blue sky again. The barometer will rise as the warm air overhead is replaced by the cold.

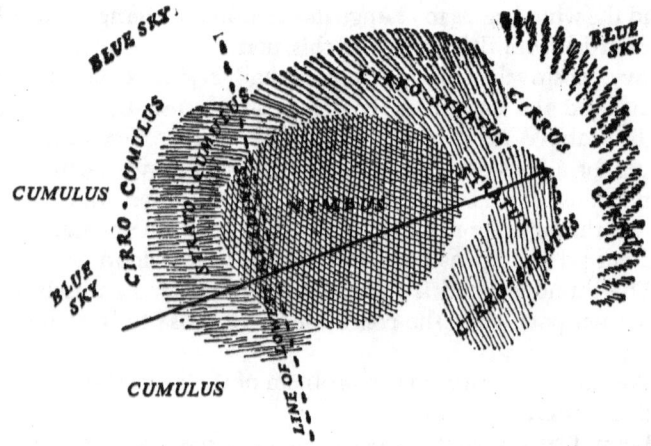

Fig. 32. A DEPRESSION MOVING NORTH-EASTWARDS, SHOWING CLOUDS TO BE EXPECTED

We have dealt here with the depression as it would seem to someone at or near the southern edge. If, however, we had been standing to the north of the depression, the wind, instead of veering from south-east through south to north-west, would have backed through east to north-east. If we had been at the centre of the depression we should have got stronger winds and a far more rapid change of wind from east to west.

At sea, therefore, the yachtsman does well to sail away from the centre of the depression. In the Northern Hemisphere the centre is found by facing the wind and stretching the right arm out sideways parallel to the ground, in line with the shoulder-blade. The centre of the depression will lie slightly behind the right arm. Hence you sail on the starboard tack to get out of harm's way. The right-hand forward quadrant (quarter-section) of the depression, looking along the path of its advance, is the most vicious, as it sweeps you round into the path of the storm. The left-hand is less unpleasant.

Most depressions pass to the north of us in Britain. They tend to travel along the sea-ways either directly from Iceland to Norway, or from the West of Ireland to Scandinavia. Their north-easterly route is due partly to the impetus given them by the clockwise winds blowing from the north of the high-pressure area of the Azores. Weather forecasters accept a mechanical principle according to which depressions tend to move in the direction of the isobars in their warm sector.

We have now to deal with the anti-cyclone which, as its name implies, is in some respects the opposite of a cyclone or depression. The anti-cyclone centres around an area of high pressure and the winds tend to blow away from its centre and, because of the laws which we have already discussed, they do so in a clockwise direction in the Northern Hemisphere and a counter-clockwise direction in the Southern. Usually, anti-cyclones mean fine weather, but in winter at any rate it does not follow that there will be blue sky. They often give fog near the coast, especially at night and early morning. Anti-cyclonic winds are light and anti-cyclones move slowly, especially the summer variety.

We have mentioned that the winds of a depression blow round it counter-clockwise in the Northern Hemisphere. More accurately, we might have said that they usually blow inwards at an angle of between 20 and 30 degrees to the lines of the isobars. Similarly, anti-cyclonic winds tend to blow outwards across the isobars.

While on the subject of winds we should mention the scale generally used in describing their force. A seaman quotes these figures in knots, but a landsman in miles per hour; for which purpose I give the approximate conversions:

Beaufort number	Speed knots	Land m.p.h.	Description	Height of waves (ft.)
0	0	0	Calm.	—
1	2	2·3	Light air. Ruffles with the appearance of scales are formed.	—
2	5	5·8	Light breeze. Small wavelets still short but more pronounced. Crests do not break.	½
3	9	10·3	Gentle breeze. Large wavelets' crests begin to break. Perhaps scattered white horses.	2
4	13	15·0	Moderate breeze. Small waves becoming longer. Frequent white horses.	4
5	19	20·7	Fresh breeze. Moderate waves take a more pronounced long form. Many white horses.	6
6	24	27·6	Strong breeze. Larger waves form; foam crests more extensive (probably some spray).	9
7	30	34·5	Near gale. Sea heaps up; white foam from breaking waves begins to be blown with wind. Spindrift seen.	13
8	37	42·6	Gale. Moderate high waves; edges of crests break into spindrift. Foam blown into well-marked streaks. Spray reduces visibility.	18
9	44	50·6	Strong gale. High waves. Dense streaks of foam. Spray affects visibility.	23
10	52	58·7	Storm. Very high waves with long overhanging crests. Dense white foam streaks. Whole surface of sea takes white appearance.	30
11	60	68·0	Violent storm, exceptionally high waves (small ships lost to view behind waves). Sea completely covered with long white patches of foam. Everywhere the edges of wave crests are blown into froth. Visibility poor.	40 or more.
12	68	77·0	Hurricane. Air filled with foam and spray. Sea completely white with spray. Visibility very seriously affected.	40 or more.

MEET THE WEATHERMAN 189

The material for weather forecasts is obtained on land, sea and in the air. Meteorological stations, often at aerodromes, record such things as barometer pressure, temperature, moisture, rainfall, clouds and wind direction and strength. This information is sent in code form to collecting centres for mapping purposes. Weather data from the upper air on temperature, pressure and moisture is assembled by means of self-registering instruments sent aloft by balloons set to burst at certain heights, after which the instruments parachute back to earth.

In addition to these maps, simplifications of which are published (twelve hours late) in the daily papers, yachtsmen make use of the B.B.C. shipping forecasts and weather reports broadcast from coastal weather stations several times a day.

Gale warnings are broadcast by the B.B.C. and from G.P.O. coastal radio stations, and cones, lights and in some cases night signals are flown or shown at coastal stations.

To understand these forecasts it pays to have a map showing the official boundaries of the weather districts. Forecasts for the areas bordering your own – and who can carry boundaries easily in the head? – may be extremely valuable.

Often forecasts of fresh-to-strong winds are more reliable than those foretelling light-to-moderate winds, which are more easily falsified by local conditions or secondary depressions. In general, forecasts of weather from south-west, which are little interfered with by land, are more dependable than those relating to winds and weather from the east. General weather forecasts are often more reliable than those of local areas. Nursery-rhyme forcasts are often no good at all. The following, for instance, should be painstakingly forgotten:

> "The weather will change when the moon does";
> "It will rain because you can see the hills so clearly"; or
> "because you can hear the trains so clearly" (both of which depends largely on the direction of the wind).

Somewhat more reliable is the jingle "Rain before seven" (G.M.T.), "fine before eleven", but not if the rain is too heavy

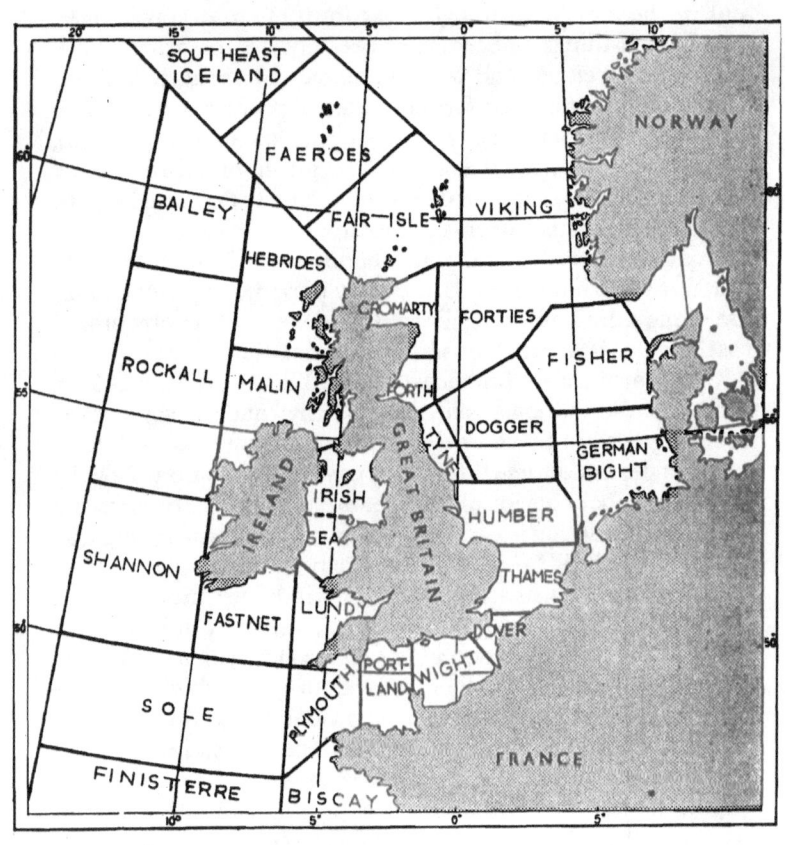

Fig. 33. SHIPPING WEATHER FORECAST AREAS
A chart showing the areas used in B.B.C. gale warnings and weather forecasts for shipping

to be driven off by the heat of the sun. On the other hand, if cumulus clouds form in the early morning and rapidly increase in size there is a good chance of rain. Red sky at night brings fair weather next day about seven times out of ten, and red sky in the morning bad weather about six times out of ten.

A halo around the moon does mean bad weather. The halo is produced by cirrostratus, which we have seen is a "bad" sign. "Mackerel sky, twelve hours dry" should be understood as meaning "Twelve hours till it rains", and not always even that. The rhyme "Short foretold soon past, long foretold long last" is sound.

These few words, of course, will not turn anyone into a weather expert (our weather is far too complicated for that), but they may help the average helmsman to guess better and sometimes even to guess right when guess he must.

CHAPTER XVI

IS HE GOING TO HIT ME?

You are out in the Channel at midnight. Everyone else is below – asleep – and you do not like to wake them. You are confronted with what appears to be four lights: two white, one above the other; one red and one green. They seem to be maintaining the same position relative to you.
    What do you do?
    Well, if you do not already know the answer to this one, the only thing to do is to call up one of the hands who does. But you should not have to think out the answer to this one. It should come to you as automatically as a blink to an eyelid.
    Here is what the lights say. The fact that green or red lights are visible show that the vessel is under way, and because there are two white lights showing, a fairly large steamer may be involved. All vessels of 150 ft. or over in length must carry two white lights when not at anchor or made fast ashore or aground. Vessels of less than 150-ft. length need carry only one light when under way, but can show two if they like.
    What else do we know?
    To anyone who has studied the traffic rules of the sea it is clear that the vessel is heading towards him. This is because both red and green lights of the same vessel can be seen at the same time. This can be the case only when the other boat is almost head-on, for the rules provide that the red light carried on the port side of the boat shall be visible only within an area extending from right ahead to two compass points abaft the port beam, and there are directions for masking the green starboard light in the same way. (Two compass points equal $22\frac{1}{2}°$).
    The fact that the vessel is head-on is confirmed by the fact that the two white lights appear one above the other. The

IS HE GOING TO HIT ME?

International Regulations provide that where two white lights are carried by a steam vessel they shall be in line with the keel, with the lower one forward of the upper one by more than three times the vertical distance between the lights, except under special circumstances, as for example when towing.

Now, if the vessel were at all sideways on to the observer, the fact that one light was in advance of the other would be obvious. But the lights are visible one above the other, so the vessel is end-on.

You should always beware when the bearing of a light of another vessel remains constant in relation to your own position – even if the other vessel is showing only a single light. A constant bearing does not necessarily mean that the two vessels are bound to hit each other – one can think up examples of vessels sailing away from each other at different speeds and keeping the same bearing – but clearly the risk of collision must be presumed to exist in the circumstances, especially when it is clear that the vessel is definitely coming towards the observer.

But it is not enough for the observer to establish that a large steamer is going to run him down; he has to decide what to do about it.

First, remember that if yours is a sailing boat with the sails up and you are not using the motor, you count as a sail boat and have the right of way over the steamer. The fact that you have a motor makes no difference, provided that you are not using it. If, however, you switch on the motor, then you technically change into a steamer, *even though you are using your sails at the same time.* This is important.

It is as well, however, not to insist too firmly on your right of way, if the visibility is poor. It can happen that a steamer's watch-keeping may be at fault, or it may be impossible for the large boat to alter course in restricted waters. All these things have to be taken into account. If you do decide to stand on your rights and wait for the steamer to give way to you, you must keep your course and speed and make no alterations which might baulk her in her efforts to avoid you. If you are not sure whether you have been seen, flash your torch on your sails and make a sound signal.

Take the above case where a steamer is coming towards you end on. What happens then if you are using the motor and so are also a "steamer"? The answer is that you must alter course to pass the other boat on your – and her – port side. Steamers using the same channel usually keep to the starboard side of the mid-channel for this reason.

Now, suppose that one "steamer" is to cross the path of another. Which has the right of way? In this case the boat which has the other boat to starboard must give way; which, to be safe, means going astern of the other vessel. At night a boat using power to which you, as another power boat, must give way, will appear as a red light on the starboard bow. (I am ignoring his white light for the moment.)

If you see a green light to port, then you have the right of way over the other steamer. If the bearing of the light seen draws ahead, the other boat will pass ahead of you. If the bearing drops back he should be able to go astern of you.

In this connection it is worth paying special attention to rule 22 of the New International Rules for the Prevention of Collision, which deals with converging vessels. These rules which came into force in January 1954 should be your sea bible.

Any alteration of course by you should be decisive – easily seen by the other boat – and should be made in plenty of time. Always make the appropriate sound signal (described below).

When, in consequence of bad weather or other causes, a right-of-way vessel finds herself so close that collision cannot be avoided by the action of the other vessel alone, she must also take such action as will best aid to avoid the collision.

Another common-sense rule is that the overtaking vessel keeps clear of the overtaken.

That covers the main points as between steamer and steamer, and between steamer and sail boat. We have now to consider the relationship between one sail boat and another. They are

IS HE GOING TO HIT ME? 195

much the same as for racing. Thus a boat that is close hauled has the right of way over one that is running free, and a vessel close hauled on the starboard tack over one on port tack. When both are free, the boat on the starboard gybe (i.e. carrying the boom to port) has the right of way over the other. The windward vessel also keeps out of the way of the leeward when both are sailing close hauled or free with the wind on the same side. (But you may not luff the windward vessel or take any risks.)

The rules as between sailing boats are easier to carry out by day than by night. For instance, you may see a boat showing a green light only approaching from port, which, as we have seen, ought to give you the right of way. But it need not if you are reaching on port and the other boat is on starboard. Nor need it if you are the windward boat or the overtaking boat. In this latter case you will see the white light (which should be fixed in the after part of the other boat) before you see the masked red and green lights.

Examples of lights shown by vessels and their meanings are given below. (See fig. 34):

1. Large steamer under way, with two white lights one abaft the other.
2. Steamer under way, with one masthead light (i.e. under 150 ft. in length).
3. Steamer towing another vessel.
4. Steamer towing two or more vessels, the stern of the after one being over 600 ft. from the stern of the towing steamer.
5. Two black balls as day signals, showing that the vessel (steam or sail) is not under command owing to accident, or other causes.
6. Lights carried by above vessel at night when stopped.
7. Day signals of telegraph ship doing cable work.
8. Lights carried by above vessel at night when making her way through the water. When not making her way through the water, no side-lights would be shown.

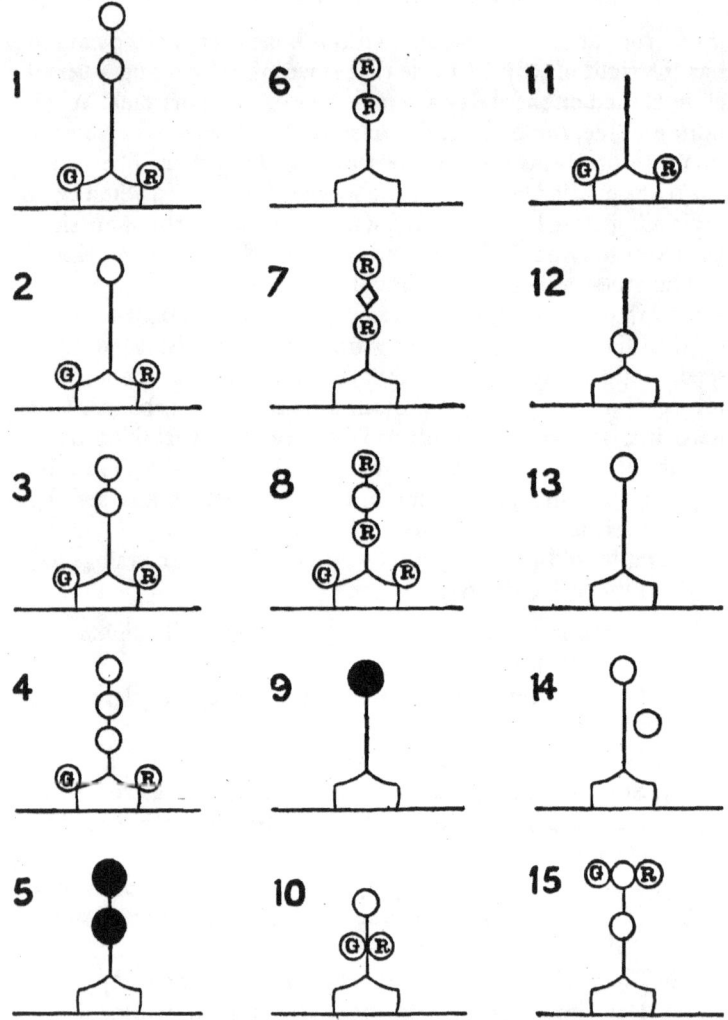

Fig. 34. LIGHTS, ETC., SHOWN BY SHIPS AT SEA

IS HE GOING TO HIT ME? 197

9. Steamer under sail only, with funnel up.
10. Small steamer or launch under way, under 40 tons.
11. Sailing vessel under way or being towed.
12. Steamer or sailing vessel, brought up at anchor. (If under 150 ft. length 1 light. If over 150 ft. 2 lights, 1 forward and 1 aft).
13. Sailing pilot cutter. A steam pilot vessel would carry a red light 8 ft. below the white light.
14. A fishing vessel with her tackle down, in the same direction as the lower light.
15. A steam trawler. A sailing trawler only shows a white light.

Many other combinations are given in various Admiralty Manuals and should be studied.

We have already mentioned sound signals.

Large steamers carry sirens or steam whistles to inform other boats, when in sight of one another, of alterations of course:

I am directing my course to starboard —
I am directing my course to port — —
My engines are going full speed astern — — —

All long blasts of 1 second duration.

When in doubt as to whether the other vessel is taking sufficient avoiding action, the boat that is keeping her course gives at least five short rapid blasts on the whistle.

In restricted visibility a power-driven vessel sounds a prolonged blast at least once every two minutes.

Signals used by steamers during a fog are as follows:

I am under way but stopped — —
I am under way but moving —
I cannot manœuvre — · ·

Long blasts 4–6 seconds; short blasts 1 second. Interval of 1 second between blasts and not more than 2 minutes between signals.

Sail boats do not use a steam whistle or siren and have to be content with a fog-horn. They use the following signals:

I am on starboard tack —	Long blasts 4–6 seconds; short blasts 1 second. Interval of 1 second between blasts and not more than 1 minute between signals.
I am on port tack — —	
I am running — — —	
I am not manœuvrable — · ·	

When anchored in poor visibility a vessel sounds a bell for five seconds at intervals of not more than a minute. There are various other regulations for vessels towing or aground or fishing.

Morse, transmitted by lamps or flags, and semaphore are not to be despised. Certain useful signals can be given by means of International Code of forty flags, ten numerals and an answering pendant. For instance:

B indicates a ship unloading explosives.
C means "Yes".
D means "I am in difficulties; keep clear".
E means "I am steering to starboard".
F means "I am disabled; communicate with me".
G means "I desire a pilot".
H means "I have a pilot aboard".
I means "I am directing my course to port".
J means "I am going to semaphore signal".
K means "Stop; you are running into danger".
L means "Stop; stand by to receive message".
M means "I have a doctor aboard".
N means "No".
O means "Man overboard".
P means (in port) "Am putting to sea". (At sea) "Your lights are dim (or out)".
Q is hoisted when entering port to show ship is healthy.
R means "the way is off my ship; you may feel your way past".
S means "I am going full speed astern".

T means "Do not pass ahead of me".
U means "You are standing into danger".
V means "I need assistance".
W means "I need medical aid".
Y means "I am carrying mails".
Z is call-sign to shore stations.

The International Code Book gives many other examples of how much can be said with a few letters. Many of the above code signals can also be given in morse. Alternative distress signals are S O S (... ——— ...) in morse; a gun fired every minute; flares at night; a small flag with a ball above or below it and a fog-horn continually sounded.

In fog or at night it is a wise precaution to hoist a radar reflector if possible higher than 30 ft. to act as a warning of your presence to ships fitted with radar and using it at the time. But it is unsafe to rely on being seen or on radar only.

Fog signals and the evidence of one's own eyes and ears is what counts because this is the only language that both ships are certain to have in common. For example, it is of no use for a ship, having seen another on her radar screen, to warn the other ship that she is altering course before both ships are in sight of one another.

Finally, as the Book of Rules says, "In obeying and construing these Rules, due regard shall be had to all dangers of navigation and collision to any special circumstances which may render a departure from the above Rules necessary in order to avoid immediate danger". In other words, we have all had the buck well and truly passed to us.

CHAPTER XVII

STOPPING AND STARTING

GETTING under way and bringing up are two of the most thrilling operations in sailing, and they often need far more judgment than is necessary when on course. For it is harder to control a boat when she is at half-speed or stopped than when she has full way on her.

Not only is steering more tricky at an anchorage, but there is less room for manœuvring and consequently more chance of damaging your own boat or someone else. "Safe in port", they say; "No such thing", I maintain.

However, let us first consider the anchor itself before going into the technique of letting it go and getting it up.

There are many different kinds of anchor on the market, but the sort most generally favoured to-day is the CQR or plough anchor, which has greater holding power for its weight and is consequently more easily handled than conventional types. Having no stock or upstanding fluke, the plough anchor is far less likely to become fouled (an anchor is fouled when a turn of the anchor chain catches on some part of it in such a way that the anchor is pulled up or tripped up by the boat's motion and so drags); and the greater the strain, the more firmly the ploughshare holds. The suggested size for a 4-ton craft is 15 lb. in the plough model, compared with 35 lb. for the conventional type of anchor.

Other figures for a boat of 8 tons: Conventional 55 lb.
                                                         CQR   20 lb.
                                        12 tons: Conventional 65 lb.
                                                         CQR   25 lb.

But it will be well worth investigating the anchorages you are likely to use before finally abandoning the conventional model, particularly if you are dealing with soft mud.

For cruising purposes two anchors are usually carried: the bower or main anchor, so called because it is in the bow ready to go; and the kedge, which is generally about two-thirds the weight of the bower.

With the anchor goes, of course, a chain. Plenty of chain is needed to ensure that the pull on the anchor in the ground is horizontal rather than vertical, for a vertical strain pulls up the anchor. The more chain you have, the lighter can be your anchor. As for thickness, a $\frac{5}{16}$-in. chain will do for a 30-lb. anchor, a $\frac{3}{8}$-in. chain for 45 lb., and a $\frac{7}{16}$-in. chain for up to 60 lb.

An anchor chain is an unlovely thing. We read one day of a man who was carrying one along the side of a jetty. The end of the chain slipped over the side and ran out, carrying the man with it to the bottom of the harbour and pinning him underneath its coils. Only superhuman struggles freed him.

Even when it is safely on the boat the chain raises problems. Its weight is best stowed not too far forward.

The last link of the chain – the one you want to keep on board – should be carefully attended to. The inboard end of the chain must be securely fastened and yet you should be able to cast it off easily if need be. Not so long ago one of the yachting periodicals recorded the story of an owner who went on a fishing expedition off the West Coast of Scotland. Having arrived at the fishing ground they anchored in seven fathoms with all their chain out. After they had been fishing for some time the sea began to get rough and they resolved to turn for home. But when they tried to raise the anchor there was nothing doing. It must have got caught round a rock. As the tide rose the chain became bar taut. And still the anchor would not budge. The owner then decided to say good-bye to his anchor and chain by letting go the inboard end. But this was impossible for the end was secured with a shackle that had rusted, and the spike with which the owner tried to loosen it broke. As the strain got worse and worse the chain burst through its fairlead and the navel pipe in the deck and started to saw through the deck. So the owner decided to try and sail out the anchor; he hoisted the mainsail and set the jib aweather. The boat lay over on her side so far that water began to lap into the cockpit. They got free only when a squall struck the yacht so hard that the anchor chain broke.

No, the proper way to secure the inboard end of an anchor chain is not with a shackle that invariably rusts from the drips off the chain. Far better to take a round turn with the chain itself round the mast, and then secure the final link with a piece of suitable rope.

Rope rather than chain is used for the kedge. Nylon or Manila are good; and coir, though cheaper and less hard-wearing, is wonderfully elastic and will absorb snubbing shocks far better than even a chain. Sisal is less durable but cheaper still.

And now for the technique of anchoring. In general, the same principles apply as in the case of a mooring. In other words, with the wind against the tide you must not expect to anchor with the mainsail up. In such cases the mainsail is lowered with the boat head to wind, and the anchorage is then approached against the tide under headsail only. Only when the ship begins to go astern is it time to let the anchor go, and then it is a mistake to be in too much of a hurry. If you let the chain go with a rush the chances are that, if using a conventional anchor, a coil or two will festoon itself round the anchor, which will then have not the faintest hope of holding. Moreover, there have been cases where the weight and force of the chain rushing out have burst through the navel pipe and sawed the ship down to the waterline.

Naturally, the anchorage chosen must be sheltered and have enough water at low-tide to keep the boat afloat. The amount of chain let out should be equal to at least three times the depth of water at high-tide. Cable and chain should be marked to show how much has been let out.

In many harbours to-day the bottom is covered with all kinds of rubbish, such as old mooring chains and even wartime débris. Under these circumstances there is a chance of the anchor becoming jammed in such a way that it cannot be withdrawn in the normal way by a vertical pull. Instead it has to be tripped (that is, pulled out backwards). Arrangements to trip the anchor have to be made before letting it go.

The usual method is to attach the anchor crown to a separate line with a light buoy for recovery.

Sometimes it is possible to lie at anchor with one anchor only, but for this plenty of space is needed. If the wind is against the tide it will be necessary to give the yacht a sheer to port or starboard to prevent her from dragging the chain over the anchor every time the tide changes. This is accomplished by giving the boat a sheer to windward when the wind is forward of the beam and turning the boat's head to leeward when the wind is aft of the beam.

However, the boat will swing far less and therefore take up less room if riding to two anchors. Moreover, in law a vessel riding to a single anchor is not considered properly moored, and if it swings and damages another boat the owner will be liable, even if he were the first in the anchorage.

Where two anchors are put out, they are disposed fore and aft on the line of the current and not on either quarter, where they may well be fouled by other yachts. The heavier of the two anchors should be laid out in the direction from which the greater strain is expected (that is, towards the less-sheltered side of the anchorage).

There are a number of ways of letting go the second anchor. If you have enough chain it is possible to let go the main anchor with twice the scope you intend to use. When the tide has carried you back to the end of this, you let go the kedge or second anchor and then haul yourself back to a mid-position. Or you can let the smaller anchor go while still under way – again with twice the scope you will need when the big anchor is down.

Under other circumstances it may be easier to take the second anchor out in the dinghy. The simplest way to do it is to lower the anchor and the bulk of the warp into the dinghy, keeping the end of the warp made fast.

Next, without standing up in the dinghy, take the anchor and secure it to the transom of the dinghy with the flukes fore and aft in order to lower resistance through the water. For securing the anchor, pass a short piece of rope through the ring at the top of the shank and round the thwart of the dinghy, to which it is made fast with a slippery hitch. Then, when you have reached the required spot, you pull on the slippery hitch without even leaving your seat and the kedge drops overboard.

Letting go an anchor is a good deal simpler than picking up a mooring, for which the boat has to be at exactly the right spot with the right amount of way on her. As with anchoring, the final approach is made against the tide. The whole art lies in judging the strength of the wind and tide and knowing your own boat. Some boats, for instance, when turned into the wind, will shoot several times their own length before coming to a standstill. Other lighter boats will carry on for a length only. Find out in advance to which class your craft belongs.

When the wind is against the tide the mooring is approached down wind under jib only. As soon as the mooring is reached, if not before, the jibsheets are slacked off to allow the tide to take way off the boat. Any other method of approaching the mooring will almost certainly mean that the bowman has to work under most unfavourable conditions.

Thus if you come up to the mooring *with* the tide instead of against, the bow hand will have to make fast at the same time as the tide is trying to swing the ship stem-to-tide. And if at the same time the ship is running *with* the wind from astern this is an impossible task.

Even when the wind is running across the tide it generally pays to play safe and reach up under jib only to the mooring.

When picking up a mooring it is a help if the hand in the bows adopts a simple method of signalling, so that the helmsman, whose view of the mooring is hidden by the bow of the boat, can know which way to steer. The bow hand holds up a boat-hook horizontally in a position where the helmsman can see it. Then if the boat is to be steered farther to port he lowers the end of the boat-hook in his left-hand, and if the boat should go to starboard he lowers the starboard end of the boat-hook. When the mooring has been reached he lowers the boat-hook altogether. Picking up the mooring is becoming easier from year to year because of new inventions. One such device consists of an ordinary wooden pole. To one end of this pole a removable cone-shaped cap can be fitted. This cap stays in place merely because of the pressure of the wood against the inside of the cone. The outer part of the cone is fitted with a ring. When the skipper intends picking up his mooring, a suitable length of warp is got ready; one end is made fast to the boat and the other to the ring on the cone. The cone also comprises a large spring clip rather similar to the most easily worked kind you find on dog-leads. When picking up the mooring the crew stands at the ready, pole in hand. He stretches out the pole, clips the cone at the end of it on to the wire loop of the mooring in the water and then tugs the pole sharply backwards. The cone, of course, comes away from the end of the pole and the mooring is now attached to the mooring rope.

This is all very much easier than grabbing the mooring with a normal boat-hook, bringing it aboard and then making fast. There is also a welcome trend towards making moorings with loops standing higher above the water and therefore easier to reach.

It is important, when picking up a mooring, to make sure that it does not belong to anyone else. Imagine the feelings of anyone who rents a mooring and who comes back after a hard day's sailing to find that someone else is in possession; someone who perhaps has gone ashore, so that there is no means of getting hold of him. Snatching a mooring in this manner is not far short of pilfering in my view.

A definite plan of campaign should be thought out before casting off the mooring or weighing anchor.

It frequently happens in an anchorage that there are boats on either side of you, in front of you, and behind you. When the wind is before the beam there may be some doubt as to whether you can clear your neighbours on either side. Sometimes you can solve this problem by sailing forward while still made fast to your mooring. This will mean some very speedy tacking, as the mooring will bring the boat up short after a very few yards in either direction; but you will gain distance forward, which is the object of the exercise. Or you can decide to drop back so as to go astern of your neighbours. You could, of course, allow the boat to drift backwards with the tide, but this would mean that for several seconds the craft would be entirely out of control, which is not a very comfortable feeling. A better way – we are still assuming that the wind is forward of the beam – is to back the jib to windward (which will blow the boat's head round) and at the same time reverse the rudder (putting the tiller to starboard in order to get the bow to starboard, and vice versa), because the boat under these conditions will be going astern.

Using this method you have steerage way from the start. Another good method of getting the boat off on the right tack is to bring the mooring some way aft. This will turn the boat away from the side on which the mooring is secured, or you can drop backwards by passing a warp round the mooring and letting yourself fall astern on this warp.

The technique when weighing anchor is not very different, except that the anchor chain will have to be hauled in to the point where it is up and down before it will break out of the ground.

Sooner or later you will probably have to come alongside a jetty. With a boat of any size this means fenders out in profusion to prevent damage. If the wind is blowing off the jetty, and we will hope that it is, you can edge up to it in the same way as to a mooring; only make sure if there is no one ashore that your crew gets on the jetty smartly with a line to the bow. All sheets should be slacked off when near enough to the jetty. If the wind is blowing on to the jetty, the best way of approach is to drop an anchor when nearing the jetty and then veer out sufficient cable to get ashore. A line for hauling the yacht to the jetty can be run ashore in the dinghy.

Often the jetty has piles alongside it, which raises the problem of how to protect the paintwork of the boat. An ordinary fend-off will not rest permanently against the pile. Therefore, as a precaution a plank, longer than the distance between the piles, should be lowered over the side of the ship and fend-offs placed between this and the side of the ship.

It is worth securing the ship astern at the earliest possible moment. Then if the bow hand is unable to make fast you can easily get the boat sailing again. Otherwise there is a chance of your being blown backwards along the quay without being able to get clear away.

When finally secured the boat should have a bow rope leading forward along the quay, and a stern rope leading aft. In addition, the boat will need "springs" – one leading from the bow aft to the quay, and another from the quarter forward. The longer these ropes are the less they will need altering for the rise and fall of the tide. In addition, there should be a breast rope leading from forward direct to the quay, and a corresponding quarter rope from the quarter.

The large rise and fall in tide that you get in some harbours lead to problems. A friend once moored his dinghy in St. Malo with somewhat too little scope, with the result that when it came to low-tide the dinghy was hanging from the jetty by its painter. An oar was lost.

Then someone else who thought they knew better, moored their dinghy near the same spot with plenty of scope for the boat to float at low-tide – so much so that when the tide rose the dinghy floated off and disappeared up the wide opening of the town drain. It just shows you never can tell.

If the harbour in question dries out, the skipper will have to take measures to see that his boat leans inwards towards the quay as she grounds. Otherwise disaster may follow.

One way of making sure that she tilts the right way is to run a line ashore some distance from the quay abreast of the mast. Attach the free end of the line to the halyard and haul taut. Slack should be taken in as the tide falls. Recipe for doing this automatically is to leave one end of the halyard free, but attached to a weight which can slide up or down the part of the halyard already made fast.

Getting away from the jetty requires less finesse than coming alongside, but it is unsafe to take for granted that there is nothing to it. For instance, with the wind aft you may find that unless you take precautions you will get bumped forward along the quay and unable to part company with it, because in order to turn the bows away from the jetty you have to turn the stern towards it. So make sure that the bow is well away from the jetty before casting off the stern lines. If space is short, you can spring her away from the jetty by bearing off forward with the boat-hook and pulling forward on a line secured to the stern. Such precautions are the more necessary when the tide as well as the wind is fair.

If the wind is blowing on to the jetty, the only satisfactory method of getting away is to take out the kedge in the dinghy and haul yourself out – unless, of course, there is a suitable buoy placed there for the purpose.

CHAPTER XVIII

SAFETY FIRST

BOAT drill has to be endured on even a transatlantic liner after the ship leaves port, so why should the helmsman of a small boat be exempt from learning what to do in an emergency, even if that emergency may never happen? And who can be sure that it will not? A foul by another boat, a broken mast, a sheet that catches somewhere it ought not to – who can truthfully say, "This can never happen to me"?

The least serious of the emergencies occurs when you run aground – unless, of course, the piece of "ground" is a rock or a sharp iron stake. Then, if the leak is small, it can perhaps be stopped temporarily by using a handkerchief or something similar as a bung; or if the hole is near the bow it may be possible in a small boat for helmsman and crew to both sit on the transom, so that the leak is kept above water-level. It goes without saying that the small boat should be provided with extra buoyancy so that it is never necessary to swim for it. And in the case of a yacht, the dinghy should be properly fitted out and flares and orange smoke signals carried in addition to the usual medical equipment, fire extinguishers, etc.

But let us suppose that you have grounded not on a rock but on more accommodating sand. The tragedy often happens when you are beating up a channel against the tide. You go in shore to get out of the tide, find you are getting along better than ever – and then you stand on a little too long. At the moment when you decide to come about, the boat which has been heeling over a little in the wind comes upright and so draws more water. Then the worst happens.

Before the boat can get under way on the new tack, the wind

blows her bow round on to the shore and she comes to a halt. Then, if the tide is ebbing, action may have to be very rapid indeed.

Sometimes the boat's head can be pushed round with an oar or spinnaker boom until she is at least head to wind, at which point the jib can be backed to windward to help her round still farther. The pushing operation will be easier if as many of the crew as possible go forward. This is because most fixed-keel boats draw less water forward than they do aft. If the boat appears to be aground on a lee shore on the side of a bank, it may pay to get the crew's weight to leeward, so that the boat draws less water and so slides off the bank. If these methods fail, something more ambitious may have to be tried. Get the sails off if there is any chance that the effect of the wind will be to drive the boat farther on. The kedge should normally be taken off at right-angles to the line of the bank, so that the boat can be hauled out as soon as there is water. If the terrain is muddy, there is a chance that it may be easier to get the boat afloat by drawing her back off the bank the same way that she came; in this case the kedge should be run out astern in the dinghy.

If the tide is going to dry right out and the boat is on the edge of a bank, take care to see that the boat falls the right way (that is, "uphill"). Otherwise, when the tide floods again there is a danger of her filling by the cockpit before the boat floats. Careful sounding with the lead or spinnaker boom will tell you how you are placed.

Having finished with grounding, let's consider a slightly more advanced case of the dinghy that capsizes. We have already suggested some of the reasons for such an occurrence. Other common causes are inexpert balancing (or overbalancing) by the crew, slowness in reacting to wind or wave effects in a sea-way, or rigging which parts under a strain.

Many capsizes can be avoided by prompt action. Never sit and wait for it to happen. For example, if the boat is blown over to *leeward* and starts to fill, you can at least save yourself from getting a wetting by climbing to the upper side. If you can once prevent the sail from touching the water, the boat will probably swing round head to wind and be all the more easy to keep upright. If the boat capsizes to windward you will almost certainly be thrown into the water as you are on the lower side. In this case do not try to climb back into the boat. It will only make things worse. Swim round behind her instead.

Your best chance of righting the boat is to stand on the centre board. The quicker the helmsman and crew clear out of the boat, the less water they will have to bail out. If the sail does touch the water there is a danger that it will scoop up water and perhaps even sink with the force of the tide. In this case there is a risk of the centre board disappearing completely from sight beneath the upturned hull of the boat, which will make it all the harder to right the boat. Therefore before leaving shore for the race let down some plate and then re-insert the centre board pin into the centre board casing. It will prevent the plate from disappearing completely in the event of a capsize.

If the boat fills as the result of a capsize, you will probably have to get the sails down. Sailing a waterlogged boat is none too good for the rigging or even the oldest mainsail, and if you have capsized the boat will be easier to right with the sails down. So that is the first step – to lower the sails. It may not be easy. The halyard cleat will probably be under water and difficult to find. But it will be easier if you have made the halyard fast with a slippery knot as shown in fig. 15A (p. 70). The alternative is to swim out to the masthead and undo the main halyard shackle.

The same applies to the jib if you want to lower that.

It will probably be necessary for both helmsman and crew to stay in the water during the early stages of bailing out. Otherwise the extra weight added to that of the water will sink the boat to the point where water comes in over the transom, as well as over the top of the centre board trunk.

When enough water has been bailed out, one of the crew can climb in over the transom and continue bailing, after which the other(s) can follow.

If, for any reason, you find it impossible to right the boat, do not attempt to swim for the shore so long as the boat has any positive buoyancy. It is nearly always farther away than it looks.

If you are lucky enough to stay upright when some other boat goes over, it is your duty to ask them if they need help and to put yourself out of any race in order to give it to them. In theory, of course, you are supposed to come up to them as if you were picking up a mooring, i.e. with all way off bow forward. But in a small boat, especially if single-handed, you will probably find it far easier to get a rope to them if you reach along close to them to leeward, and throw the rope or painter when you are abeam and then round up.

There are some other precautions which you can take before going sailing on a blowy day. The first is to tie in the bailer. It is one of the few items of gear in a modern dinghy which does not float, unlike the paddle, jib stick and anchor buoy.

The best way to avoid other kinds of trouble at sea with your gear is to see that it is in good order. Failing this, rapid action may ensure that one single mishap does not lead to a score of others. For instance, if the mainsheet parts, turn the boat into the wind at once while she still has way on, otherwise it may be difficult to get the boom back on board. If the windward shroud goes, get the boat on the other tack as quickly as possible. If it is the forestay, put the helm up and get the boat running, so that the main strain comes from aft.

A halyard, or on larger boats a topping lift, will sometimes do duty instead of a stay. If the boom breaks, do not attempt to come up into the wind, for under these conditions the sail will flap the boom dangerously. Keep the sail as full as possible while you bring it down.

The loss of a mast is one of the most serious misfortunes that can happen. If there is a heavy sea on or one is near a lee shore, it may be better to cut all adrift, for otherwise the mast may ram the boat and stave in the planks. Otherwise the mast can be brought alongside and partially salvaged.

Sailing in a heavy sea without shipping water calls for great skill. Briefly, this involves turning the boat as near bow on to the wave as possible if the wind is forward of the beam, and turning the boat stern to wave with a following wind. When the wind is on the beam you can take your choice; though too many turns in either direction will take you off your course.

Undoubtedly, the worst time comes when you have to run in a strong wind before a heavy sea. Then, if you are over-canvased, you will really regret not having reefed down in time, for the boat will yaw from side to side despite any frantic efforts on your part, and there is always the danger that she may try and round up, beam-on to the wind, with disastrous results.

When beating into a sea on a windy day, you cannot point as close to the wind as you can in calm weather. You have to keep her moving fast; and if you do not do so you will lose all way when you head into a wave, and that means trouble. When you go about, wait for a smooth between the waves.

The best time to reef is, of course, before you leave port. The weather forecast and barometer will give an idea of what kinds of wind to expect, but you must be your own judge, too. Offshore breezes are more difficult to gauge than on-shore breezes. This is because the wind coming towards you over land may be diverted by some hill or other feature, so that you feel a good deal less of the wind on shore than you will notice at sea. Moreover, if the wind is offshore, the waves will to some extent be masked and the sea will look calmer than it is.

At sea you get a better idea of the wind's strength when sailing into it than you do when either reaching or running.

We have already referred briefly to reefing and to the two methods, roller reefing and points reefing. But there is a limit to reefing. Possibly your mainsail will have three sets of reefing points and no more. Or, if you use the roller reefing method, you will find that after a time you get to the point where any more reefing will lead to a ruined sail.

In a yacht at sea, under such circumstances, the mainsail is taken down and a trysail hoisted instead. This is a loose-footed sail, i.e. the foot of the sail is not attached to a boom. To balance it (for the main and jib must always be proportionate in size) we use a small storm jib.

If the wind increases still further in force, you may have to take off all sail and ride to bare poles, some experts advise using a sea anchor. This device is shaped like the windsocks you see on airfields, and it is streamed over the bow with plenty of warp, preferably coir, which floats and which therefore makes it unnecessary to buoy the anchor. A good way of preventing the warp from chafing is to lower some anchor chain and attach it to this. The sea anchor has at its sharp end a ring to which a tripping line is attached. Without the tripping line it would be impossible to recover the sea anchor.

The most difficult problem when caught out in a blow is to decide whether to ride it out or make for port. If you have plenty of sea room it is probably safer to ride out the storm. It is no good making for port unless you can enter it easily at all states of the tide. Even so, an entry on the ebb (i.e. with the wind against the tide) may prove very unpleasant if not dangerous; and if there is a sandbar the seas at this point will probably be heavier than those outside. Most boats can survive large waves at sea provided these waves do not break. Trouble comes when the waves break – through being undercut by shoals or the tide or the wake of the ship.

At sea, if you want to jog along down wind under full control, it may be possible to do so by hoisting the storm jib and running before the wind with the sea anchor streamed astern. Then in the lulls the yacht can proceed on her way with the anchor tripped, and if she seems like getting out of control the trip line can be slackened and the anchor will hold the yacht stern on to the waves. Or you can run down wind without a sea anchor under bare poles.

It may happen one day that you have to beach your boat on some unfriendly shore, or rescue someone who has got cut off by the tide under some cliffs. If you have an anchor with a long enough line you can drop it over the bows and approach the shore gradually, veering the line as you go. Even if the line is too short for this you can still drop the anchor over the side. It may not hold, but it will drag along and still accomplish the most important purpose, which is to keep the boat bow on to the seas. If you have no anchor, get the boat stern towards the shore, and then whenever a large wave looks likely to cause trouble row a few strokes to seaward.

It goes without saying that every ship should carry on board a supply of spares and the knowledge of how to use them, but so much depends on the size of the yacht and on the journey that is to be made that we do not attempt here to set out a list. Various methods of signalling for use in cases of distress are referred to in an earlier chapter.

Finally, there is the problem of what to do if someone falls overboard. In general, the rule is, no matter what course the boat is sailing, she will have to be gybed. This rule is based on the fact that the man in the drink will have to be picked up with the boat to leeward of him, and gybing is the simplest way of getting into that position. Immediately the cry "Man overboard" is heard, the helmsman should throw a life-belt as near as possible to the man in the drink – taking care, of course, not to hit him. The life-belt, like the life-jacket, should be coloured yellow rather than white, and should be horseshoe-shaped, as this type is very much easier than the ring pattern for the man to get into. Before casting, the helmsman should put into action the calcium smoke pot and flare (if any) attached to the life-belt. The life-belt should have attached to it a yellow dye marker, such as was used in the war by the R.A.F. for day spotting, and if in tropical waters a shark-repellent device. Some life-saving equipment is fitted with electric light apparatus which starts to work automatically in the water, or should do if nothing has corroded – a high possibility with electrical apparatus exposed to sea air for any length of time. The life-belt should be kept handy to the helmsman's reach; it should not be "securely lashed" or made fast in any way that means that seconds are going to be wasted freeing it. Three suitably placed wooden pegs are all that is necessary.

I said that the quickest way of reaching the man in the drink was to gybe the ship, and so it is. But this does not mean that this must be done right away. Indeed, it could not be if the ship was running with spinnaker drawing. It may, in any case, be better to keep the yacht on a noted course and to drop a second life-belt for marking purposes. This narrows the area of search. The helmsman, or a member of the crew detailed for the purpose, should try to keep an eye on the man in the water. With these precautions it should not be necessary to send a man aloft as spotter.

Having found the man in the drink, the next thing is to get him aboard. On some occasions the dinghy may be the best bet. But lowering the dinghy and rowing about in a heavy sea are not lightly to be undertaken. If the victim can clamber into the small boat, well and good. But if he has been swimming for some time the chances are that he will not be able to lift himself, plus the weight of his wet clothes, aboard unaided; and in this case the weight of two men at one end or one side of the dinghy will be too much for the craft. If the victim is able to climb over the transom, the rescuer can help balance things by retiring to the bow of the boat. A rope looped into a bowline and slung over the side may help to make a primitive kind of ladder.

If the victim is unconscious, the best that can be done by one oarsman in a small boat is to pass a line round him or through the loop of his life-harness (mentioned below) and tow him ashore or to the parent ship. Take care to see that the man's head is above water during the towing operations.

If it is decided to pick him up without lowering the dinghy, the yacht itself must be edged up to him in the same way as it would be for picking up a buoy. If the auxiliary is being used, make sure to switch it off before there is any danger of the rescuee being struck by the propeller. Switching off is better than leaving the motor in neutral, where an accidental push on the gear lever can lead to trouble. It is also safer not to use the boat-hook on the man in the water – safer, at least, for his good looks.

The ordinary yacht's ladder used for climbing aboard a yacht is not much good in a sea-way and is all too likely to be washed away. Impromptu ladders take time to set up and are not always in the right place when you want them. Manhandling is probably the easiest way on a large boat; a spare halyard can be used to lift the rescuee aboard, after which he should be given warmth, artificial respiration (if necessary), and then brandy. But it is far more important to prevent the man from falling overboard in the first instance than to snatch a chance of bringing him back alive later.

These are the precautions:

Any cruising boat should be provided with life-lines rigged to powerful stanchions. The Royal Ocean Racing Club of Britain and the Cruising Club of America wisely insist on these in the rules governing their races. The stanchions should, if possible, point inboard rather than vertically. They should be strong enough to hold the weight of a man falling against them when out of control. There should be a pulpit or solid framework in the bow of the boat to support the crew while changing sails.

Crews with any experience will remember almost automatically to keep one hand for the ship when moving about the deck.

In rough weather it should be made a rule for crews to wear a life-jacket. A jacket of kapok, which provides a warm lining and keeps the wearer afloat for some hours, is all that is needed for shoal water and river racing. When ocean racing, however, something extra is needed. The ideal life-jacket has some automatic flotation such as cork or kapok, plus an inflatable airbag or collar worn in front so that the chest rather than the back is buoyed up, and, if possible, the neck and HEAD as well. In rough weather it pays to keep the bag partly inflated if this does not restrict the wearer's movements too much. Then if he is knocked on the head while falling overboard he will still land right side up. Kapok has come in for some criticism lately because its buoyancy can be destroyed if it becomes soaked in oil. Therefore the safest kapok vests are those with the kapok sewn into waterproof pockets.

In shark waters the life-jacket should have suitable shark-repellent devices and a reliable form of lighting device. In addition, each crew member can wear light canvas "life-harness". The harness should consist of a strongly built canvas framework with a strop or loop attached to it near the wearer's chin, so that he can be lifted out of the water or towed face uppermost. When the ship begins to pitch and toss it should be an order that any crew going on deck must wear jacket and harness, and if working on a job that needs two hands for any length of time he should fasten a lanyard attached to himself at one end and to the rigging at the other. One convenient arrangement is to have the lanyard pass from the chest loop referred to above through a press-stud strap at the waist, and from there to the rigging. Then when working on board the upper part of the lanyard is held close to the body, where it does not get in the way. When any strain is put on it the press-stud opens up, giving the lanyard its full scope. Just under six feet should be long enough, *provided that you do not wind it around yourself* – a dangerous form of amusement. In heavy weather, and if the crew is sufficiently numerous, it should be arranged for watches to be taken of two men at a time.

To make spotting easier, all life-saving equipment should be coloured a bright canary yellow. White, among the shadows and foamings of the sea, is extremely hard to see. Inflatable rubber dinghies with tent hoods are easier to launch off a ship than ordinary wooden ones and safer to jump into. All lifeboats or rafts should be fitted with radar reflectors.

The radio telephone is becoming more and more useful as a safety device.

In such ways the risks taken afloat can be cut to the bare minimum.

CHAPTER XIX

GOING CRUISING

You may well ask why it is necessary to have a separate chapter on cruising, seeing that we have already dealt with most branches of navigation and seamanship. The answer lies in the fact that to begin with, at any rate, you will probably be going cruising as a guest aboard someone else's boat and not aboard your own. This raises a new set of problems. On your own boat, for instance, you can be as firm-jawed and dictatorial as you like. Of course, if it becomes widely known that this is your practice you may find it hard to get crews, but that is your affair; and if, through any carelessness, you damage your own boat, then it is your headache. Quite a different situation arises if you are invited to sail on someone else's boat. In the first place, being their guest you will have to fall in with their ways, their timetable, their method of sailing, their times of getting up and going to bed. In short, you will have to be easy to live with. This holds good not only in a privately owned yacht, but equally in club and other boats to which the crew contribute part of the cost.

The best recipe is a sense of humour combined with a good deal of patience.

Before you accept any invitation to go on a cruise you must get a clear idea of how long it is going to take and whether the skipper intends to keep to this time plan. It is rather trying, for instance, to find that instead of getting a free cruise as you planned, you have, because of delays here and there, to buy yourself an expensive air ticket back from Bilbao or some such place in order to be at the office on time.

Your second step should be to establish with your host what will be required of you and whether it will be within your capacities. If you have been on only one or two cruises of the kind before, say so. No one will think the worse of you, and it is only fair to your host not to let him count on an experienced hand, only to find that he is one short.

Next, we take the question of sea-sickness – an unattractive subject, but not to be shirked. Many of us suffer from it, especially at the beginning of the season. It is not safe to conclude that because you sail comfortably without a thought of sea-sickness in a small boat, or because you are never ill crossing the Channel in one of the Railway Executives' comfortable packets, that you will have no trouble at all helping to make tea in the galley of a pitching ocean racer. The safest thing as I said earlier is to have a proven cure for sea-sickness. Most of these contain either hyoscine or one of the anti-hystamines, a good example of which is the British brand known as Avomine. It is well worth trying to find out in advance which of the remedies available suits you best. Some of them, though admirable, produce drowsiness and are therefore unsuitable for anyone except unemployed passengers. Doubts that it will be all right on the night cause you unnecessary anxiety and may lead you to feel worse than you would otherwise be. If, after all, you have to be sick, try and reach the *after* part of the *lee* rail.

In general, cruises are not so luxurious as you might imagine from seeing pictures brought back from them. Often your first introduction to your floating home will be a visit to the yard where she is fitting out, in order to get to know the boat and, incidentally, to sweat blood doing some of the jobs needed before she can be put into the water.

Before each cruise there is sure to be tidying-up work to be done, if not repairs left over from the last trip. There is much rowing to and fro to pick up bread, milk and sometimes water if this cannot be piped direct into the freshwater tanks. And freshwater can weigh extremely heavily.

One of the most useful contributions you can make to the success of a cruise is not to bring too much luggage. In most cases there will be no room for the normal suitcase. It may look fine on your bunk, but what is going to happen when you caulk down at night? Put the suitcase on the floor? It will probably be slap in the way of half a dozen lockers. And how would you get to bed at all if everyone dumped their suitcases the way you do?

If possible – this is for men only – limit your clothes to at most one suit of shore-going clothes, i.e. reefer, flannel trousers and appropriate shoes, and nylon shirts and pants which can do duty indefinitely if washed out at night.

Some hard-hearted skippers, if racing, refuse even this much baggage allowance to their crews and insist that they bring sea clothes only. We will discuss questions of *what* later. The *how-many* for short cruises should be one complete change of clothing before each main sleep. They should be packed either in small overnight bags or a long, narrow sail bag which is easily stowed or hung up. Take an extra duffle bag, empty, for bringing home wet clothes, with some extra clothes if much work has to be done on the bowsprit. We hope we have said enough to allow the women members of the party to work out for themselves how much is needed for their comfort. Their outfit will probably not be very different from the sea-going male wardrobe.

As has already been hinted, most cruises are far from leisurely affairs and are snatched from the short time that can be spared from some office or factory – or regiment. This means leaving on the dot to catch the tide and not tarrying at some anchorage over night, but pressing on regardless. Watches are set. They may be of anything from one to four hours according to the weather and visibility, and you may have a companion to talk to or you may have to "go it" alone. The worse the weather the shorter the watch, and the worse the visibility the greater the need for more than one pair of eyes on deck.

If, as is probable, the boat is larger than you have been accustomed to, you may find yourself steering for the first time with a wheel instead of with a tiller. This at first is strange.

Make sure in your own mind which way to turn the wheel in order to vary the compass course. If you are standing behind the wheel it is easy to imagine that you are driving a car and you will find that the ship behaves in rather the same way. But on some boats the wheel is *behind* the helmsman. In this case it may be easier to hold it by the bottom spokes and steer as though you were dealing with a tiller. Often you will find that when using a wheel there is less correction to be done than with a tiller, which can move out of true without your noticing. Avoid overcorrection. If there is no readily distinguishable mark on the wheel it is worth tying a fine cord round the "spoke" which is uppermost when the rudder is dead centre. You will then know at any time how far over on either side you have put the helm.

If you are doing your trick alone, find out in advance under what circumstances the skipper likes to be called. Some, for instance, like to be told of any other ship approaching to a distance of under a mile. They may not wish to take the wheel every time, but they like to know; since the responsibility for avoiding the other boat is ultimately theirs.

If the night is clear you may prefer to sail the boat on her course by means of a star lined up with the rigging or some other part of the boat. This is fair enough, provided you remember that the star – or rather the earth – is moving, so that the bearing will not remain absolutely constant. A periodic check with the compass is therefore indicated.

On any cruise it is important to be punctual on watch, and indeed better still to be ready before you are due on, so that you have a chance to make the off-coming watch and yourself a brew of cocoa.

During the day you will have to seize any opportunity you can to get a shave. It is a trying ceremony but worth it in moral uplift. Batteries for electric razors are apt to take up rather a lot of space though there are exceptions and some people swear by clockwork models. Don't use too much fresh-water, even when helping to wash up.

Finally, don't be ashamed to get some sleep after lunch or whenever else is possible. Most of these cruises mean at least two night crossings and a good deal of wide-awake jollification at the other end.

Lately there has been a growing interest in dinghy cruising and at least one boat, Ian Proctor's "Wayfarer", has been specially designed to sleep two people on the floor of the boat with a shelter above them rigged over the boom. A trip of this kind needs careful planning not only of the courses and distances, but of the food and clothes to be taken and the methods of launching, beaching and otherwise securing the boat.

And one must be tough – mighty tough to be sure of enjoying this kind of cruising in our summer weather.

Now as to what to wear. It is hard to be precise, for your clothing has to cope with heat and cold as well as dampness. The small-boat sailor probably has a worse problem than others because of the acrobatics he goes through and because of the wear on the seat of his pants.

First, let us imagine that we have fine and sunny weather. We shall assume that the day is warm, the sky is blue and that the kind of boat you are sailing on does not involve getting wet. In such conditions shirts and shorts will do equally well for men and women. But beware early in the season of shorts or shirts with short sleeves. It is most unpleasant to feel your arms and legs being burnt bright scarlet and not to be able to do anything about it.

For shoes, the general preference seems to be for those blue canvas ones, the soles of which are covered with a forest of rubber spikes. One can now buy very comfortable ankle boots with these soles which keep out the wet. These, in my opinion, pick up far less grit on shore than rope-soled shoes. Crepe rubber should be refused, since it is treacherously slippery on wet decks.

Now for the hat. Many never wear one at all, from which it might appear that the cooling breezes of summer help to ward off the dangers of sunstroke. Personally, I find linen hats, which look so suitable for sailing, are rather hot, and even a nicely shaded green under-surface to the brim does not help to get rid of this disadvantage. However, if the wind is not going to be too strong and you feel there is a likelihood of your getting baked, by all means stuff one in the pocket. For glare, the American-style peaked cap is useful. It makes you look like a jockey, but is very practical. Underneath the peak of the cap is a polarized shade, which filters out the glare from the water as well as some of the direct rays of the sun. The shade can be lowered or raised in a moment, rather like the visor of the old-fashioned war helmet.

At the beginning of the season you may find that it is worth taking along a pair of gloves in case any unexpected strain takes the skin off your fingers. These should be of the string type, as used for riding. It pays to cut off the ends of the fingers if you are likely to have to do up or undo shackles and the like.

Both shirts and shorts should have as many pockets as possible. In the shorts you will need a knife on the end of a lanyard – for who can say that you won't want it some time in an emergency, to cut something or cut yourself free from something? You may need pockets, too, for course-cards, handkerchiefs, money.

Now let us take another type of weather – cold and dry, such as you might get in April at the beginning of the season, or October at the end, or all through the British summer for that matter. You will probably find it more comfortable to replace the shorts by an old pair of flannel trousers. These should, if anything, be on the short side rather than on the long side, to avoid catching in the hundred-and-one projections on the average deck. For the same reason trousers without turn-ups are better than those with. Further, it pays to have some kind of elastic cuff at the end. With the trousers goes some kind of woolly, and if you are going to keep this on it will be possible for you to wear braces. These are far more efficient than a belt in preventing a gap forming just over the waistline, as it often does otherwise.

If the wind is very cold you can put on a second woolly, preferably without sleeves, for freedom of movement soon becomes a problem. An "arctic" vest of the knotted string type adds several degrees of warmth though one wouldn't think so at first sight.

If you need something wind-proof, a jacket is indicated. It should be of ample length. Some jackets are held together with zip-fastenings, others with snap catches, toggles or metal latch backs. Zip-fastenings are fine if they don't rust or corrode. Other fastenings are surer – until the material gets softened up and they pull away. So you can take your choice. The sleeves of the jacket should have elastic cuffs to prevent the shirt cuffs underneath from getting wet. Kapok lining is extremely warm, though troublesome to dry when once it is wet.

Finally, we have to provide for a rainy day. This means oilskin or something similar if you are to keep dry. Some old-fashioned materials are stiff to move about in, and, through condensation, make you almost as wet inside as you would have been outside without it. A full-length oilskin coat allows a certain amount of natural ventilation, but oilskin trousers and jacket very much less, for the trousers to be efficient must have no flies or other openings, and the coat must be bound to one with some kind of belt and a snap fastening at the lower hem of the coat to prevent it from flying up. However, there has been considerable improvement in recent years and many of the plastic-coated waterproof materials are relatively light and flexible.

When buying oilskins see that the jacket pockets have vent holes, otherwise water will collect in them. When choosing blue serge-type material, ask for the kind which does not show spray marks.

When dinghy racing, sometimes the wettest part of sailing, I find that a compromise helps. Mackintosh trousers prevent, or should prevent, one's seat and most of the nether regions from getting damp (but the trousers must be kept up with shoulder straps). A buoyancy jacket (if necessary with a waterproof smock over the top) does for the top half. It is probably worth having a towel round the neck to catch the drips, but, as one is sitting so often sideways on to the spray, it may be possible to have the jacket partly open in front for air-conditioning purposes. The jacket should be bought plenty large.

There seems to be no remedy that I know of to prevent waterproof trousers from wearing out in the seat when used for dinghy sailing. Nor is there much hope of keeping the feet dry, for rubber boots are clumsy and unsuitable in many ways for dinghy work – notably when the feet have to go under the toe-straps for sitting out. Short ankle-length sea-boots which I mentioned earlier in this chapter are especially useful in an emergency when cruising. Otherwise, imagine what happens, for instance, when you are called out of your bunk on a wet night to help change one of the headsails. You spend some time lacing up your canvas shoes, and by the time you have finished unlacing them you and your shoes and feet are soaked. Boots take no time at all to put on, and keep you dry. They should be bought in a size larger than the one which fits you, so that they can be shaken off easily if necessary under water, for a man in waterlogged sea-boots may find it hard to swim well.

For wet-weather headgear, I suppose it will have to be the sou'wester, unless something better comes along in the plastic line. Unless you have something as stiff and heavy as a sou'-wester the chances are that the rain, instead of dripping from the peak down the back of your jacket, will send a cascade of spine-chilling liquid straight down your back. Pixie hoods, which eliminate this particular worry, offer no protection in front.

I know that this sounds rather a wardrobe, but would point out that many old clothes, otherwise unusable, can be pressed into use at sea.

CHAPTER XX

PILOTAGE AND NAVIGATION

So far we have been steering by sight chiefly from buoy to buoy, but something more is needed if we are to go off shore. We need, in fact, at least seven accomplishments:

1. We have to know how to distinguish the navigation, as distinct from racing, buoys in our harbours and estuaries.
2. We shall have to understand the symbols and figures shown in the average chart and the business of converting the true bearings to magnetic, and vice versa.
3. We shall have to know how to allow for the deviation of our own particular compass from magnetic bearings.
4. We shall need to steer compass courses, having regard to the effects of the wind and tide on the boat.
5. We shall want to find our position on the chart by taking bearings on objects seen.
6. We shall have to calculate our position on the chart by dead reckoning, especially when out of sight of landmarks.
7. We also need to know something of the system by which the ship's position can be calculated, when out of sight of land, from the position of the sun, moon or stars.

Let us take it all step by step.

First, buoys. These are the regulations *at the time of writing*. Conical buoys indicate shoals on the starboard side of a channel to a vessel entering from seaward. They are painted black, or black-and-white check. There may also be a top mark raised on a stick above the buoy – a cone or triangle pointing upwards; or if the buoy is not at the entrance to a channel, a

UNIFORM BUOYAGE SYSTEM
(Proceeding with Main Flood Tidal Stream)

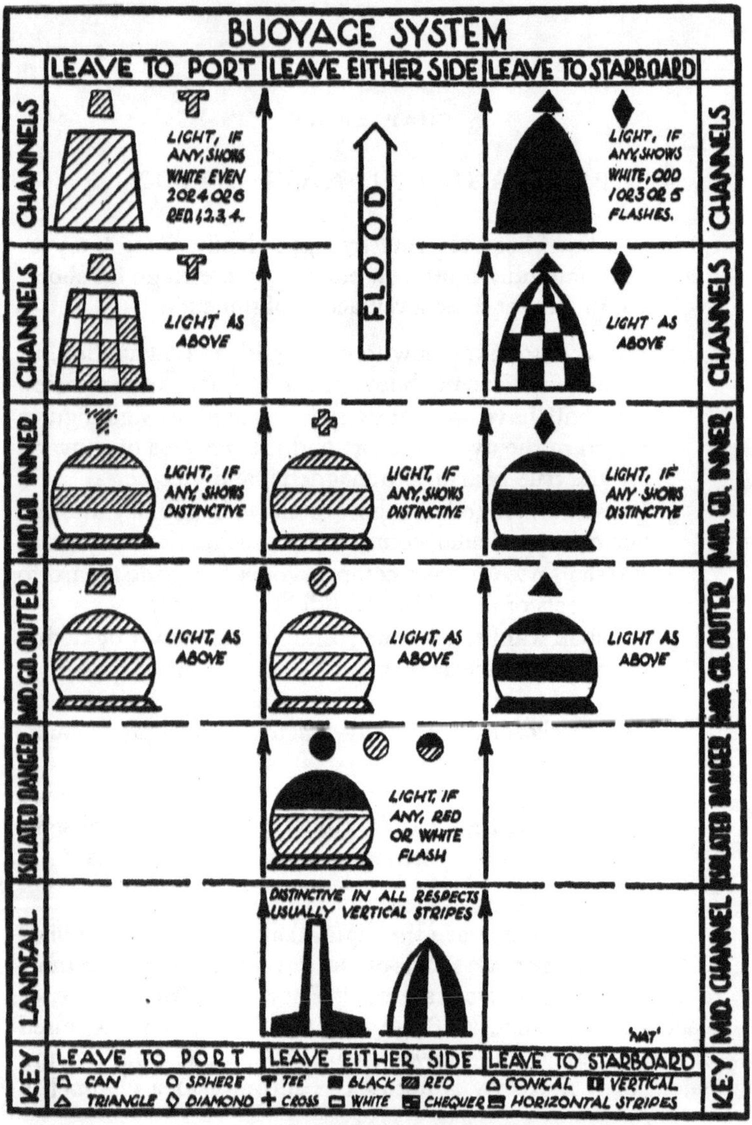

Fig. 35. COASTAL NAVIGATION BUOYS
From a supplement to Reed's Nautical Almanack 1958.

diamond. These buoys must be left to starboard. If lit, these starboard hand buoys show one, three or five white flashes.

Flat-topped can buoys indicate shoals on the port side of a channel for a boat entering from seaward. They are coloured red or red-and-white check with wedge-shaped top marks. The top mark can be T-shaped if the buoy is not at the entrance to a channel. Such buoys must be left to port.

If the buoys are lit or have sound apparatus this will be shown on the chart. Port hand marks show red flashes (any number up to four) or two, four or six white flashes.

Spherical buoys mark obstructions in the middle of the fairway. They are painted with horizontal stripes: red and white if the main channel runs to starboard or if there are two channels of equal importance, and black and white if the main channel runs to port for a vessel entering from seaward.

The red-and-white spherical buoy to be left to port may have a top mark showing either a T or a wedge. If so, the T marks the inner end of the obstruction or mid-channel shoal, and the wedge the outer end.

In the case of the black-and-white spherical buoys to be left to starboard, a cone-like top mark indicates the outer seaward end of the obstruction, and a diamond top mark the inner end. If the obstruction is an isolated one the danger mark is spherical, coloured with wide black and red horizontal bands separated by a narrow white band. Top mark, if any, is a sphere painted black or red or half-black and half-red horizontally.

If the channels on either side of the mark are of equal importance, the top mark for the outer-end buoy is a red sphere and for the inner-end buoy a red St. George's Cross. These middle-ground buoys, if lit, will show only white or red lights, and the colour and length are arranged to avoid uncertainty as to the side on which the mark is to be passed.

Mid-channel buoys marking the deep-water line of the channel may be either red and white or black and white with vertical stripes, and a shape which is neither spherical, can, nor cone. The top mark is often a St. Andrew's Cross. A series of buoys on the same side of a channel are frequently numbered consecutively, counting from seaward.

Red can-shaped buoys with the word "Watch" on them indicate that there are lightships in the neighbourhood.

Yellow-and-red buoys indicate a military target area. Yellow-and-red conical buoys to be left to starboard, and yellow-and-red can buoys to port.

Green buoys bearing the word "Wreck" are just what you might expect. They are cone-shaped if the wreck is to be left to starboard, can-shaped if the wreck is to be left to port, and spherical if it can be passed on either side. Wreck light-buoys to be left to starboard show a triple green flash every ten to fifteen seconds; those to be left to port a double green flash every ten seconds; and those passable on either side one green flash every five seconds.

Lightships are normally stationary, but if for any reason the lightship is out of position she will cease making signals or showing her ordinary lights. When out of position and not on tow, she will by day hoist a large black ball at each end of the vessel and fly the International Signal PC. By night she will show a fixed red light at each end of the vessel, and in addition will show a red light and a white light or a red flare and a white flare simultaneously every fifteen minutes.

Shoals in smaller channels are marked with poles, brooms, withies, beacons, or fixed posts with a lattice-work top mark such as a globe or triangle. The various fog signals emitted from navigational marks should be learnt, but remember not to rely on your ears alone. Sometimes the folk on shore may be late in starting the fog signal, or a strong wind may blow the effects away. Often there are freak conditions which allow the navigator to hear better when he is several miles from a buoy than he can when close to it. Bells, etc., worked by wave motion may make no noise in very calm weather.

Buoyage systems in use outside the United Kingdom should be studied if cruising outside home waters.

We next need to know how to read a chart. It may show a

PILOTAGE AND NAVIGATION

large stretch of coast, or a small section of it, or just one particular harbour, which you will certainly need if you are to enter that harbour. All three kinds of chart are used when cruising. One of the most important points to note at the outset is whether the chart has been corrected to date and whether the soundings given are in feet or fathoms. An amazing amount of information can be gathered from a not-very-eye-catching chart. For instance, there are abbreviations for more than fifty different types of sea bed. You can check the quality of the bottom for anchoring or other purposes by putting tallow on the under-surface of the sounding lead, which is then said to be "armed". The different kinds of coastline – cliffy, sandy or shingly – are pictorially shown. Be it mangroves or marshes, you can see them illustrated on the chart, and be warned or encouraged. Church, Buddhist temple, mosque or Moslem tomb, there are signs for them all. Rocks awash at chart datum or with less than six feet of water at the datum of the chart, or small isolated rocks in exposed positions, or rock ledges on which depths are known in general to be less than six feet, are shown as a cross or a cross with a dotted circle around. It is worth learning everything you can about the symbols used on charts.

Take the dotted lines, for instance. If they run continuously they indicate the one-fathom line. Dots broken into groups of two show the two-fathom line, and so on. Those things like the teeth without the comb may mean fishing stakes. There are six important symbols describing wrecks and indicating whether they are dangerous or not. Radio stations are carefully distinguished from radar stations. The behaviour of lights – fixed or alternating, flashing or occulting (an occulting light is one which has one or more eclipses at regular intervals, the total eclipse period being less than the duration of light) – is also dealt with.

A sheet showing the symbols and abbreviations used by the Admiralty is published by the Stationery Office, and is probably worth a special place near the chart table.

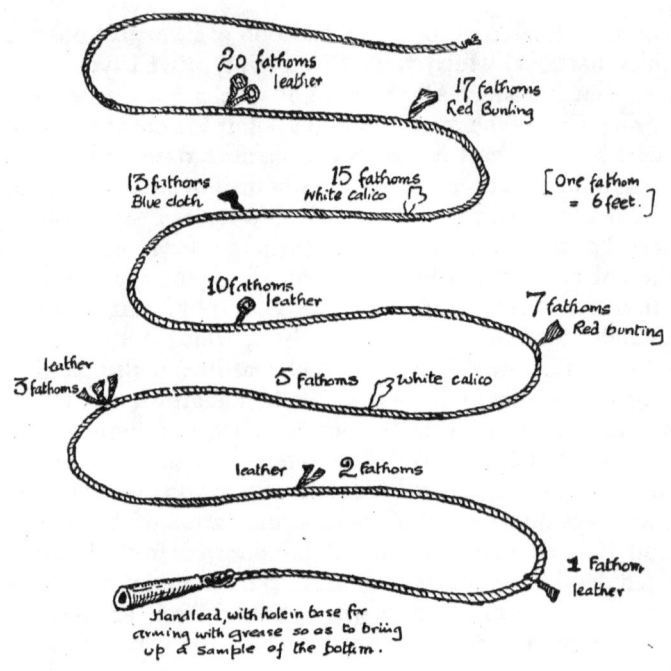

Fig. 36. LEAD LINE FOR SOUNDING

The picture you see above shows the good old fashioned lead used for sounding for depth in waters up to 20 fathoms.

You will find it particularly useful
(1) For checking bearings in a fog
(2) For seeing that you have enough and not too much water for anchorage
(3) For making sure that you are not drifting while at anchor in a blow

The lead should be kept in a handy spot where it can easily be reached by the helmsman.

Before using see that the lead line is properly coiled and free to run out. Swing the coil once or twice to get the balance of the thing and let her go well forward.

This is to ensure that the line is perpendicular by the time that it reaches the bottom.

Your own lead line may not need to be as long as the one shown.

Most of the charts you are likely to buy are drawn to Mercator's projection. The advantages of this type of representation are impressive. To appreciate them, first imagine a globe. Then take two places on it – London and Oslo, for example. The shortest distance between these two cities is on the path of what is called the great circle (that is, a circle bisecting the earth and passing through these two capitals). But if you were to draw this circle you would find that it would cut the various meridians of longitude, not at one angle but at different angles. In other words, it would be impossible to set a constant course from London to Oslo.

But suppose you use Mercator's projection; you find on your chart the direction of a line from London to Oslo; you keep your boat on that course – cutting the meridians each at the same angle – and you duly arrive at Oslo. True, your Mercator course is not quite as short as if you had taken the Great Circle route and would be hard to plot on a globe, but on a map drawn to Mercator's projection it is "plain sailing".

Mercator's projection is, of course, a distortion of the lines you see on a globe. You can imagine it being made as follows: A transparent globe has the lines of longitude and latitude painted on it in black; fitting round the globe is a long cylinder of tracing paper. In the centre of the globe is an electric light. The shadows thrown on the cylinder of paper will show the meridians as parallel lines and the distance between degrees of latitude to be larger at the Poles than the Equator.

It follows that special precautions have to be taken when measuring distances, since the scale on Mercator's projection varies with the latitude. Suppose, for instance, you want to find the distance between A and B on your Mercator chart. Set the dividers at half the distance and find the point on the scale at the side of the chart exactly level with your half-way mark. Count off one-half of the distance you are going above this point on the scale, and the other half below, and add the results together to get the correct distance figure.

We have now to consider the compass on which so much

navigation depends. The compass is in essence a magnetized bar balanced horizontally so that it is free to pivot. Being a magnet it is affected by the presence of any other magnet, and if it is placed alongside a second magnet one of its ends will be repelled and the other be attracted by either end of the second magnet.

Now the earth is a magnet of a sort, with one pole somewhere deep in the earth to the north-west of Hudson's Bay (some 1,200 miles from the true North Pole) and the other to the north of South Victoria Land. So one end of our compass, being affected by the earth's magnetism, tends to point towards the magnetic north, and the other end towards the magnetic south. As neither of these places mentioned is at the real North Pole or real South Pole but deep in the earth, there are variations between magnetic north as shown by the compass and the true north as shown on the chart. As can easily be imagined, the amount of variation between true and magnetic changes according to the geographical position of the observer. Over the magnetic pole the compass needle would point, if it could, directly downwards, as there is no longer any horizontal pull. In Greenland the compass points 50 degrees to the west of north, and in British Columbia 30 degrees east. Equally, there are certain lines, called agonic lines, on which magnetic and true north coincide. One agonic line passes from Hudson's Bay through Ontario, Ohio, Carolina, the Bahamas, South America, and through the River Plate to the South Atlantic. Another runs from Sweden across Poland, Turkey, Egypt, Northern India, Siam, Sumatra and Western Australia.

The difference between magnetic and true north should be shown on each chart for the place mapped on the chart.

But the amount of variation between true and magnetic north in any one place also varies almost continuously during the year. In practice we ignore daily variations, but charts show the annual change in compass variation.

There still seems to be no really satisfactory explanation of the origin of the earth's magnetism, or of why it changes year by year. One theory is that there is a cycle which repeats itself every 480 years, but as the experts have not been recording much longer than that the theory remains unproved.

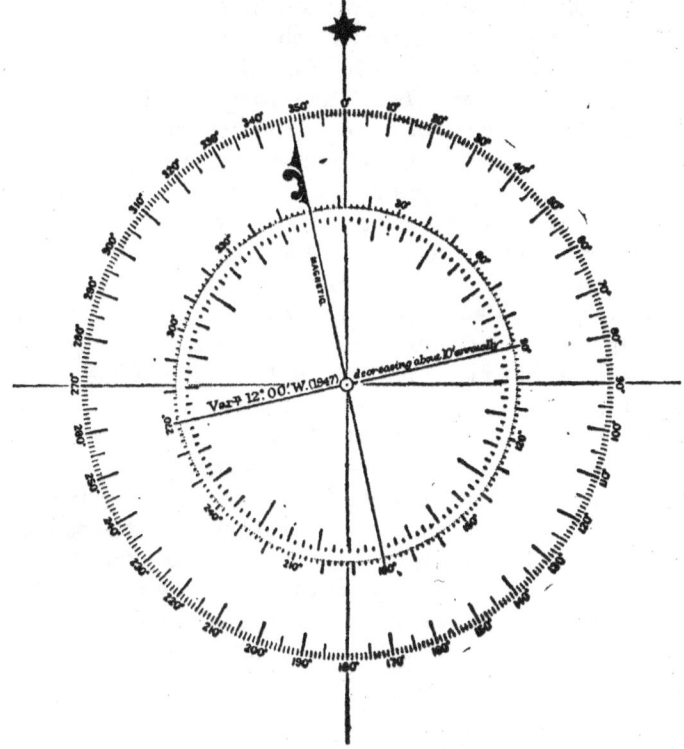

Fig. 37. COMPASS ROSES
showing variations between magnetic and True North on a typical chart

We have now allowed for geographical and annual variation of the compass. There remains one other adjustment to be made before the compass really speaks the truth. This is called adjustment for deviation. The magnetic field of a compass installed on a boat will be affected by the influence of metal objects on the boat, the influence varying according to whether the objects in question are north, south, east or west of the compass. A compass-adjuster can smooth out these deviations with the aid of small magnets, or you can plot the deviations yourself. For this purpose choose a calm day. Pick two landmarks in line with each other in such a position that it is possible to know your exact bearing from them – your chart will probably give some examples. Then swing the ship round and note the difference between your true bearing converted to magnetic, and that shown by the compass, at each of sixteen positions of the ship's head. You may be able to swing her round with the engine or get someone to row her round. Note the differences on a card. It will then be possible for you to convert easily from compass to magnetic or vice versa.

Suppose, for instance, that when you "swung the ship" you noted that when the ship's head pointed due west magnetic, the magnetic bearing of the landmark which you knew from the chart should have remained constant at 5 degrees west of north is shown as true north. It follows that the deviation is 5 degrees clockwise on a west magnetic bearing.

Suppose, later, that you wanted to sail on a course which the chart tells you should be due west magnetic. If you took the compass's word for due west magnetic, you would sail off on a course 5 degrees north of west. But you do not wish to do this. So instead you have to sail a course which, according to the compass, is 5 degrees south of the magnetic west. Then everything will be all right.

In other words, you convert magnetic course to compass by correcting easterly deviation counter-clockwise, and westerly deviation clockwise. A good way of memorizing this is to learn by heart the sentence: "Magnetic to compass westerly clockwise" or, if it is easier for you, remember this by a sentence beginning with the same initials: "Mr. Churchill wants Conservatives."

Conversely, when you wish to find out what magnetic course

you are sailing by looking at the compass, you reverse the process, applying westerly deviation counter-clockwise and easterly deviation clockwise.

Once you have worked out your deviation table you have to be careful not to upset the compass. For instance, moving the anchor chain aft or forward might produce further deviations. *So can any metal object such as the starting handle of the motor if left near the compass.* If the worst comes to the worst, you can re-check you deviation at sea with the aid of a heavenly body.

And now for the instrument itself.

When steering on board we do not, of course, use a bar compass, but a circular card which is kept floating level in a bowl; the direction of the ship's head is indicated by a mark on the bowl called the lubber's mark. If the part of the compass card marked north is opposite the lubber's mark the ship will be going north, and so on.

The older compasses are based on a system of dividing the horizon into thirty-two points. Many mariners still steer mainly by points.

First, there are the cardinal points, north, east, south and west; and the intercardinal points, north-east, south-east, south-west and north-west. These intercardinal points are subdivided into eight others, and those eight into sixteen others.

The points system is quite convenient for sailing under conditions found in the average cruising boat. At night, for instance, in a small boat the helmsman does not want the compass to be too well lit, for he has to keep his eyes open for lights at sea, and if his eyes are dazzled by a strong compass light he will not be able to keep watch properly. Now the points on the compass card can be clearly shown and he can thus keep the ship on course even if the compass is not very well lit.

On the other hand, the points system is not precise for navigation purposes; for the circle, as we learnt at school, is divided into 360 degrees, and thirty-two will not divide evenly into 360. It is difficult to lay off an exact course under these conditions. So helmsmen are getting to rely more and more on well but not dazzingly lit compass cards showing degrees (0 degrees to 360 degrees) rather than the points of the compass.

As already explained, you will find on your chart two roses or circles of degrees showing the difference between the true bearings and magnetic bearings of the area covered, together with a note of the annual variation. For making full use of these roses you need various simple instruments such as a protractor for measuring angles, or parallel rules, dividers, pencils and soft rubber. (You will also need a magnifying glass, binoculars, a hand bearing compass, a torch and an eight-day clock, plus a sextant and a deck watch if you are thinking of celestial navigation.)

Now, suppose that the course you have selected on the chart runs upward at an angle of 45 degrees with the bottom of the chart. What magnetic bearing should this be? To find out, we place the parallel ruler along the selected course and roll or slide it over to the magnetic rose on the chart and read off the magnetic course; or you can use the protractor, a rather different instrument from the one we knew as children. It consists of a transparent, plastic ruler-like arm attached to a transparent disc marked with compass degrees. The disc can be rotated.

Suppose that you want to go from A to B. You put the centre of the disc over point A and turn the protractor arm till it runs through the centre of the nearest compass rose on the chart. We will suppose that the centre of this rose happens to be placed at an angle of 135 degrees magnetic from your point of departure. This bearing will be indicated by where the arm cuts the rose. Now turn the disc on the protractor until it, too, makes an angle of 135 degrees with the arm. The disc will now be in a similar position to the magnetic compass rose. Hold it firmly there, and swing the arm round along the course you wish to steer. The reading shown by the arm on the protractor disc is your magnetic course.

We have now reached the stage where we can lay off our accurate magnetic course from the chart and can convert this

PILOTAGE AND NAVIGATION 239

by allowing for deviation into a compass course. But you may have also to provide in advance for the effects of the tide and wind.

We have already looked into the tide and its effects, which are shown in tidal atlases and in some charts. Frequently, on a trip of some twelve hours the effects of the tide cancel each other out as far as steering is concerned. At other times some calculations are necessary. Thus suppose you want to travel true east and the tide is setting you south-eastwards, you will have to steer somewhere north of east in order to make good your proposed course. In order to find out how much to alter you will need to know your speed through the water. For this purpose we use an instrument called a log. It consists of a log line attached to a spinner, which revolves as it is drawn through the water and records the revolutions in sea-miles on a counter. When you stream the log make sure that the counter is set to zero, and note the time and place. When you take in the log detach the line from the rev-counter and let it go free into the water while you draw in the spinner, otherwise the line will kink itself up before you get it aboard. Now the log shows you the distance travelled through the water, and you can calculate your speed in knots through the water by reading the log at half-hourly intervals and multiplying by two.

Now suppose we are out in a fine breeze. We know that our course will be probably a point or two north of east. The log (or a good guess of yours subsequently verified by the log) shows that on our course we are moving at approximately six knots through the water. We also know from tidal information that the rate of the tide for the next hour will be three miles across our path and to the south-east (true). We can now arrive at an approximate course to steer by means of a simple diagram. Assume that A is any point in the true course AB which we wish to make good. AC represents the effect of the tide during an hour's sailing. Now, on the same scale, we draw a line from C six sea-miles long (representing the distance sailed through the water in an hour), so that it exactly reaches the true-course line at B. CB is then the course which, after allowance for variation and deviation, should be steered from A in order to arrive at B. No matter what the log says, AB should theoretically be the course made good at the end of the hour. On the chart you will probably prefer to represent the course steered by the line AD (parallel to CB) and the effect of the tide by DB (parallel to AC. AD can be checked against the log reading after one hour).

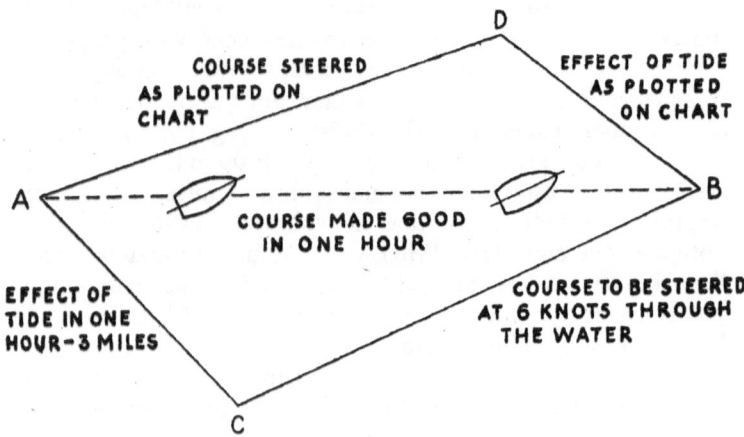

Fig. 38. ALLOWING FOR THE TIDE

Allowance for the effect of the tide must always be made when converting log readings to distance made good. Thus if the tide is directly with you the tidal rate must be added to your log reading, and if it is against you it must be subtracted when translating log reading to the dead reckoning course plotted on the chart. The popular sailing almanacs have special tables by which, if you care to, you can allow for the set of the tide without making any diagram. These tables also allow you to calculate the ship's speed in a tideway over the ground.

Finally, to make good your chosen course you may have to

PILOTAGE AND NAVIGATION 241

make an allowance for leeway (that is, the distance the wind blows you to leeward). Much depends here on whether your boat is old or new. Older boats sag away freely, modern ones less so. You can get an idea of leeway by seeing whether the ship is going where she is pointing or whether she is being blown sideways. The wake of the ship will show how far this is the case. When beating, the angle between the head of the boat and the wake may be 2-5 degrees. It is not usually necessary to make any special additional allowance for deviation when correcting course for leeway.

What is the next problem? It is to discover from a landmark your position at sea. Suppose, first, that you see a church steeple marked which you recognize on the chart. You must first take a bearing on it to discover whereabouts in relation to it you are. It is not always possible to take a direct sight bearing with the normal steering compass, which is usually fixed in a more or less sheltered position, but you can get a fairly good idea in your mind's eye; or you can turn the ship directly towards the point in question and take the compass reading at the moment when the ship's head points directly towards the landmark; or use a hand bearing compass or similar instrument.

This reading, converted for deviation and magnetic variation, tells you that at a certain moment you are somewhere on a line drawn at a certain angle from the landmark in question.

How do we find our whereabouts on this line? The simplest way is to have another, or better still, two other landmarks not in direct line. These will give you other lines cutting the first bearing line. Their point of meeting shows your position. If possible the landmarks should be at least 20 degrees apart. If only one suitable landmark is visible you can take two bearings of it from different angles, plotting your course made good in between them. If, for instance, you take a note of your position when your bearing is 45 degrees from the landmark and again when the bearing is 90 degrees, your distance from shore at the time of the second bearing will be equal to the course you have made good in the meantime. The same would hold good for any isosceles triangle. Thus you could take the bearings at 60 degrees and again at 120 degrees, or at 50 degrees and then again at 100 degrees. In other words, you double the bearing for your second reading and work on the course made good.

Perhaps, however, the weather is bad and just when you want to take a second bearing clouds or fog get in the way. Even under these circumstances the navigator is undefeated. Let us suppose for instance, that he gets his first bearing at 45 degrees; he misses it at 90 degrees but is able to get it at 120 degrees. What he does is to assume on the chart where he was when he took the 45 degrees bearing (A in Fig. 39). He might equally have assumed some other point on the line DF such as H, for instance, or E, but he did not. From A he plots the course made good until he gets the second bearing of 120 degrees. At that point, according to his dead reckoning, he will have reached B. But B is short of the line DE where he should have been to get a bearing of 120 degrees. Therefore he did not start at A but somewhere else on the line FD. Equally, he did not finish at B but at some other point on the line GJ, which is parallel to his original bearing FD. This point must be C, which he would have reached from the starting point E. This result is known as a running fix. The same system can, of course, be used for taking single bearings from two different landmarks seen at different times, in which case the fix is said to be obtained from transferred position lines. A note of the time and true bearing of each fix should be made for entry on the chart.

Next, we have the problem of keeping track of your position by what is called dead reckoning (that is, plotting a course on the chart without regard to land bearings or shots of the sun, but simply from readings worked from a given point of departure). Almost everything else depends on your proficiency in this. You will presumably start from a point you know (if you do not there is little hope for you). This position which you know should be pencilled in on the chart as a dot with a circle

PILOTAGE AND NAVIGATION 243

round it. Alongside should be your time of departure (marked G.M.T. or B.S.T., as the case may be), so that your speed can afterwards be calculated. Diagrams to allow for the effect of tide and leeway can be made on tracing paper placed over the chart or graph paper, and the resulting magnetic and compass

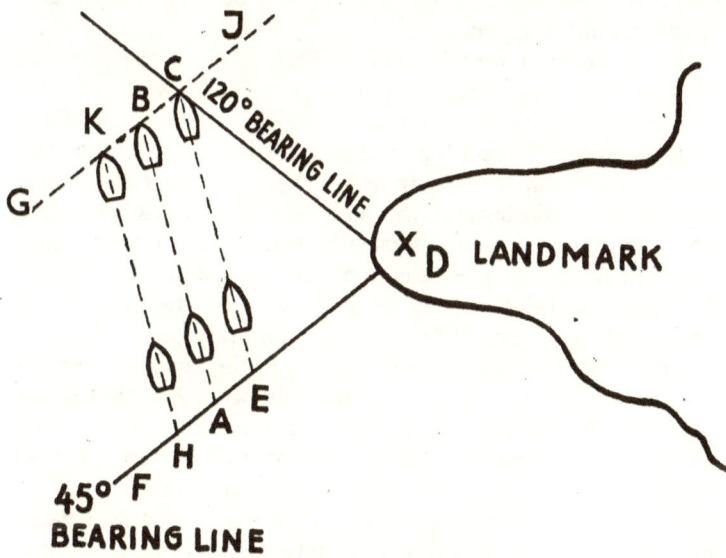

Fig. 39. A RUNNING FIX
HK, AB, EC are 3 courses which the yacht could have sailed from the line FD. EC is the true course

courses entered in the navigator's log. Thereafter, a plot on the chart should be made of every change of course in terms of true bearing, together with the time of change and log reading. The true course in degrees and estimated distance made good should be noted on the chart. This technique will give you your dead reckoning position. Dead reckoning should be worked out at least once an hour and as often as every half-hour if in restricted waters.

Any position calculated by dead reckoning is an estimated position, and to distinguish it from a fix we enter it in the chart as a dot with a triangle around it and the letters E.P. Every estimated position should be disregarded whenever a certain fix is obtained and the fix treated as a new point of departure.

Finally, we come to the art of getting bearings when out of sight of land altogether.

To begin with we will cheat slightly and use the radio for this purpose. One system employs a portable set which is tuned in to any of the many radio beacons in Britain, France, Holland and elsewhere. The set is placed so that its centre line is parallel to the centre line of the ship and is then tuned in to the wavelength of a radio beacon, the position of which is known. The call-sign of the beacon is usually transmitted two or three times in morse for identification purposes. When the beacon has been identified, a loop receiver on top of the set is swung round till the signal fades right off. The position of the loop pointer will then indicate the bearing of the beacon. To get a fix the procedure is repeated, if possible, with several beacons. The makers claim that fixes within 2 degrees at ranges of up to fifty miles can easily be obtained. For good reception the set should be placed as high in the ship as convenient.

Another system is called Consol. This is the English name for the long-range World War II navigational system. It was extensively used by the Germans on U-boats and long-range aircraft to give assistance in their Atlantic campaign and was called "Sonne" (meaning sun, because of the resemblance o the radiation pattern to the rays of the sun). An improved British system has been put into operation in the United Kingdom at Bush Mills in Northern Ireland which, together with a beacon at Stavanger in Norway, gives coverage to North-West Europe and the British Isles within a radius of 1,000 to 1,500 miles. There are other beacons at Seville and Lugo in Spain, and at Ploneis in France. This system, like the loop one already described, has the advantage that it can be received on an ordinary wireless set. The bearings obtained by Consol are a good general guide to position but distortion can cause errors of several miles to creep in. So if possible it is worth making an independent cross-check.

When using Consol, your receiver is first tuned in to the frequency of the desired station and a series of dots (or dashes) followed by dots (or dashes) is heard. Periodically, the series of dots (or dashes) appear to merge with the series of dashes (or dots), giving a short, steady note. To obtain the bearing the number of dots and the number of dashes heard in a complete cycle are counted or timed with a stop-watch (the signals are made either every second or every half-second, depending on the station in use). The total number of dots and dashes heard in each cycle should add up to sixty; but in practice, since the change-over is masked by the steady note, one or more characters are lost and the total count is usually less than sixty. The number of lost characters is obtained by subtracting the total count from sixty and assuming that half the missing characters are dots and the other half dashes. The bearing can then be found by reference either to special charts or to tables.

There are two other well-known radio aids to navigation – LORAN and DECCA. Loran (Long Range Navigational Signals) can be picked up by a vessel with a radio set fitted with a special receiver, but the signals sent out from shore stations are meant for ocean navigation only.

The Decca system is very much more accurate but requires more expensive equipment and charts than the average yachtsman can afford.

Radio bearings and fixes should be entered on the chart in the same way as other bearings as true bearings taken from the boat.

Finally, there is celestial navigation.

With modern tables and almanacs navigation has been so greatly simplified that there is no need for anyone to feel that they are unable to tackle it.

It cannot be dealt with fully here, and the following is not intended for instruction but merely as a guide to the gist of astro navigation. The sun only is considered.

At any given second of time there is a spot on the earth's surface immediately under the sun (known as the G.P.) and this place can *always* be found out from almanacs. If the sun is right overhead you *must* be on this spot. If you move away in any direction the sun gets lower in the sky and you are somewhere on a circle with its centre at the G.P., and from all places on this circle the sun has the same altitude. All you ever get from a sight is part of this position circle; and the circle is usually so big that a section of it appears on your chart as a straight line.

How do you know where to draw this position line on your chart? Firstly, direction; the position line is drawn at right-angles to the azimuth. The azimuth is the bearing of the sun from you, and it can be taken by compass, or more accurately and quickly from tables. To take one special case, when the sun is due south, at noon, the position line is drawn due east and west, and the fact that lines drawn east and west are marked on your chart as parallels of latitude is one of the reasons that a noon sight is so easy. (Another is, of course, that you can tell when the sun is due south, without taking the time accurately, by watching it through your sextant till it starts to drop.) When it is at its highest it is due south of you. At that moment your zenith distance (90 degrees minus your altitude reading) equals the angle between you and the G.P. of the sun measured at the centre of the earth, and *since you can find out from the almanac by how much the sun is north or south of the equator, this amount (known as the declination) added to or subtracted from the zenith distance gives you, in the case of a sight taken at noon, your latitude* (see diagram 40). THIS PRINCIPLE IS TRUE OF ALL SIGHTS, THE DISTANCE BETWEEN YOU AND THE G.P. OF THE SUN MEASURED AS AN ANGLE AT THE CENTRE OF THE EARTH EQUALS YOUR ZENITH DISTANCE. Unfortunately it is not possible to put a compass on the earth and draw off your position circle (though for amusement you can try it on a globe).

For this purpose take a sight of the sun not necessarily at noon, and the time accurately and work out the sun's G.P. Both the latitude (declination) of the sun's G.P. and the longitude

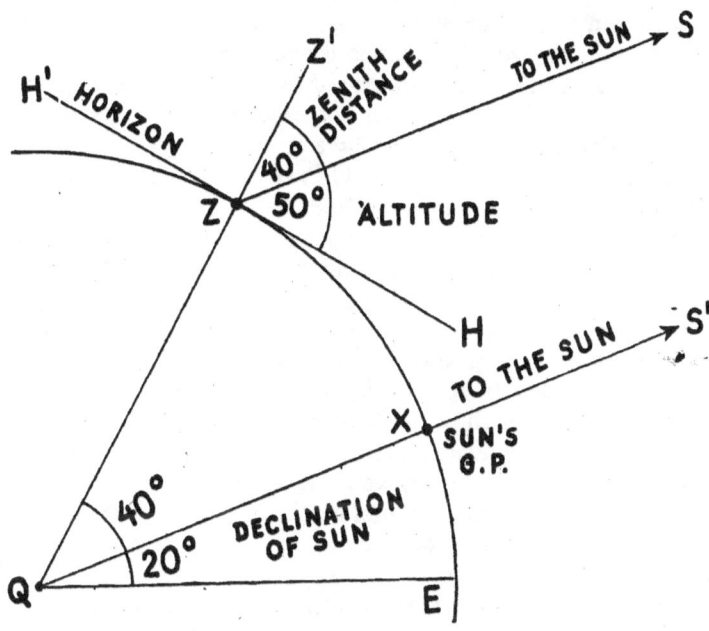

Fig. 40. CALCULATIONS FOR A NOON SIGHT

Z = Observer
Q = Centre of earth
QE = Line of equator
    Angle SZH = observed altitude (say 50°)
       ,,   Z'ZS = observers zenith distance (90°—altitude) = 40°
Z' = Line of observer's zenith perpendicular to horizon
H'—H = Horizon

N.B. The angle Z'ZS = angle Z'QX since ZS and QX are parallel lines cutting the same straight line Z'ZQ.
          X = Sun's G.P. (from almanac)
    Angle XQE = Sun's declination (from almanac) say 20° N.
        ZQX = Z'ZS = 40° (see above)
∴ Observer's latitude (XQE + ZQX) = 20° + 40° = 60° N.

measured westwards all the way round the earth (known as the Greenwich Hour Angle) are easily obtainable from the almanac.

Then put one arm of the compass on the G.P.; if the altitude of your sight was 50 degrees your zenith distance will be 90 degrees minus 50 degrees equals 40 degrees. Now as we have already seen the zenith distance is the same as the distance between you and the G.P. measured as an angle at the centre of the earth – and since 1 degree corresponds to 60 miles of the earth's surface, your sight must have been taken 40 × 60 miles, that is, 2,400 miles from the sun's G.P. If you set the compass at this radius with one arm on the G.P., the other arm will pass through your position, though this answer won't be accurate enough to help you navigationally. So we use another method.

We have already seen that when we DON'T know where we are we can tell our distance from the sun's G.P. by observing the sun's altitude (though this by itself is of little value).

Equally, however, if we DO know where we are, we can find out how far we are away from the sun's G.P. from tables.

So in practice we pretend we DO know where we are at the time when we take the sight, and we then work out from tables how far off the G.P. would have been from this assumed position at that moment.

We then compare this result with what we got at the time of the sight from our sextant by direct observation in order to get our position line.

The difference between the two results is the distance our position line is away from the assumed position.

For example, if the altitude reading of the sun observed with the sextant works out at more than the sun's altitude calculated by tables from our assumed position, when we must have been nearer to the sun's G.P. than we assumed – by one mile for each minute of arc of difference. Equally if our true altitude is less than the calculated figure, we must have been farther away from the sun's G.P. than we assumed.

PILOTAGE AND NAVIGATION 249

Here is how it works on paper:

1. After taking the sight we assume what our position was on the chart *at that time*. It will be as near as possible to our estimated position by dead reckoning, but the longitude

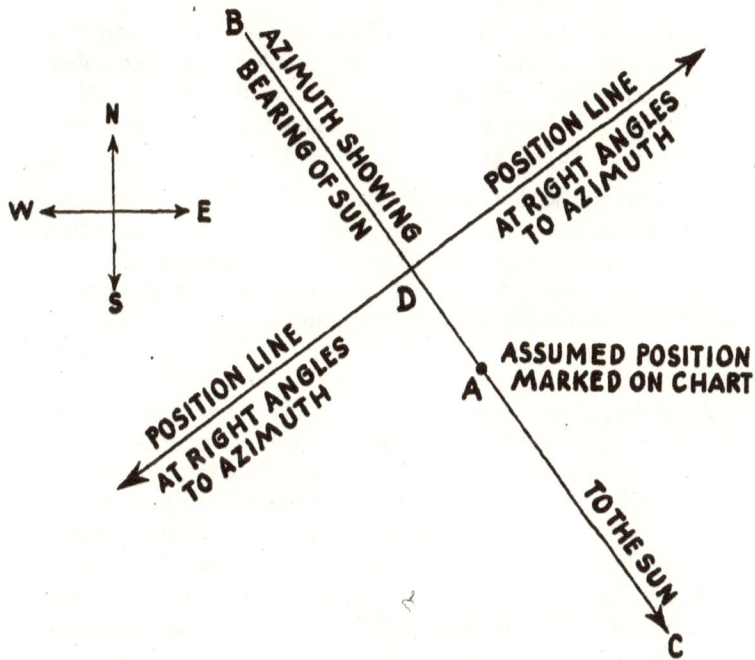

Fig. 41. POSITION LINE OBTAINED FROM AN ASSUMED POSITION

A = our assumed position
BC = azimuth of sun from tables (based on actual time of sight and an assumed position).
AD = distance on chart representing (say) 4 sea miles, equivalent to 4 minutes of arc, being the difference between (1) sun's altitude calculated from assumed position and (2) the true altitude from observation. In the example the calculated altitude is larger than the true.

and latitude may be shaded up or down slightly to make the use of the tables easier.
2. Mark in the assumed position on the chart.
3. Work out from the tables what the azimuth of the sun was from the assumed position at the moment when the sight was taken. Draw in the azimuth to run both sides of the assumed position.
4. The position line can then be drawn in at right-angles to the azimuth line. The difference between true and calculated altitude tells us whether the position line should be nearer to the sun than the assumed position or farther away. (See fig. 41.)

Thus we know that we are somewhere on this position line, but the azimuth does not pinpoint our position accurately. That is why it is impossible to get a fix with one sight.

But if we can find a second position line or bearing from some other source – this second sight, taken in conjunction with the first, gives a definite fix. We can get this fix either by taking simultaneous sights of the sun and moon, or by getting a later sight of the sun or of the moon, stars or planets at dusk or dawn if there is a good horizon, and get a transferred position line fix in the same way as described earlier. Radio or land sights can, of course, be combined with celestial sights for getting fixes. Do not forget to take the time and read the log for dead reckoning purposes every time a bearing or fix is obtained.

Almanacs, we should mention, give the same kind of information for the moon, the stars and the planets that they give for the sun, and the procedures are the same in principle.

We will next examine the sextant, the instrument used in obtaining the altitude of the sun and other heavenly bodies. It is simply a device for measuring angles and its work is done with the aid of mirrors. When observing the altitude of the sun, for instance, you look at the horizon with the naked eye and move the sextant until the reflection of the sun shown in a mirror is exactly level with the horizon as seen by the naked

PILOTAGE AND NAVIGATION 251

eye. This movement carries the pointer of the sextant along a numbered scale. When satisfied that the sun is "bang on", you read off the angle shown on the sextant in degrees, minutes and seconds.

When using the sextant for sights, small adjustments have usually to be made to convert the observed reading to true figures. One adjustment is for the height of the observer's eye

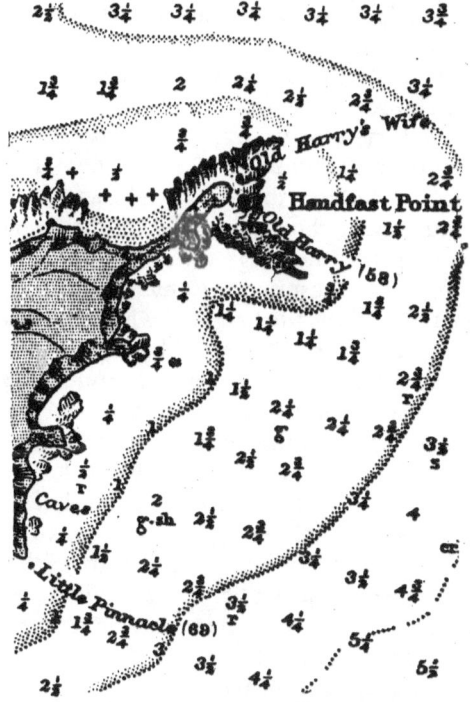

Reproduced from Admiralty Chart No. 2172 with the permission of the Controller, H.M. Stationery Office, and the Hydrographer of the Navy.

Fig. 42. FROM A TYPICAL ADMIRALTY CHART (SLIGHTLY ENLARGED)
showing part of the Swanage area of the Dorset coast

above sea-level – this is sometimes referred to as the dip of the horizon. Another correction has usually to be applied when shooting the sun or the moon to ensure that the altitude is measured from the centre of the body (not yours but the one in the sky). The amount of altitude to be added if you are observing the lower edge of the sun or moon is in the almanacs for each day of the year. A third allowance has to be made in the case of the moon for what is called parallax. We have hitherto assumed in our calculations that rays of light from heavenly bodies striking the various parts of the earth are parallel. This is a safe assumption in the case of the sun, planets and stars which are remote from the earth, but not in the case of the moon. The necessary corrections of parallax by altitude and latitude are in the almanacs for each day of the year.

For coastal navigation the sextant allows you to fix your position by measuring the angles between three objects ashore and so obtaining true bearings without the complications of conversion. Also, by measuring the angle between the base and the top of a single object, the height of which is known, you can determine your distance off shore. This information, together with a compass bearing, gives you a fix using one landmark only. Or, reversing the process, you can find by means of tables how small an angle the sextant must show to ensure that you are an agreed safe distance away from the chosen landmark. The heights given are based on the level of high-tide, so that the object will sometimes appear larger than it really is – giving additional margin of safety. The centre of the light glass is treated as being the top of a lighthouse. When trying to keep your distance, remember that tides passing across the mouth of a bay or inlet tend to set the ship in shore.

When shooting sights of heavenly bodies, the navigator goes on deck with an accomplice bearing a watch set to correct time based on Greenwich, and takes four or five sights at intervals of about a minute. If plotted on graph paper, one edge of which shows time and the other the altitude reading, the result of these readings should be a straight line. When shooting sights, the navigator anchors the lower part of his body to something firm and waits to take his sight until he can be sure that he is holding it straight, and that it is the horizon he sees and not a wave top. Then he shouts "Now", and his accomplice takes the time.

APPENDIX

ON BUYING A BOAT

MANY otherwise excellent works on sailing deal in one of their earlier chapters with the mechanics of buying a sail boat. Deliberately, I have not followed this practice.

My view is that all too often a yacht is picked and paid for before the new owner has sailed enough to know what he really wants.

Therefore my advice on buying marks the conclusion rather than the beginning of this work.

In the case of small boats such as we discussed in an earlier chapter, little damage need be done if the tyro chooses a type which he later finds is unsuited to his style of sailing. But few can afford to throw away even a little money in these hard times; and when one enters the realm of cruising yachts a mistake in choice can come expensive. I therefore once more urge any prospective buyer to try out as many different types of craft as possible, so that he may not be disillusioned by any one of them.

Only sailing experience can tell him whether he is going to be happier in a yacht which has limited accommodation but is fast and handy, or in a boat that is roomy and steady enough to sail herself but sluggish to manœuvre and slow on a beat. A fast boat may be just as seaworthy as a sedate one, but nothing can give it the degree of spacious comfort you get, say, in a Dutch barge. A fast boat needs a tougher crew and, if properly sailed, will require more sail changing – not to speak of a larger wardrobe of dry clothes for the crew. A slow boat, on the other hand, can often be brisked up with the aid of a motor.

A well-designed hull which behaves equitably in a sea-way is the most important thing of all, for of all the features of a boat the hull is the least alterable.

For cruising, my prejudice, if the budget permits, is strongly in favour of a boat with full standing headroom below and a light and well-ventilated cabin. It does not pay to economize on galley-space, chart-room, toilet facilities or even on clothes' or sail storage lockers. But if these comforts are achieved only by means of a bulky superstructure or unseaworthy design, the victory is a hollow one.

The size of boat chosen will depend partly on the money available and partly on how many people there are to help sail her. There are limits to the sail area and weight of ground tackle that can be handled by one man alone. A man and wife between them should be able to manage a craft measuring up to 25 ft. on the waterline, provided that the design and sail plans are moderate.

Having decided on your requirements you can now begin to cast about for the right boat. The would-be buyer can, of course, himself put a "wanted" advertisement in the yachting papers, but it is none too easy to frame one's requirements in words which are specific and yet not too rigid. Also, you may get many more answers than you have time to deal with. Often the boat that catches your eye in an advertisement happens to be remote from your home town. You will probably find it quicker to go to the manager of a reputable local yard or to a recognized yacht broker.

Let us suppose that by one or other of these methods you have found a boat which appeals to you. Do not at once rush in and make an offer. Have a look first at *Lloyd's Register of Yachts* and learn something of the history of the yacht – when she was built, and where, and who designed her. If this life history is encouraging you can make an offer subject to a satisfactory surveyor's report. Your offer will, of course, be rather less than the price named by the seller.

At this point you should ask the seller for a detailed inventory listing the equipment, fittings, furnishings, bedding, crockery, etc., which he is prepared to include in the sale price. This is a "must", unless the new owner is prepared to face a heavy charge for replacements.

Examination of the yacht by a qualified – and we emphasize the word qualified – surveyor may cost £8 or more, but it will be money well spent, and may save you from being landed with a bill for renovations costing many times that sum. Even if the hull be sound, the surveyor may discover other repairs which will have to be done and which can be taken into account in the subsequent bargaining.

It is usual for the buyer to pay the cost of surveying. This is logical, because if the yacht be sound there is no reason why the seller should be called on to pay anything for the trouble he has presumably taken to keep her so; and if the yacht is unsound and the deal called off, then the unlucky owner has suffered quite enough in depreciation in the value of his boat without having to pay for the bad news out of his own pocket.

If the owner refuses to agree to a survey or to have the boat slipped for the purpose, it should be concluded that he probably has a very good reason for his refusal and the deal should be called off. Equally, the buyer should insist on seeing for himself how the boat handles at sea, and that her gear is well designed and simple to operate and her sails in good shape.

If the surveyor gives a good report and the boat survives her sea tests, the price can be agreed on and the sale concluded.

If the yacht is registered (and it should be if any foreign travel is contemplated) the seller must produce the certificate of registration – the equivalent of the ship's passport – showing that he is the sole owner. The seller should sign an official Bill of Sale* recording the transaction before a witness, and confirm on it that the boat is free of all encumbrances (for clearly the new owner is going to find himself in a weak position if the yacht has been mortgaged or its owner has run up a large bill for repairs or storage at the shipyard which has to be satisfied before the yacht can be removed).

After receiving the Bill of Sale and paying the money, the new owner forwards the Bill of Sale, the Registration Certificate and a formal declaration* (signed before a Registrar of British Ships, a Justice of the Peace or a Commissioner for Oaths) that he is now the new owner, to the Registrar of Shipping at the Port of Registration of the yacht in question, who will then register the transfer.

Expert advice should be sought from a reputable insurance broker on the type of insurance required for the yacht and, if necessary, for her crew.

* These forms are obtainable from H.M. Stationery Office.

www.ingramcontent.com/pod-product-compliance
Lightning Source LLC
Chambersburg PA
CBHW020644230426
43665CB00008B/314